Caspian Diary

J.M. Sandler

For Rebecca

SHE WAS MY MOTHER

Like the heroines of her beloved poet, Ferdowsi,
she possessed mystical wisdom, remarkable empathy
and uncommon courage. She was as brave as she was
beautiful, as wise as she was humble, and as eloquent as
Persian Poetry

Indeed the Idols I have loved so long,
Have done my Credit in Man's Eye much wrong:
Have drowned my Honor in a shallow Cup,
And sold my Reputation for a Song.
Omar Khayyam

- The Final Chapter -

It is the first day of spring 2008. It is a day that all Iranians around the world celebrate Noe Rooz: the inauguration of a new year and a new cycle of life.

Noe Rooz signifies the rebirth of optimism and hope, and so it is on this day that I have come to Los Angeles for the last time in anticipation of celebrating my own rebirth. I have come to redeem the life that has been hostage to a yearning I have sustained with diligence and hope for decades. This hope, this existential longing to belong, has consumed my life, and now I have come to free myself from its grip. I am here to reconnect with or otherwise abandon interminably, the family with whom I share a bloodline and a common ancestry.

They are all here in Beverly Hills, transplanted from Iran after the revolution. They live in their massive and opulent mansions, guarded by their hefty arrogance and nurtured by narcissism that is blinding. Their homes are in proximity to one another, much like they were in Tehran, and a million light years away from where I have been and who I have become. They flaunt their golden affluence, their lifestyles of "The Rich and Famous" and yet claim to be exilic victims. They commiserate often but more decisively now, during this time of an historic presidential election, about how they had been the silent quarries of the revolution; and how determined they are not to become casualties in this country's new age of political transition. Their purpose is abundantly clear, but the essence of their grievance escapes me. Nonetheless, I have come here not to indulge my urge to question or to protest. I am here to make peace...to quench my longing and soothe my ache of loneliness.

I HAD LEFT my homeland nearly forty-eight years ago, long before the mass migration of the Iranians of the Post Revolution. I had come to America alone and impecunious at the age of seventeen, bearing a heart full of hope and a suitcase full of unbearable memories. I was a rebel with a cause, determined to make right the shattered and shameful life that I had lived behind a veil of lies and secrecy. I had come to a land where only a few could pronounce my name or speak my language. "Persia" was a noun of an obscure origin and "Persian" was an adjective that identified exotic cats and expensive carpets. With the exception of international scholars and students of history, most Americans spoke of "Iran" and "Iraq" interchangeably to express their disdain for an oil-rich country in a far away desert that was siphoning their dollars with its exorbitant oil prices.

Indeed, in the decades prior to the revolution, Iran witnessed unprecedented affluence and prosperity.

Many Iranians, wisely paranoid and aptly dubious of the lasting stability of the regime, tucked away their assets in Swiss banks during Iran's economic splendor. However, once in the safe protection of their new country of "exile", they gradually invested their immense fortune and reinvented themselves.

I, too, had reinvented myself in this new land by tucking away not a surplus of assets but the dividends of my shame. My immigrant life had been an unrelenting struggle to keep at bay the intrusion of my past by clinging to the hope that each day would be better than yesterday. But now, for some time, yesterday had become the core of my present, infused with a new stratum of pain. It was twelve years ago when the salves that time and I had meticulously laid to shield me from my devastating past were recklessly scraped away... soiled by those I had loved and trusted...and now, I was here to mend the wrong and resurrect my faith.

EARLIER TODAY, I had boarded a flight at JFK airport hoping to arrive in Los Angeles before dusk, but the flight was delayed, and now, at 2 a.m., as I cautiously maneuver the unfamiliar Hills of Beverly in my rented car, I suddenly find myself walled by a foreboding blanket of darkness. I can't see what is ahead of me, nor the road from where I have come. Gravity will have me tumbling down the twisted road if I let go of the brake, and it will hurl me down into the prowling oblivion if I go forward.

In the distance, I see the vast panorama of the Los Angeles skyline; the flickering lights feebly bidding to rise and unite with the alluring sparkles of the regal homes high up in the hills. I know the Iranians of less fortunate means who live down in the valley, but the illustrious Hills belong to my relatives- the multitude of family members who do not know of the journey that has brought me here.

I have reached the summit of a winding incline and as I sit precariously perched over the rigid cliff, I think of how eerily symbolic this predicament is to the life I have lived. I am alone and in peril; desperately fatigued by a life-long quest to resurrect my family; chasing a dream that has been obstinately elusive and unyielding... And now at this moment, vulnerable to the grief and heartache that still awaits me, I contemplate pressing the car forward and over the cliff... letting it tumble down and rouse the silent canyon to claim my last breath and my life's final chapter. But what of the mission I have come to accomplish? What of the pledge I have made to redeem myself and claim my mother's honor?

No, ...I can't give up. I can't succumb to despair and die. I have to summon the pride that has always given me strength to persevere... I must let it pull me through one more time.

I tug at the emergency break and turn off the car. Then I wrap my arms around myself and wait for the sun to rise.

⁇

-Loss of Innocence-

My earliest childhood memory is vivid, elaborate and concise. It haunts me in my waking hours and creeps inside my head at night to summon me from sleep, screaming and crying for help. It is an image of me as a toddler, lying on my back underneath a brass bed. I am clad in a white dress that is pulled up high to expose my naked body from the waist down. My face is partially veiled behind the white embroidered bed skirt, yet my body lies bare below my neck.

A tall, disheveled woman is pacing the floor of a bedroom that is covered with an intricate Persian carpet. She casts her eyes first towards me and then, with restless anticipation, towards the door. Soon, there is a knock on the door and the woman ushers three young men into the room. The men talk to the woman briefly, and then each one walks deliberately towards me. I see each man approaching me and lowering his body close to me.

This searing image fades abruptly at this point, but a wrenching sensation in my stomach remains. I do not know what has happened, but I remember hovering outside my body, watching, and at the same time lying there underneath the bed. This memory, inexplicable yet vivid, is so traumatic that it is buried deep in my subconscious and does not surface until a ghastly night, shortly after my thirteenth birthday.

IT IS Noe Rooz, the spring of 1956, and my father's cousin, Mehran, has invited us to his villa in Shiraz for the holidays. Shiraz is a beautiful city in southwestern Iran, renowned for its magnificent historic treasures, and celebrated infinitely for its beloved poets Saedii and Haafez. We have never been to this popular destination and now my mother is delighted for the opportunity to take my siblings and me along to see the legendary city of literature, culture, and fragrant flower gardens. She has, nonetheless, a much more important agenda: to keep a careful watch on yet another potentially ruinous business venture that her husband intends to embark upon.

For years, my father has not been able to generate an income. My mother's modest salary from teaching high school mathematics by day, and then tutoring students at night, has been the only stable source of income that has paid our rent and provided a substandard meal menu for the family. Since my father has no capital to invest, my mother fears that once again, in his inebriated state, he will make financial promises that he can't fulfill. Although her pride has never allowed her to speak explicitly of our financial hardship, she knows that she can appeal to Mehran's sensibility not to have my father borrow money to invest in a risky endeavor.

Despite an age difference of more than a decade, Mehran has always had a unique affinity for his older cousin. The two men share a distinctively loyal relationship that consists of indulgence in *aragh* (vodka), cigarettes, backgammon, and boundless anecdotes of their reckless escapades. Tonight, as my mother and I wash and put away the dishes, I can see that she is listening intently but inconspicuously to the two men's random conversation, attempting to assess the soundness and feasibility of their new business scheme.

It is about midnight when my mother and I take my eleven-year old sister Ruhie and six-year old brother Jafar into a spare room, where we had arranged their makeshift beds earlier. I pull a couple of sheets and a pillow from the closet and put them in the far corner of the room where I will sleep. We have done this routine many times before, having to stay overnight at our relatives' homes because my father was too drunk to walk on his own.

My mother waits until I am settled under the covers, then she turns off the light and goes to an adjoining bedroom where my father, in his alcohol - induced vigor, would assault her and demand sex.

Some time later, long after the blanket of darkness has taken the night, I am lurched from the depth of sleep with strokes of a hand on my genitals and the panting breath of someone fondling me. I leap up to my feet screaming, overcome by fright and a nauseating chill.

"Maman, Maman...." I bellow, weeping.

As I gaze my eyes at the door, waiting for my mother to rush in, I see the slithering shadow of a man fading into the darkness. I hear his cacophonic grunt and recognize his familiar grumble...I know the man who has just molested me is my father. In an instant, I am swept into a black hole and something inside me caves in. I am numb and yet I feel riddled with indescribable terror and pain.

"What happened, Azadeh *jaan*? Did you have a bad dream?" My mother wraps me in her arms to quiet my quivering body.

I lift up my head ...wailing and gasping for air. I can't speak. Words elude me and ordinary language can't describe the crippling wave of shame that has taken my breath. I cover my face and drop my head to my chest, forcing my eyes shut to avoid looking at my mother.

"Did you have a bad dream?" She lifts my head up prompting me to look at her and then asks me again, this time with hopeful anticipation.

"Was it a bad dream?"

I can't disappoint her. I see her tormented face; the stare of resignation and imposed detachment; the face that I had seen so often when she had stood by helplessly watching my father flog, beat, and torture me. She could never stop him, and she had nowhere to run. I gaze at her with sadness and empathy. She has been in pain for so long... I can't burden her with mine. Perhaps denying the truth will surreptitiously alter the reality.

"Yes," I nod avoiding her eyes, "it was a bad dream, Maman."

She breathes a sigh of relief and pulls me into her arms again. I snuggle close and bury my face in her warm bosom... the familiar sweet scent that always gives me comfort. I love my mother…. I love her more than anything and better than anyone else.

"Try to get some sleep, *azizam*, my beloved."

"I'm so sorry I scared you, Maman."

I pull the cover over my head and cry quietly. The dark and menacing space where my hell had taken root earlier is now, oddly, a sanctuary that I want to protect; and the only place where I feel protected. I am safe in it, and safer for being alone with it…alone to talk to myself in a language that no one else can understand.

AS I LAY ALONE and disconnected from the world, the dreamlike memory of my infancy flashes through my mind…vivid and ominous as if I had witnessed it here, just moments earlier. Suddenly, there is an odd and eerie awareness…a paralyzing familiarity that sends chills through my spine and leaves me drenched in a cold sweat. I feel as if I am about to die. I wish for death to come so that I will no longer have to search for the meaning of my dreadful life.

I wrap my arms tightly around myself and pray to take my last breath.

- Uncommon Passage -

That faithful night in Shiraz would be neither the end nor the singular beginning of the trauma that would alter my life and shape my destiny. I would have to live a thousand lives and suffer a thousand deaths, relying only on my diary to keep my secrets safe and my sanity in check. But most often, as life was too shameful to reveal even in my diaries, I made up stories about heroines who survived their tragic lives and reached far beyond ordinary human capabilities to save themselves and rescue those they loved.

The day I graduated from high school, I knew that I would have to become the heroine of my own stories; I would have to save myself so that I could save my mother and my siblings. I knew that I would have to leave home and go far away...as far away as *Amrika* where my past could not get in my way. I knew that I would have to pursue my education; achieve pride and success so immense that my shameful past would be all but obliterated and only then, would I be able to save my family.

ON MAY 19, 1960, at age seventeen, as Iranians rejoice in anticipation of Queen Farah's delivery to the Kingdom, a son who would become the Crown Prince, my parents and my siblings cram into my Uncle Moshe's 1957 Ford and head for Tehran's Mehrabad Airport. Today, I will be boarding an Air France plane to Paris en route to New York's Idlewild (JFK) Airport. In my suitcase, I have packed selected photographs of my family and friends, love letters, memorabilia, and the two dresses I have sewn with the surplus fabric donated by my beloved Aunt Atefeh. In a handbag, I carry my red diary and my two letters of admission: one from the University of California at Berkeley, the other from UCLA. Inside a small pocket of my handbag, I have tucked away the sum total of my financial assets: five fresh twenty-dollar bills that are to sustain me indefinitely through my capricious journey.

Since my graduation from high school a year earlier, I had worked at Iran's *Banque* Melli and saved money to pay for my plane ticket to *Amrika*. All year, suitors had been pursuing me, perhaps unaware of our financial and family crises. One prominent *khastegar,* suitor had appealed to my parents through mediation with our family patriarchs and even my employer. He had promised to provide me with a life of abundant love, leisure, and luxury. My mother had declined the suitor's request for *khastegari* meeting and informed the matchmakers that she would not allow her daughter to be a "child-bride" even for an illustrious prince. "She is going to *Amrika* to study

19

medicine," she had broadcasted, "she is going to be an educated woman: free and independent; not a man's voiceless property."

AT THE AIRPORT, family members have come to wish me farewell and to offer me gifts of hope and remembrance. Many are tearful and some are looking on in silent disbelief. Young girls never leave to go to a far away land without a chaperone or sustainable wealth. Going abroad is the exclusive right of the privileged who send their children to elite boarding schools in London, Geneva or Paris.

"Where is she going?" I hear the murmurs of some relatives. "Who is going to look after her in *Amrika*?"

I have shared so many memories with each and every one and now I am leaving them all behind- most likely never to return home or to see them again.

As my departure time approaches, everyone is rushing to take a picture with me and then once again, the hugs and tearful goodbyes resume.

"*Azadeh jaan, Khoda negahdaret basheh*, may God hold you in his embrace."

I thank them all, and some I hold in a long and tearful embrace for the second or third time. This is our Persian tradition of saying farewell. We are a people of hyperbolic passion and incurable sensibility.

My father hands me a small envelope.

"Look inside. This is an antique signet ring engraved with the head of a king from the Sassanian Dynasty. It is worth a lot of money. I want you to show it to my brother, Abe. He knows antique dealers in New York. Ask him to sell it and give you the money."

My father has always talked about treasures and transactions that would bring him prosperity. I want to believe that this is not just another one of his fantasies.

"Keep it safe." He demands, smiling with the pride of a venerated aficionado of Persian antiquity.

I place the envelope in the small pocket of my handbag, next to the twenty-dollar bills.

"Thank you, Papa. I will show it to Uncle Abe when I see him."

My father's youngest brother, Abe, had moved to America two decades earlier in search of a better life. He had married a petite and pretty woman named Henrietta and had two small children. A year earlier, he had come to Tehran for a visit, pompous and proud of his good life in the new country. He had brought Chiclets gum for all the kids and nylon hosiery for the women to give us a taste of the splendid goodness that *Amrika* had offered him. Abe spoke in a grating and nearly incoherent amalgam of illiterate English and colloquial Hamedani. Amidst his glory of impressing the family with trivia, he did not miss the opportunity to boast about his knowledge of academia, even though he had never been anywhere near it. He seemed to take personal pride in the fact that I had been accepted to such elite universities as UCLA and Berkeley, and that I planned to pursue a medical degree. He had assured my mother that once I arrived in *Amrika*, he would guide me and look after me.

AS BOARDING begins, my mother reaches out to hold me one last time. She squeezes me tight, hesitant to let go. Her face is soaked with tears.

21

"Take this with you, *azizam.* My memoirs are all in here." She hands me a large frayed folder bound by a weatherworn cotton string.

"We will be reunited soon." She whispers softly and without conviction.

I wipe my eyes and kiss her face again and again.

"We will, Maman *joon*...we will."

I hold my mother's memoirs next to my heart. It is all that I will have of her until I see her again. I know she wants me to read her diary and know the true story of her life. I know she needs my voice to speak for her someday.

I walk the tarmac with the pride of a soldier ready for combat in a battleground very far away. I feel immense sorrow in my heart but unyielding strength in my resolve. I walk towards the steps that lead to the propeller plane and my gait weakens momentarily as I begin to climb the stairs, but I quickly regain my posture and put my foot firmly down to ease my next step.

I look back and wave goodbye, yet once again. I have said farewell and embraced everyone I loved, except for Vaheed, the boy who has long confessed his undying love for me...the boy I have loved in secret, because neither the cultural mores, nor my mother's strict rules of chastity would ever allow me to display any signs of amorous intention towards men.

I had met Vaheed two years earlier when I was fifteen and he was nineteen. My father had known his family when he worked for the French Railroad Company in Southern Iran in the late 1930s. After the death of her husband, Vaheed's mother, Ella had moved to Tehran with her two sons and daughters and had become reacquainted with my father. Unbeknownst to my mother, one evening my father had invited the family to our house for dinner as a gesture of friendship but with the devious intention to borrow a rather large sum of money. Once Maman discovered the truth, she was plagued with shame and anguish. However, she wanted to maintain an affable relationship with the family, hoping that one day she would refund their money.

Ella's young daughters, Mona and Dalia, perhaps unaware of my father's clandestine duplicity, became my friends. They enjoyed a liberal European lifestyle and freely socialized with their male friends. They often invited me to their mix-gender parties and insisted on teaching me the popular American and Ballroom dances.

Although I was permitted to dance with Vaheed, holding hands with him would have been perceived as the prelude to kissing him; a sin tantamount to losing my virginity. My mother often chaperoned our social gatherings but even in her absence, her authority loomed as a monitoring conscience that shadowed my every move. There were a few stolen moments, however, when in a crowded room, away from the watchful eyes of my mother, Vaheed would take my hand and pull me so close to him that I felt the beat of his heart and the heat of his passion permeate through my body. He would caress my face so softly that it would send chills down my spine and rapture me in ecstasy, craving for more. Sometimes, he would run his fingers through my hair, as he fixed his glance at me with his sensual dark eyes, and serenaded me with words that made my heart throb with desire.

"I love you, Azadeh. I love you beyond anything I could ever have imagined." He would exclaim. "My love for you will never ever die!"

When I last saw him two days ago, he told me that the news of my travel to *Amrika* had devastated him. "Please tell me you are not serious, Azadeh." He protested. "You are seventeen...just a child. How can your mother let you live alone in a foreign country?"

I could not tell Vaheed why I was leaving. I was not quite sure of any answers myself. I knew only that I had to leave. I could not listen to the pleas of my own heart or to his. The scars of shame were so deep and insidious that they eclipsed even the magic of his love.

He could see the flood of tears coursing down my face.

"What about us?" He bellowed. "I love you, Azadeh and I know that you love me, too."

"Please Vaheed *joon*, please forgive me," I begged, "You should love someone else. There are so many girls who are in love with you and would welcome your embrace."

I lit a cigarette to quiet my despair. I regretted everything I had said.

"No, my darling. I will not ever love anyone but you."

"I must go Vaheed." I wiped my tears away, trying to be strong... the longer I stayed, the harder it was to say goodbye.

"I will wait for you, Azadeh... Promise me that you will not give your heart to anyone else.... promise me that you will not let America's liberal culture blemish your *nejabat*; your chastity."

My heart was aching insufferably, but I couldn't circumvent the brutal reality. I had to say goodbye. I asked him to come to the airport so that I could see him one last time.

"I can't bear to see you leave, Azadeh. The pain would be intolerable."

He walked away in silence. Yet I knew he was weeping.

AS I CLIMB the final step to enter the plane, I take one last look, hoping to see Vaheed in the crowd, but he is not there. He has kept his promise.

Inside, a young stewardess clad in blue uniform welcomes me with a smile.

"*Bonjour, Mademoiselle.*" She checks my ticket and leads me to a window seat in the back of the plane. I thank her and cozy up to my chair in anticipation of experiencing my first flight. From my window and through the haze of my unbridled tears, I can see the restless faces above the necks that crane from side to side to take one last look at me before the plane takes off. I know the betting chatter that has ensued as each one claims to know where I am seated. They could be looking at anyone but it would not matter, because everyone on that plane is a numinous member of their own family; sharing the same aching heart as they say farewell to a loved one. I know that they will all wait anxiously until the plane ascends and disappears into the sky. It is the ceremonial valediction to someone who will be badly missed.

The propelled engine begins to roar and as soon the plane is airborne, my exhilaration of leaving the ground and soaring into the sky is dulled by the gravity of all the things that I am leaving behind... everything that had kept me grounded yet captive at the same time.

The snowcapped summit of the Alborz Mountains are quickly disappearing and giving way to floating white clouds. There is no time for reflection and no relief to come from remorse. I am on a solitary journey from which I cannot return. I must remain calm and strong and move forward. But first, I have to walk through the darkness of my past to let the enlightenment free me from it.

I put a blanket across my feet and open the pages of my mother's diary. I need to read it and put together the pieces of her tragic life that has long become my own.

- Dowry of Deceit -

My mother, Esther, was born in Rasht in 1923. She was the youngest of four children: a nine-year-old brother, Azad, a six-year-old brother, Nader, and a three-year-old sister, Narges. Her father Khalil Kalimipoor was a tall, handsome and exceptionally learned man whose ancestors, the Yuhudi family of rabbinical scholars, had fled the Spanish Inquisition and settled in Kashan. Her mother, Tova Hamedani, a sophisticated and feisty young woman, had lost her parents at a young age and lived in Hamadan with her older brother, Yaghoub, until the day of her wedding at the age of nineteen.

In 1913, the newly married couple visited Rasht, a major city in the Gilan province, approximately 24 km (15 miles) south of the Caspian Sea. In the early 1900s, the lush and fertile region of Gilan on the bed of the Sefid River was the market and processing center for rice, tea, peanuts, and silk. It boasted a unique history of commerce and culture because of its proximity to the Caspian Sea, the strategic Gateway to Russia and Europe.

The industrious couple settled in Rasht and began to export local goods and commodities. Their endeavor proved to be highly successful and earned them access to travel, theater, and a vast library of arts and literature. The children were introduced to classical music early on, and when Khalil discovered Esther's fascination with the violin, he bought her a Stradivarius that she ambitiously played and treasured throughout her youth.

Khalil and Tova were highly respected in their community. They were revered for their aristocracy: a culture of philanthropy and excellence in education, which they instilled in their children and promoted in the region. They reportedly owned a horse-drawn golden carriage that was made available to Kings and dignitaries whenever they visited the Gilan province. However, their generosity and hospitality was not exclusively bequeathed on the privileged. Their home was a sanctuary for the poor, where they regularly fed the homeless and the hungry.

Tova (Khanom jaan), Azad, Khalil (Rasht: Circa 1918)

Shortly after Reza Khan claimed his title as the Shah and the ruler of Iran in 1926, tragedy usurped the tranquility of my mother's family. Azad, the first-born son, a prodigy with good looks and extraordinary talents; a boy so cherished by the community that he was named the Caspian Son, died suddenly at the age of twelve, leaving his family shocked, shattered and inconsolably grieved.

THE SYSTEMATIC persecution of Jews in Hitler's Germany compounded the family's sorrow and distress. In 1933, my grandfather Khalil, fearful that the anti-Semitic uprising would be filtering down from Europe, changed the family's last name to protect their Jewish identity. He had predicted that Hitler would invade the rest of the continent and eventually plague Russia and the Middle East, but he did not live to witness the accuracy of his chilling prophecy. Seven years after the death of Azad, Khalil at age forty-two died after a brief illness, leaving his devastated young widow with the grueling task of collecting his debts. Since all business transactions of the time were consummated by the proverbial handshake, my grandmother had to search near and far for witnesses to bring before the local magistrate in order to authenticate the legitimacy of her claims against delinquent merchants.

Seventeen-year old Nader, who had just graduated from high school when his father died, was a brilliant scholar with a passion for science and medicine. Although he had briefly considered attending the newly inaugurated college of medicine in Tehran, he decided instead to remain in Rasht to teach so that he could oversee the collection of his father's fortune.

For the next two years, while fourteen-year-old Narges and eleven year old Esther attended school, their mother was often absent from home, as she continued her exhaustive and valiant effort to appear in court each day and present her case before the magistrate.

IN THE MIDDLE EASTERN culture of the 1930s, women were groomed to marry at a young age; and with rare exceptions, they were neither expected nor encouraged to pursue higher education. A woman's eligibility for marriage declined rapidly after the age of eighteen and commonly ceased once she reached the age of twenty-one. An unmarried woman in her early twenties was referred to as *torshideh*, old and soured. This was a label that brought shame and humiliation upon the young woman and her family. A girl's desirability for marriage was assessed based on her age, the reputation of her family, the size of her dowry, her beauty, and her ability to produce male children-the reliability of which was determined by the women's ancestral record of producing male progenies. Although a suitor's hierarchy of these characteristics might have varied, the requirements remained the same. Traditionally, children lived with their parents until they were married. Men were the exclusive guardian of their family's name, fortune, and reputation. They remained home as bachelors until their sisters were honorably married. Girls married in chronological order with priority always conferred upon the oldest daughter to preserve her honor. This was a mandatory and revered custom, a decree as sacred as a girl's virginity on the night of her wedding. Once the girls were married, then the parents would determine who would be a suitable bride for their son. They would select an appropriate candidate and ask the girl's parents to grant them the traditional visit of *"khastegari,"* the official request for their daughter's hand in marriage. Although this formal visit was assumed to be the first step in initiating the matrimonial process, often a less formal 'behind-the-scenes' agreement and negotiation had already taken place. In such cases, the groom's family offered valuable gifts of gold and jewelry, symbolic of their son's ability to provide for their daughter.   In turn, the girl's family offered the groom *jahazi,* a dowry that was negotiated based on the suitor's qualifications and the woman's desirability.   Ultimately, the larger the dowry, the more respect and reverence the bride would receive.

My mother and her sister Narges had been raised in a progressive environment and by enlightened parents who had fostered in all their children the desire to pursue higher education. The girls had lived an exemplary life and were highly admired in the community for their academic excellence, beauty, noble upbringing, and effervescent personalities. Matters of matrimony had never been discussed or entertained, as it was patently clear that the girls would continue to achieve the highest academic goal they desired. Nader, however, now the patriarch of the family, was of the opinion that women had neither the aptitude, nor the justification to pursue higher learning.

"Tahseel, education," he insisted, "is wasted on women because their role in life is to be good housewives and produce sons who would be praiseworthy." What Nader condemned even more vehemently was the valued tradition of giving a

woman *jahazi.*

"This tradition is *mozakhraf,* pure rubbish. The priority of every young woman should be to 'trap' a man who would be willing to marry her without a dowry." He vowed not to offer a single dinar, a penny, to suitors who come for his sisters' *khastegari.*

At the age of nineteen, Nader was a formidable foe to anyone who challenged him. He stood tall, strong, and strikingly handsome; with penetrating blue eyes that accentuated his chiseled face and exuded authority. His remarkable acumen was unparalleled by his contemporaries or even by his elders. He was calm and emotionally remote; a man of few words who would never engage in ordinary and mundane conversations- particularly those with a sentimental undertone. However, once prompted by an inquiry about science, mathematics, history, politics and finance, he immediately captivated his audience with his extraordinary knowledge and expertise, never failing to awe them with a comprehensive answer or a winning debate.

It was Nader's unwavering judgment and equanimity that demanded his mother's respect and convinced the weary and grieving woman to defer to him all financial and domestic decisions. She was widowed and alone at a young age and knew that ultimately she would have to depend on Nader to take care of her. This was the traditional duty that every son was expected to fulfill.

WHEN MORDAD, a 27-year old unemployed man took the trek of *Khastegari* with his entourage from Hamadan to Rasht in 1936, no one suspected that it was the thirteen-year-old, Esther and not her sixteen-year-old sister, Narges, who was the object of his matrimonial pursuit. Mordad's three older brothers and his only sister were already married but he and his two younger brothers still lived with their parents. He had seen Esther's picture at the home of her uncle Yaghoub in Hamadan and had become instantly infatuated with her. Once advised of Nader's intention to turn away any suitor who expected *jahazi*, Mordad was prepared to play his hand skillfully to his best advantage.

What Mordad lacked in the form of discipline, accountability and income, he compensated for with an effusive and charming personality. He wore a stylish chapeau and a confident smile. He was warm and engaging; adept with the gift of storytelling that he sprinkled with anecdotes in fluent French. He had fully rehearsed his proposal to assure his future in-laws that he had his own fortune and did not expect a dinar of *jahazi*. To buttress his claim, Mordad had brought with him a two-tiered diamond necklace and a diamond studded engagement ring, both purchased with money he had borrowed from friends and relatives.

Tova was unimpressed by the seduction of the jewels and the charm of the vociferous suitor. "Esther is just thirteen. She is a child..." she objected, "and her engagement would jeopardize, if not obliterate, her older sister's chance for marriage."

"*Hazrat -e-* Tova Khanom, your Excellency, Lady Tova," Mordad appealed slavishly, "I swear to you that I will be completely discrete; I will not announce my engagement to Esther khanom until her older sister is honorably married."

Tova was not satisfied with the suitor's promise and Mordad knew that he would have to solicit Nader's approval to win Tova's consent.

"*Jenab Hazrat-e Agha-e* Nader Khan, your High Excellency," Mordad indulged Nader benevolently, "I exalt you for your courage not to conform to petty traditional rules. You know that any other suitor would expect at least a minimal *jahazi* from you, but I am prepared to decline it, even if you offered it to me."

"*Merci, Agha-e* Mordad." Nader was immensely pleased.

"Are you sure Nader Khan that this decision will not damage the girls' reputation and their future welfare?" Tova appealed to her son warily, troubled by his hasty verdict, but careful not to challenge his authority.

Mordad seized the prevailing moment of silence to clear his throat and produce a pack of Gorgaan's out of his pocket. He deftly ejected three cigarettes. He offered one to Tova, another to Nader, and took the last one for himself. He removed a single match from the matchbox and held it between his thumb and his right index finger. He then swiftly ignited it with a single strike against the matchbox that he held in the palm of the same hand. It was a skillful display of dexterity that did not go unnoticed; it offered Mordad the timely diversion, and warranted Nader's bemused attention.

The odor of burnt sulfur permeated the room as the suitor first lit Tova's cigarette and then Nader's, looking him in the eye to gauge his reaction to his mother's question. He then lit up his own cigarette, took in a very long drag and slowly exhaled. A large plume of smoke exited his mouth and his nostrils, leaving him engulfed in a shroud of seduction and mystery. At this moment, Mordad looked just like one of those sophisticated Hollywood stars that young Nader had seen and admired on the movie screen.

"I assure you that I will postpone my marriage to Esther Khanom until her older sister is married." Mordad repeated his pledge, one more time for good measure.

Nader was clearly impressed with the suitor's charm and his adroit presentation.

"Well, Khanom?" He never addressed his mother or anyone else with the common and endearing salutation-"*jaan*". It just wasn't his style; and it set him apart from all other mortals.

"You see," he asserted confidently, "We have no reason to decline Mordad khan's *khastegari*."

The suitor smiled victoriously, and Nader was profoundly relieved. The men shook hands, sealing the destiny of the thirteen year-old Esther; officially eradicating her freedom, dreams, and dignity.

By the time the *Khastegari* was concluded, Nader was addressing Mordad as his trusted brother, "*baraadar-e geraami*," and lighting up Gorgaan cigarettes with him as a sign of solidarity. He assured him that his sister would be honored to serve him for as long as she lived.

THE NEWS of the successful *Khastegari* spread in Hamadan like wildfire. Tova's brother, Yaghoub, a wise and well-respected man with daughters of his own, was stunned and infuriated by the news of his

36

young niece's engagement. He immediately sent a messenger from Hamedan to Rasht to deliver his severe condemnation of his nephew's unconscionable action: "How dare you force a thirteen-year-old child to marry an unemployed playboy fourteen years her senior?"He wrote, and demanded that the engagement be dissolved immediately. But his warnings would go unheeded. Nader persuaded his mother that her brother was simply misguided.

For weeks, the two sisters cried and pleaded with their mother to revoke the engagement and send back the jewels. But Tova, the woman who had stood boldly in court before judges to recover the family's fortune, could not challenge her son's will.

IN THE FOUR YEARS that followed her engagement to Mordad, Esther reconciled herself to the fate that was chosen for her. She went on to finish high school at the age of sixteen and began teaching mathematics, just as her sister had done two years earlier. Mordad, who had finally secured employment with a Railroad company in the Persian Gulf, came to see his fiancé on holidays and took her for rides in his rented car. When he was away, he wrote to her of his unbearable despair.

"My beloved Esther, I am lonely and longing for us to be together as husband and wife."

Esther wrote to her fiancé about her joy of teaching and encouraged him to be patient and productive. For Nader, however, it was paramount that Mordad's interest did not ebb because of distance or delay of his intended wedding. He wrote to him regularly: "My esteemed brother, Esther counts the days to become your bride and your devoted loving wife."

Then to the rolling Heaven itself I cried,
Asking, "What Lamp had destiny to guide
Her little Children stumbling in the Dark?"
And- " A blind understanding!" Heaven replied
Omar Khayyam

- Destinies Sealed -

The year 1939 was a pivotal time for my mother's family to change the course of their destiny. This was the year that Nader could have attended the newly established Medical school in Tehran and set his sisters free. They were earning salaries that afforded them financial security and independence. They dressed in high fashion clothes and made frequent trips to Bandar Pahlavi: the popular seaport near Rasht and the hub of intellectual homily. They joined their friends and colleagues in cafes and teashops to recite poetry and debate the political and social inferences of Russian and European literature. This was the singular, most cherished year of the girls' youth: the time for them to choose their own path and purpose as their father had always wished. But Nader did not want to leave Rasht. He declared adamantly and acrimoniously that his obligation to his family had deterred him from pursuing his medical studies when in fact; his true passion was to take charge of the family fortune and invest it for his own benefit.

Tova (Khanom Jaan), Esther, Narges
(Bandar Pahlavi: C. 1939)

That summer, Mordad contracted Malaria in the southern city of Ahwaz and promptly terminated his employment with the railroad company. He joined his family who had moved to Tehran and wrote to Nader that he wanted to get married immediately. Nader acquiesced. He, too, was moving to Tehran to invest in the lucrative business opportunities that Reza Shah's industrialization had amply promised.

When Tova's brother, Yaghoub, decided to move his family to Tehran, he tried once again to intervene on behalf of his young niece. He told Nader, in no uncertain terms, that he was outraged by his rapacious scheme to deny his younger sisters their inheritance. He warned him that his lack of foresight and unilateral decision would condemn the girls to a life of disgrace and devastation. But Nader, inspired only by his own greed, was neither concerned nor threatened. He was determined to achieve his goal and hoard his father's entire fortune.

Unable to persuade his nephew to reverse his decision, Yaghoub asked Esther if she would come to live with his family in Tehran where she could attend college. Yaghoub was hopeful that if he assumed responsibility for the young girl, Nader would be willing to annul the engagement and leave open the opportunity for suitors to pursue Narges. She was, after all, three years older than Esther and approaching the critical age of twenty. She would soon be banished by matchmakers and labeled as torshideh- a pitiful spinster no man would want to marry.

"It is too late *Daii jaan*, my beloved uncle," Esther

41

had wept, "I am no longer pure and unblemished. Mordad has kissed me... I have no choice but to marry him. Otherwise, I will cast shame and dishonor upon my family."

Yaghoub had wiped his niece's tears and held her in a loving embrace.

"Esther *jaan*, I admire your *nejabat* and chastity, but kissing a man should not sentence you to a life that is not of your choosing."

In the arms of her uncle, and for a few brief moments, Esther had felt safe and cherished ... just as she had felt long ago in the embrace of her father, Khalil.

"I value your love and your wisdom, *Daii jaan*. But Nader Khan is now like a father to me. I must trust and obey him."

Yaghoub knew that Nader was not at all like his father, Khalil.

ESTHER'S MARRIAGE to Mordad was a catastrophe that began on the day of her wedding and consumed her life and vitality each and every day that she lived.

Following their modest wedding, Mordad, still penniless and unemployed, bartered the services of his pregnant wife for food and shelter that his youngest brother and cousin, both serving inactive military duty, could provide. Esther spent her days attending to housekeeping chores: cooking meals, washing, mending, and ironing the men's clothes and uniforms.

At night, after dinner, Mordad drank *aragh*, smoked cigarettes, and played cards with the men until he was intoxicated, incoherent, and feeble on his feet. He then staggered into the bedroom demanding that his exhausted wife soothe him and satisfy his sexual needs. Sometimes, in the middle of the night, he would leave the house to look for prostitutes. Twice, he had gone to a neighbor's house, bribing their maid with pocket change and threatening her with blackmail until she had surrendered. The maid had cried to Esther and begged her to make him stop, but any questions or complaints would only escalate the abuse and the threats. Esther was terrified that her husband would contract syphilis and bring harm to her unborn baby, but Mordad was too drunk and ignorant to care.

At age 18, Esther gave birth to a boy she named Teymour. It was a difficult delivery. So many women died in labor every day, and so many infants perished during or after birth. But once Esther held her son under her breast to nurse him, all her fears and anguish seemed to be obliterated. She promised God that she would always revere him, and pledged that she would never be sad again. But, it was not long before her faith would fail her and her promise would be broken. The baby died in her arms six months later, leaving her heart with a gaping wound that would never mend.

- A Night in Paris -

It is almost 7 p.m., when the Captain announces that we will soon be descending to arrive at Anvalid (De Gaulle) Airport. We had left Tehran nearly ten hours earlier and now, after a two-hour stopover in Beirut and another in Rome, we have finally arrived in Paris.

Since I have missed my connecting flight to New York due to unusual delays, Air France is providing me with transportation and an overnight stay at a hotel in Paris. This is a treat that I would never have imagined even in my most prolific fantasies.

Within twenty minutes, I am escorted outside by an airline representative and led to a taxi that takes me to the most magnificent hotel I have ever seen. I cannot keep my eyes off the glorious edifice that stands before me ...it looks like a castle I had once seen on the movie screen...except this is in splendid regal colors.

Inside, everything looks exquisite in Louis XIV décor, and I am thrilled that my suite has its own luxurious bathtub, shower, and toiletries. I am mesmerized by what I see. I guardedly tiptoe around the room and touch everything to make sure I am not dreaming. I call out my own name several times to rouse myself, lest I had fallen asleep. Then, I see my reflection in the mirror and quickly remember the reality that looms ahead. But for now, I cannot let this day and the city of Paris slip away. This rare and unprecedented generosity of fate will expire in a few hours and I have to rush to embrace it. I shall behold the rapture of the city of lights for one brief night and let it illuminate the darkness that surrounds me.

Downstairs, I consult with the concierge and mark the city map with the address of the hotel and the wondrous sites that I hope to see.

I walk the streets of Paris, dazed and dazzled. I embrace all the sights and sounds that I can see and hear until exhaustion takes me over. When I return to the hotel, I write cheerful notes on post cards that depict the sites I have visited. Then I get my luggage and wait for the taxi to return me to the airport and to my new reality.

On board the Pan Am flight destined for New York City, I settle into my seat with a mixture of anticipation and anxiety. I will soon reach a far away continent to begin a new life, but will that life be better than the one I have left behind? I take a deep breath and reach for the still unread diaries at the bottom of my valise. Now I need to search for the missing fragments of my life...those concealed in the chronicles I have kept since childhood.

Tir   1332:   June   1954

My Dear Diary,

I always wanted to start writing to you on a happy day or a special occasion, but there is never a truly happy day in my life. That is why it has taken me so long to write to you. You see, even my birth was not a happy event. I was born on a cold February night and a time my mother recalls as "famine" ...a time of extreme poverty and hunger. Although Reza Shah had declared neutrality in the war, the allies nonetheless invaded Iran in 1941, presumably to protect the vast resources of our oil from the enemy. The occupation by the Russian troops in the North and the British army in the South caused severe shortage of food that affected mostly the poor.

My mother was still grieving the loss of her first-born son when she discovered that she was pregnant again...just when the troops invaded our country.

By the way, my name is Azadeh and I am eleven years old. I was given two names when I was born. The one on my birth certificate means "the glow"; it is the name that I have hated all my life...so much that I can't even bear to write it down. My other

46

name is Azadeh. This is the name I like. It means freedom. I want to be free ...free to hope...and free to find a way to escape the treacherous life I live.

The name Azadeh was given to me in memory of my mother's older brother, Azad; the beloved prodigy who died at the age of twelve. My grandmother Tova, my Khanom jaan, says that her son's spirit had come to her in a dream, and wanted me to be named after him.... So the family calls me Azadeh, but every one at school knows me by my other name. All my female cousins have Persian or European (Farangi) names and go to private Jewish schools, but my siblings and I have Arabic names and go to public schools.

When I was born, my father was still unemployed, and the relatives who shared the house with my parents had left for military duty, so we were hungry and on the verge of being homeless. This was when Maman began to pawn everything to save us from starving.

Maman has told me that when I was nine-months old, I nearly died because of severe respiratory distress and high fever. I was hardly breathing when in the middle of the night she carried me to the house of a daroo saaz, pharmacist and begged him to give me a dose of the penicillin that had just arrived in Tehran for the first time. The compassionate daroo saaz had taken us to his apothecary and administered the miracle medicine that saved my mother from mourning the loss of her second baby. Then, when I was just over a year old, I dipped a twig into the howze (pool not designed for swimming) and chased it as it plunged under the water. Maman had rushed to the yard, pleading for God's mercy. She says it was a miracle that she was able to pull me out just before I sank to the bottom. I wonder if my deceased uncle, Azad, has been watching over me. My grandmother says it is because I am named after him. I have to believe in something so that I can go on living, a reason why I live this life of misery.

When I was two and half years old, my mother gave birth to my sister, Ruhie. My father was outraged. He wanted a boy and this child was not only of the inauspicious gender, but possessed the unflattering curly black hair and dark complexion much like his own. These are not good features for women to have. They are certainly not popular with Iranian men.

"I'll call her Sooskechi, the Little Roach." My father had croaked once he laid eyes on the baby.

My mother had recoiled with horror.

"She is ba namak, salty."

Maman was trying to enhance her baby's image, as one would do to augment the taste of food.

Some time after the birth of my sister, my father's brothers offered him a job that required traveling. My father insisted on taking me on his road trips. I do not have any vivid memories of these excursions, but always hear him gloat about how much I loved sitting on his lap as he drove from city to city.

"My baby loved me so much ... she would get sick as soon as I said I was going away."

I will never know the truth about my travels with my father, but I know that I squirm and get a sinking feeling every time he tells the story.

Two years after my sister's birth, we were evicted from the apartment house on khiabahn-e yakhchal, the avenue of Ice. It was an appropriate name for a place that held so many bad memories. My mother wanted us to live in a nicer neighborhood, but we had no money and she had already pawned all of our valuables: the rugs, the wedding gifts and all her jewelry were gone, save a delicate gold watch she always wore on her wrist. It was a gift from her beloved uncle, her Daii jaan Yaghoub. He had given it to her just before her wedding.

> "Esther jaan: Let this watch remind you that
> Life leaps with each increment of time.
> I hope that you will know when it is time
> for you to set yourself free and
> change the course of your destiny."

My mother wore this watch with special pride. This yadegaari... this memento, was a precious symbol of hope from her beloved uncle who cherished her and tried to protect her from the ravages of her brother's greed. Now, with nothing else to sell or pawn except for her watch, my mother could no longer conceal our poverty from the family. It was then that my father's parents offered us shelter. They lived on a massive property: a compound with an eight-foot brick wall and a large wooden gate that surrounded a vast yard and a large pool in the middle. There were two houses on the far ends of the compound; each consisted of two floors connected by a stairwell that extended from the yard. In the house at the far end of the yard lived one of my elder uncles, his wife, and their five children. The other house was occupied by my grandparents, my youngest uncle Moshe, and his wife Atefeh. The servants' quarters that was located near the gate would become our home for the next three years. We had two small rooms and a kitchen. The floors were bare, the furniture was old, and there was a musty odor that never went away. We had no hot water and the only faucet in the kitchen delivered a jolt of electricity that made my mother shriek every time she washed dishes.

In the winter, we sat on the floor around a korsi (a low square table with multiple blankets hanging over it, and a pot of burning coal underneath). At night, we stretched our feet under the korsi and pulled the covers up to our necks to keep warm and fall sleep.

Once a week, my mother, sister and I walked to the public bathhouse and luxuriated in the copious warm waters for a nominal fee. We scrubbed our bodies, washed each other's back, and chatted with acquaintances who had come for their weekly bathing. Sometimes, if not often, the woman's chatter was all about matchmaking... about who was eligible for Khastegari and which young girl would be an appropriate mate for a man who was ready to get married.

Soon after we moved into my grandparents' house, my mother was pregnant again. She worried all the time about our persistent poverty and wondered how she could feed another baby. She had been thinking of resuming her teaching career but now, pregnant and with two young children, she had no option except to rely on the charity of her husband's family.

Living on the compound with my uncles, aunts, cousins, and grandparents was the best time of my childhood. Every day, my little cousins and I gathered in the yard to play. Out there, the world seemed like a big happy playground. But as soon as my father came home, nothing was safe anymore. He drank all night and we never knew what would unleash his rage or who would become the target of his craze. Most nights, however, Maman was the chosen victim of his brutality.

I adored my Uncle Moshe and Aunt Atefeh. They were the kindest and the best family anyone could have. My Uncle Moshe was always delighted to see me. He'd pick me up and shower me with kisses. He tickled me and had me roaring with laughter until I was breathless... begging for mercy...and yet wishing for more.

"Pedar Sookhteh, toe shaitooni kardi", an endearing expression, save its translation, 'you naughty girl...your father is toast!' It is the inflection of the words in Farsi that reveal whether you are being teased, admonished or ridiculed. When Uncle Moshe held me in his arms, I felt safe and happy. I thought nothing bad could ever happen to me. I wanted to have a father just like him.

I was four and a half years old when my mother altered my birth certificate to make me older and eligible to attend first grade. My birth certificate still bears the smudge where my birthdate was changed. I don't know why my mother wanted me to start school at such a young age, but I know that once I did, my father could no longer take me on his road trips and I never again became ill when he announced he was going away.

I remember my first day at Firoozkoohi Elementary School. It was the middle of the school year and no one looked familiar. I was one of the tiniest girls in the class of twenty-five girls. In our class photo, I sat precariously at the end of a long bench looking like a little toy doll in my black school uniform, surrounded by two rows of first-graders who were all older and considerably larger than me. Apparently, neither the smudge on my birth certificate, nor my miniature stature had raised any one's suspicion about my true age. I have *always been the youngest and the smallest girl in my class, and now as I notice that all the girls, even the younger ones are growing taller, I am sure that God is punishing me. I know I am not like every one else...there is something different about me...something even beyond my empty belly and my small stature. I am not like other girls, that's why I am more comfortable being alone and on my own.*

Dabestan Anooshiravan Dadgar (Tehran: C.1948)

Our first-grade teacher was a stocky woman who wore a double--breasted suit, thick stockings, and a silk scarf around her head. She carried a wooden ruler in her hand at

54

all times and was fast on her feet to whip us at the slightest infraction. Her favorite method of punishment, however, was to grab an ear and twist it until it turned purple.

I don't know what criteria she used to determine which method of punishment would be appropriate, but once she smacked me so hard that the ink pen in my hand pierced through my upper lip and left me with an indelible tattoo. On another occasion, when I accidentally dropped my pencil, it instantly prompted her outrage.

"You undisciplined child, pick up your pencil immediately and sit up straight." She shrieked in a guttural voice so harsh that it delivered severe torture of its own.

"Khaili bebakhsheed Khanom. Forgive me Madam." I was very sorry but it didn't matter. I knew I was at her mercy. I closed my eyes and waited. ...And then when she withdrew her hand from my twisted ear, I felt such excruciating pain that I expected to find my severed ear resting on the ground. But I was too afraid to look, for that too, would have warranted another round of harsh punishment. I sat still and took a sigh of relief only when I heard her footsteps fade away. Soon, my stomach would be growling and the pangs of hunger would mitigate all the pain of injustice.

In 1947, my mother gave birth to her fourth child, Flora. She was a stunning baby with blue eyes, black hair, and silky alabaster skin. Although everyone had hoped for a boy, the exquisite beauty of this baby was so astounding that no one would utter a single word of disappointment. Then one day, just three months after Flora was born, an older cousin came to pick me up from school. I had always walked to and from school alone and was surprised to see him waiting for me.

"Why did you come to pick me up today?" I asked.

"Berim, berim, let's go." He held my hand and hastened his pace.

As we approached the compound, I could hear my mother's heart-wrenching cry from outside the gate. Inside, in our barren living room, I saw my aunts and cousins... some crying, others trying to comfort my mother. My sister Ruhie was whimpering and looking bewildered. She ran to me and wanted comfort. I held her hand and walked over to my mother who was weeping over Flora's bassinet.

"Chi shodeh, Maman, What happened?" I looked over her shoulder and saw the empty bassinette. I started to cry.... I knew something bad had happened to Flora.

Maman stared at me for a moment, and then began to scream with an ear-piercing squeal.

"Oh, God of Abraham, why do you take my children? What have I done to disappoint you...what have I ever done to deserve so much pain and punishment?" Maman was rambling and inconsolable.

"Flora is gone...the child is dead," someone announced to a newcomer, and I knew what that meant. Just a few months earlier, my grandfather who lived in the compound had died. I never saw him again. I knew that when people died they disappeared, never to be seen again. Our Babajoon was a very old man and spent most of his time in bed moaning, but I knew that young people and little children died, too. Maman and Khanom jaan often talked about the death of twelve-year old Azad, my six-month old baby brother, Teymour, and my young grandfather, Khalil. And now Flora, too, was dead.

Maman looked exhausted and sick. Her eyes were swollen from crying and she was staring at something I couldn't see. I sat down and quietly prayed that God would make her well and never take her away. Then I lay down next to her and cried until I fell asleep.

In a few days, when my father returned from his trip, he was ranting about his brothers, cursing them for staying in their cozy office and making him do all the traveling.

"Do you know why I have to work for my binaamoos, immoral brothers?"

I knew this was the familiar tirade that always led to my mother's torture. I stood in the corner, crying and trembling.

"Do you know why, Jendeh khanom, the elevated prostitute...why I have to work so hard?" He gulped down his aragh..."It's all because your damned brother didn't give you a jahaz. He knew you were worthless."

Maman was begging him to stop, but he was oblivious and his diatribe would not end unless he passed out.

"Oon dowzd-e bisharaf, oon pedar sag e-poolparast; that immoral thief, that bastard, the money worshipper who's God is Gold... He stole your father's money...every dinar of it, and gave you nothing."

"Stop, Mordad." Maman was screaming. "Khafeh show, jendeh, shut up whore."

"Flora is dead." Maman shouted and finally got his attention.

In a moment, my father's deafening roar interrupted the fleeting silence. His eyes narrowed...he looked like a raging beast, aiming to leap on his quarry.

"Chi migi jendeh? What are you saying whore?"

I ran to Maman to catch the blow of my father's fist before it struck her, but it was too late. He had knocked her to the ground and was beating her.

"Maadar mordeh, maahdar jendeh, your useless mother should die...that whore." He slammed my mother against the wall.

"Bache-ta koshti; you killed your child?"

"Please Papa stop...please don't hurt her." I pleaded with all my might. But I could see through the flood of my tears that my father wasn't done. He pulled me away and began striking my mother again.

"I am going to kill you." He roared.

I was certain that my mother's death was imminent but I was helpless. My sister was crying. She was hungry and wanted me to give her something to eat. We had no food in the house, but I remembered a box of sweets someone had brought over that day. It was on top of a freestanding hutch in the kitchen. I pulled open each drawer slightly to use as a makeshift ladder and climbed it. But as I reached the top, the hutch toppled over and crash-landed on the kitchen table. My parents rushed in. My father was foaming at the mouth, and my mother was

59

limping with bruises on her face and arms.

"You are bleeding." Maman saw the blood that was flowing from my leg. A shard of broken glass had lodged in my calf and left a deep gash.

"Khodaye maa rahmkardeh." Maman was thanking God for his mercy... for not letting the hutch land on my head and kill me, but I was thankful that my father had been distracted from killing her. Then, as she began to tend to my wound, I heard my father's familiar drone ... the disturbing grunt that meant the night of torture was not over yet.

"I'll finish you both later." He promised as he left the kitchen.

EVER SINCE the overnight trips with my father ended, he has become more abusive towards me. He looks for any excuse to punish me and I often oblige him because it distracts him from battering my mother.

"Get out of my way whore." He elbows her, "I have to teach this wretched child how to behave."

My father jostles me on the bed, clasps my ankles together in one hand, and then holds them against his chest so that I am completely restrained.

"*Boro, boro souskechi, boro suzan biar.* Go little cockroach, go get me a needle." He beckons my sister who is happy to please him. This is the only time she can count on my father's praise and attention.

"*Aafareen bacheh*; well done, child."

He keeps my ankles fastened together in one hand and pricks the soles of my feet with the needle that he holds firmly in his other hand.

"Ghalat Kardi...ghalat Kardi? Are you sorry for the wrong you have done?" He chants the question repeatedly with each thrust of the needle into my skin. Sometimes, he arms himself with a belt or a kabob skewer to whip me or to strike the soles of my feet. My body twists and contorts with every sting of the needle and with every whip, but I know that if I try to be silent and pretend not to feel the pain, I can endure it better. It is as if denying the pain will make it go away. I imagine myself standing outside of my body and peering through the doorway, right alongside my helpless mother and bemused sister.

Dear diary,
Ever since flora died, Maman has been sick and I don't know what to do for her. She cries all the time and still doesn't feel better. Papa has gone away again, giving us reprieve from his tyranny but leaving us without money. A few days ago, I begged Maman to let me go to baghalli, the corner grocery shop, to get some bread and cheese. I knew we had no money but it was not uncommon for us to buy things on credit.

"We already owe him so much, azizam. I don't know how I can ever pay him back." *Maman reminded me tearfully.*

"But Maman, we have nothing to eat and

we are all so hungry."

"Maybe he will extend us the courtesy once again." Maman finally conceded.

I ran all the way to baghalli in anticipation of quelling the growls of my hunger.

"Salaam, Agha -e Tabrizi" I greeted the shop owner who had seen me with Maman on many occasions.

"Salaam khanom koochoolou, Hello little lady, haleh shoma chetoreh? How are you?"

"Merci Agha" I thanked him and told him that my mother had sent her regards.

"She is a very fine lady...it is a pity that she lost her baby."

"Yes, Sir. She has been crying a lot and I've come to buy some lavash bread and paneer, feta cheese for our dinner."

"Have you brought money koochoolou?"

"Bebakhsheed, Agha. Forgive me Sir," I lowered my head, "mazerat mikhaam, maa emrooz pool nadareem; I am sorry, we have no money today."

Mr. Tabrizi walked to the back room and returned with a tattered notebook. "Look." He began to thumb through the pages, and then pointed to a long column of items with numbers written across them.

"Little girl, do you know how much your mother owes already?"

I felt ashamed and was about to turn around and run away... But I had to get us something to eat.

"Maybe we can just have some lavash, bread." I pleaded ruefully.

Mr. Tabrizi paused, and then suddenly closed the book as if regretting what he had done.

"Your mother is a good woman. I am sure she will pay me someday." He touched my shoulder and gave me a sympathetic smile. Then, he handed me a shirini bereji, a rice cookie and said, "nooshejaan, go ahead and enjoy it."

I knew my mother had come here on many occasions to buy food on credit. We had been surviving on the humanity of a kind stranger.

"Salaam Agha -e docteur Rashti." The grocer cheered, as a man walked in. "Khosh amadeed, you are welcome here."

I was sure that this man was a very good customer...someone who always paid for his groceries.

Agha Tabrizi disappeared behind the wall again, this time announcing that he was going to bring out some tea. When he returned, he removed a steaming cup of tea and some sugar cubes from his tray and placed them on the counter within his friend's reach. Then he smiled at me again and began to cut up some paneer.

"Agha -e docteur Rashti," he asked his friend somberly, "When you lived in Rasht, did you know the Lahijani family?"

"Of course. I went to school with the son, Nader, who now owns a very lucrative business on Khiaban Ferdowsi. The family had an outstanding reputation and a substantial fortune. But sadly, the father died at a young age after losing his favorite son."

"So, you know the mother of this child, Esther Khanom-e Lahijani?"

Docteur Rashti nearly jumped out of his seat. "Mother of this child?" He paused to take a long look at me... his eyes wide open with surprise.

"This girl is the daughter of Esther Khanom-e Lahijani, you say?"

"Indeed, she is." Mr. Tabrizi exhaled.

"I remember her well...a poised and beautiful young lady. She was teaching high school mathematics, I recall, at the age of sixteen...quite brilliant, I'd say. All three siblings were brainy intellectuals and well bred. The young boy who died could have been the next Einstein.

"So, how did this child's mother become so destitute? She can't afford to feed her children. Last time she was here, she wanted to give me her gold watch, but I wouldn't take it."

Agha-e Rashti looked pensive. He was shaking his head to echo his disbelief. Then he lit a cigarette and took a long drag... he was quiet for a while.... pondering.... perhaps searching his mind.

"Aah... Now I remember. The brother, Nader, took charge of the family's fortune and married off his younger sister, this child's mother, before the older one was taken. It was a calamity. The older girl was so disgraced, no one sought to marry her; and the man Esther khanom married was ill suited for her. You can say that the proverbial juhoodi greed; gluttony for gold and money was fully reincarnated in this case. The brother made his sisters ghorbani. He sacrificed them to pad his own pocket.

The two men must have forgotten that I was there, or perhaps didn't think I would understand their grown-up vocabulary. They were engrossed deeply in discussing Maman's family while I stood quietly, albeit nervously, eavesdropping on the their conversation. I had been nibbling on my cookie and savoring it, but then I almost choked on the last bite when I heard agha-e Tabrizi call my uncle those awful names

65

that papa calls him all the time.

"Ah...there you are little one, khanom koochoolou. Take this home with you." Mr. Tabrizi handed me a chunk of paneer and two sheets of Lavash.

"Khoda komak koneh- I hope God helps you." He said and then, he turned to his friend and spoke in a language that I didn't understand.

When I got home, I told Maman the whole story and she cried for a very long time. I often wonder if our relatives know how we live. They have big houses with furniture and lots of food to eat. I don't think they know about being poor or hungry, but I am glad they don't exclude us from their festivities. I love going to their parties and weddings because everyone is happy... and being near them, breathing the same air, makes me feel loved and happy; that's when life seems worth living. Whenever we are at a wedding or a party, everybody insists that I get on the stage to dance and sing. They shout:

"Bravo, Azadeh...sing something in Arabic...how about a Turkish song... now sing an Indian song." Then they cheer: "Dance for us, Azadeh... dance for us."

Of course, I oblige them. I have a full repertoire of popular Persian songs by

Delkash, Vigen, and Marzieh to keep me singing all night.

Singing, dancing, painting, and writing are my favorite things to do...they help me postpone worrying about all the things that I don't have and all the things I can't do.

Azadeh: The Entertainer (Tehran: Circa 1949)

Family Picnic (Karadj: Circa 1947)

The Worldly Hope men set their Hearts upon
Turns Ashes-or it prospers; and anon,
Like Snow upon the Desert's dusty Face
Lighting a little Hour or two- is gone.
Omar Khayyam

-Ashes of Greed-

It is the year 1945, and at age twenty-eight, *Daii jaan* Nader has amassed a considerable fortune importing building materials from Europe. He has purchased a luxury three-story residential building in the upscale Northern section of Tehran and lives on the top floor with his mother and his spinster sister. His tenants occupy the other two floors of the building.

Aunt Narges, in spite of her '*maraz roohie*', spirit disorder; a convenient euphemism for her alleged insanity- has resumed her teaching career in Tehran and is earning a respectable salary. At work, she is distracted by her rigorous academic schedule, but at home her anguish is renewed. Every night at dinner, she reminisces about their youth and reminds her brother of the shame and humiliation that he has brought upon her.

"Do you see the ashes of your greed, my esteemed brother? Do you see what you have done to your sisters?" she laments, "Esther and I are both *badbakht*, doomed... you gave my beautiful sister to *aashghal*, garbage; a man who is not worthy even of her discarded toenail, let alone her grace and intellect.

70

You devastated her life, and ruined my chance of ever getting married."

Nader Khan, absorbed in reading the newspaper, avoids eye contact with his sister. Occasionally, he turns his attention to his plate to fill his spoon, or to glance at his mother who is choking on her food. For some time now, *khanom jaan* has been stricken with an undiagnosed malady that causes her to gag when she attempts to swallow food.

Narges recoils as she watches her mother place a morsel of food on her spoon, then return it to her plate unconsumed because even the smallest bite can throw her into a suffocating swirl.

"Look at our mother...this is what you have done to her." Narges cries. But Nader khan will not grant his sister an iota of validation that might her feel worthy.

"And you, *khanom jaan*...Why didn't you stop that malevolent and devastating transaction?" Narges looks to her mother for redemption and support, but *Khanom jaan* has none to offer. She has already turned blue and nearly breathless from choking on her food.

Now, Narges rushes to take her mother to the bathroom where she will regurgitate everything she has managed to eat.

This is the typical nightly discourse at the family dinner table: a pathetic scene that has become routine.

When *Daii jaan* Nader finally speaks, it is always to remind Aunt Narges that she needs to be more vigilant in seeking treatment for her nervous disease. Then, he lights up a cigarette, drinks his tea, and

71

retires to his bedroom to sleep. It is time to close the curtain on what he calls "the nightly theater of absurdity and female hysterics."

IN THE NEXT few years, Aunt Narges' bouts of depression and episodes of rage intensify as her search to recover her dignity fails. There is indeed no medication that can eradicate her shame without obliterating her mind and her intellect. She refers to herself as the "spinster of the Board of Education," doomed to live in disgrace and sentenced to die alone and childless.

"You see, Esther, at least you have your children. You will never be alone."

Maman tries to console her sister, but she knows that words will not mitigate Narges' angst and loneliness. When she suggests a short tip to the nostalgic shores of the Caspian Sea, Narges is delighted and the sisters look forward to a week of rest and reprieve. However, it is not long before Aunt Narges becomes restless and persnickety. Just two days after our arrival, she is enraged because I have used her scissors to cut my hair. She suddenly charges at me and pulls it out of my hand, missing my eye by a millimeter. Later, as I lay on my stomach to read, she pummels me with her fist so ferociously that I hear my ribs crack and feel the air rush out of my lungs mercilessly. I lay on the ground in pain, trying to catch my breath, certain that I will never be able to walk again. Once Maman pulls her away and helps me stand up, I pledge to avoid proximity to both my aunt and to scissors for the rest of my days.

As soon as we return from our harrowing holiday,

we learn that we are about to be homeless again. Uncle Moshe's wife has had a baby and needs to hire someone to help her with chores and the care of our ailing *Naneh* Deena, my father's mother. We have no choice but to vacate my grandparents' compound and relinquish the servants' quarters to the housekeeper.

Maman has run out of excuses to explain why everything valuable in our home has vanished. She used to say that she pawned them for protection; keep them safe from the thieves. But I never believed it... I knew that it was not her possessions but her dignity that she was trying to protect. Now pregnant once again and on the verge of being homeless, Maman has no choice but to tell her mother the truth.

"I have nothing of value left to sell, khanom *jaan*.... nothing except for my gold watch." She reveals tearfully.

"Take this bracelet." *Khanom jaan* removes her ornate 18-carat bracelet that her husband had given her on the day of their wedding. "This bracelet no longer suits me. Keep your watch. I know how much you cherish it."

IN JUNE 1949, when my mother is seven months pregnant, we move to a new apartment. We have two rooms on the third floor of a three-story building. There are two other rooms on the same floor, occupied by a couple with a small child. We share with this family the kitchen, and utilize the entrance hall as a common sitting room. Our landlords, Mr. and Mrs. Ebrahimi live on the main floor with their three sons. They are the gentlest and the most generous people we have ever known.

73

Our building is on *Koocheh* Tulu, a cul-de-sac on Khiaban-e Shah, the main motorway for our King. We are a short distance from the house of the Prime Minister Mossadegh, and less than a kilometer from the row of Royal Palaces and the Shah's primary residence, Palace Ekhtessasi. At the end of our cul-de-sac stands a massive structure that houses the hardware and engineering plant of the telephone company. Its entrance is located several blocks away but its imposing and permanently locked gates seal the dead-end of our street. On the other corner of the cul-de-sac is a massive barn that houses stacks of firewood and piles of coal on display for sale. Its large and tattered wooden gate sits directly on Khiaban-e Shah, where the King's motorcade and the Royal traffic often traverse. But neither the Royalty nor the neighbors seem offended by this incongruous setting. Our cul-de-sac is a remarkable amalgamation of different ethnicities and religions, all living side by side in harmony and genuine friendship. Our landlords, Mr. and Mrs. Ebrahimi are Jewish as are we. The other tenants are Aashuri, Christian and Zoroastrian. On the corner of Shah and Tulu is a colossal house that belongs to a reclusive Baha'i family. They do not socialize with anyone, but they are kind, affable, and quite civil.

The expansive estate to our left belongs to the Mokhtar family. *Docteur* Mokhtar is a highly decorated General and a skilled surgeon. He was born and raised in Turkey and studied medicine in Paris. He is a Sunni Muslim, but his wife is from an eminent line of religious Shia Imams. In 1949, *docteur* Mokhtar tended to the Shah's injury from a bullet discharged by a would-be assassin. Since then, he has become an honored friend and the private physician of the Royal family. In spite of his position and prestige, *docteur* Mokhtar, ruggedly handsome and always impeccably groomed, is a man with uncommon humility and great compassion. Everyone loves and respects him, and I gloat when he speaks to me affectionately in his charming Turkish accent. *"Bacham, shoma chetor hastid?* How are you, my child?"

General Mokhtar's family lives a life of privilege and status. They have several cars, a maid, a butler, and a military driver. Their six-bedroom house is filled with precious carpets and furnishings. Their magnificent garden is adorned with fragrant flowers, ponds, waterfalls, and fruit trees. My sister and I often watch with envy the abundance of goods, the trays of fruits and sweets, and the jugs of fresh milk that are delivered to their house daily. We rarely can afford to buy milk, meat or fruits. Rice, bread, and occasional eggs or chicken is all that we can afford. *Docteur* Mokhtar's children wear clothes that are made in *Amrika*; and they have real dolls to play with. Maman makes our dresses with donated materials, and I make our dolls with paper and sticks. We are poor but proud to be in a country that allows us to live amongst such diversity of lifestyles and religions without prejudice. I feel safe walking on the streets any time of day or night, secure that no one will harass me; and confident that if I ever get hurt, everyone will instantaneously come to help me. Sadly, this sense of trust and security is so palpably absent from the home in which I live.

TWO MONTHS AFTER we move to our new residence, in August of 1949, my mother gives birth to a long-awaited son they name Jafar who is instantly the focus of everyone's attention. Our entire family, friends, and neighbors gather in our small apartment to attend his *Milah*, the ceremonial circumcision decreed by our Jewish Law. We hardly ever have anyone come to visit but suddenly, there are so many guests that we have to empty out our bedrooms and borrow chairs from our neighbors so people can sit. Everyone has brought generous gifts of gold coins and money... perhaps enough to pay for this event and some future bills. There is abundant food, refreshments, and even special entertainment delivered by the munificence of our landlord's son, Esa who plays his accordion and makes us dance and sing.

Later that night, long after everyone is gone, my sister and I wake up to my mother's heart-wrenching cry.

"No Mordad... no...Please don't."

I rush to my parents' bedroom and witness a most chilling scene. My father is chasing my mother around the room, trying to snatch my brother from her bosom, and threatening to toss him out of the window.

"*Sedash kam nemisheh*, his wailing doesn't fade. Shut him up so I can sleep." My father growls and stumbles as he launches at my petrified mother clutching her baby.

My heart drops to my feet. I am helpless to stop him...but I know that I have to do something.

"*Bedineed* Papa, look." I grab his bottle of *aragh* and hold it up over the window, threatening to toss it away. As my father stumbles towards me, I tighten

76

my grip on the bottle, bolt out to the next room, and slide under the low-lying bed.

"*Bia*, come get it." I dare him.

"I'll get you later, *tokhm-e-sag*, seed of a bitch." My father curses and grumbles as he leaves the room.

My sister is whimpering in the closet, and I hear my mother's cry as she hums a lullaby and nurses her son to sleep.

I stay silent and motionless in my hiding place until I drift into a safe swoon.

-Khastegari-

On a fall day, soon after my brother's *Milah*, my mother dresses me up and tells me that we are going *Khastegari* for her beloved brother, my *Daii jaan* Nader. A matchmaker has found a girl who meets my uncle's scrupulous specifications: she is light-skinned, underprivileged, uneducated, and naïve.

We pick up *Khanom jaan*, and take a taxi to Sar Chall, the Jewish ghetto on the outskirts of the city. This is where the seventeen year-old potential bride for my uncle lives.

As Maman and my grandmother discuss with the girl's parents the terms of engagement and the wedding, she briefly appears at the door, as if on cue, and stares at us sheepishly. Her name is Marjan. She has light complexion and appears quite malleable and meek. She is, indeed, an appealing candidate to fulfill my uncle's needs. Moreover, her mother has delivered three sons and that, according to folklore science, makes her *pesar za*, fertile with a male cultivating uterus. Her parents explain that at age seventeen, Marjan is in tenth grade Home Economics track of high school, designed to prepare students for housekeeping and marriage. They assure us that they would have no objection to having their daughter leave school before the year's end so that she can get married. In fact, they would very much prefer a brief engagement and an expedient wedding.

ON A DECEMBER NIGHT in 1949, *Daii jaan* and Marjan are married in a modest ceremony. Just a few weeks earlier, *Daii jaan* Nader had delegated Maman to present Marjan with an engagement ring and had instructed her to arrange for a suitable wedding; one that would expose neither his fierce frugality nor his immense fortune. However, to keep with tradition, as he was now on the receiving end, Uncle Nader had sanctimoniously accepted the small *jahaz* that the bride's parents had provided for their daughter's nuptial bliss.

Now, three months after the wedding, the celebration of Marjan's pregnancy is truncated by skirmishes between the three women living under the same roof. Although it is customary for the bride to live with her husband's family, the prospect of Marjan's peaceful cohabitation with her in-laws proves to be untenable because of the vast chasm in their class and culture. Every day, Narges and *Khanom jaan* are astounded by the plethora of odd behaviors that Marjan exhibits. They echo their concern and displeasure to Nader Khan privately while Marjan sleeps or is occupied in the kitchen, eating.

"She hides there, thinking no one can see her. She stuffs her mouth with bread as if she is expecting famine." Narges reports with outrage.

"Why doesn't she say good morning, Nader khan?" *Khanom jaan* weeps with indignation. She insists that Marjan's lack of respect is deliberate; designed to create conflict. After all, hadn't her mother raised her with proper decorum...had she not taught her daughter that lack of courtesy towards others, especially elders, is insolent and unacceptable."

"It is alright Khanon.... Don't let it bother you." Nader advises his mother. He, too, has noticed his wife's peculiar behavior, but he is not at all concerned. He does not care about his mother's aristocratic pride and expectations. What matters most to him is that Marjan remains subservient and yields him sons as brilliant as he is.

"Couldn't you have found someone with culture and good manners?" Narges asks her mother, "Was a vagrant girl from the gutter the best my brother could wed?

Narges can't reconcile the fact that a girl with such unremarkable heritage has become the recipient of good fortune, while she and her sister are condemned to a life of despair.

At dinner, Marjan pushes her plate away and puts it within the reach of her husband who is savoring his meal.

"Here Nader Khan...take my share. You like your mother's cooking."

Ever since Nader had discovered that his wife's

80

cooking was unappetizing and tasteless, he had asked his mother to cook their dinners. Marjan could never duplicate the flavorful Rashti dishes that *Khanom Jaan* prepared.

"I am not hungry... Stress has destroyed my appetite again." Marjan rubs her pregnant belly. "*Bebineed* Nader Khan, look at me.... I swear to you, if this baby doesn't come out right, *beman marboot neest-ha*, it is not my problem." What she means is that she can't be blamed for it.

"You are a good actress, *Madame*, but I saw you eat enough for five babies." Narges retorts with derision.

Marjan despises her in-laws vehemently but knows that she has to make meticulous plans to persuade her husband to get rid of them. She has learned from her masters of housekeeping the valuable skill of *kharkardani,* how to turn a man into an obedient mule. She knows how to get what she wants without appearing weak. She knows that Nader Khan does not like "feminine theatrics."

"*Azizam*, you need to relax after a hard day at the Baazaar. Instead, you come home to bear the burden of your mother and your sister. They'll give you ulcers and ruin our family. They are your enemy."

Nader lights a cigarette and ponders the words of his pregnant wife.

"I swear Nader Khan, I'd rather live in a chador, a tent...but with you alone." Marjan proclaims artfully.

Nader displays a faint but encouraging smile. "*Dorost misheh*, it will be alright." He assures her, "I'll find a solution."

"*Kaii migi misheh*, Nader khan, when?" Marjan asks delicately, "Better be soon...promise me, it's gonna be before you get me pregnant again."

There is a rational and reasonable remedy to mitigate much of the domestic conflicts in *Daii jaan's* household by allowing *Khanom Jaan* and Narges to live independently on a separate floor of the three-story dwelling. But he is not willing to relinquish the rental income, even though Narges will pay her own share.

IN AUGUST 1950, Marjan gives birth to a son they name Javid. The *Milah* is a joyous event. Everyone is relieved to know that the family's name will be passed on and preserved by Nader Khan's male offspring. Although my mother has never surrendered her maiden name- the only choice she has been able to maintain since she began teaching at age sixteen- nonetheless, the privilege of passing the family name on to the next generation remains a distinct privilege that only a man can claim.

Today, as Nader watches his infant boy lay naked to be circumcised, he is triumphant to have fathered a son in his own image, one who will bear his name and possess his intimidating intellect. But as he surveys his son closely, he notices for the first time, the boy's striking resemblance to Marjan. Suddenly, his skin pales and a bitter chill obliterate his glee. What if his noble son has inherited all of his wife's genes and none of his?

He lights up a cigarette and swiftly walks away. He cannot allow for this ghastly thought to haunt him any longer.

☑

- The New Deal -

On August 19, 1953, we are suddenly in the middle of a war zone, witnessing first hand the battle between the loyal soldiers of the Shah's army and the insurgents of the newly energized revolutionary Toudeh party. Recently, the country's decade-long dispute over the Nationalization of oil culminated in massive uprisings against the Shah, leading to his departure, and subsequently to the democratic election of Prime Minister Mossadegh as the leader of our country.

For two days, while the war escalates just steps away from our home, we take shelter in the basement of our building, where children huddle together and the elderly pray for our safety. The ominous and steady sounds of mortar crossfire are terrifying. We hear them fly overhead and pierce through the walls of the building. Our lives and the future of our country are in the hands of people we don't know and can't see. It is unclear who our friends are and who will be our enemy. We are running out of food and water and don't know if at any moment, the doors will burst open and we will all be killed. We have not seen *docteur* Mokhtar and his family and don't know if they have fallen in the hands of the revolutionary army.

Eventually, in less than few days, the sounds of war and gunfire diminish, and the radio announces that a swift CIA-sponsored *Coup-d'état* has ended Mossadegh's regime and returned the Shah to power. The former Prime Minister and our short-term democratic leader, Mossadegh, is promptly arrested and sent away to live in exile. Once peace is fully restored, *docteur* Mokhtar returns home with his family and entire entourage- all seemingly unharmed.

AMIDST the backdrop of our national turmoil, three years after Uncle Nader had promised his wife to put an end to the saga of their domestic *mêlée*, he finds a suitable collaborator waiting at his office doorway. Peymaan, a thirty-five year-old frail, poor, and uneducated man has come looking for work. He is simple - minded, unskilled and the perfect prey for *Daii jaan*'s scheme. Peymaan needs a job desperately and Nader needs a desperate man who wants to please. With his extensive business empire and Real Estate holdings, Nader can utilize Peymaan's limited capabilities to do menial jobs for him. In turn, Peymaan will marry his spinster sister without a dowry.

"Narges Khanom is a teacher and makes a good living. She will have a considerable pension when she retires." Nader guarantees.

The wedding brings more relief than joy to both families. Peymaan is deeply grateful and for Aunt Narges, this union, albeit indecorous and pejorative, is the only chance she will ever have to claim a modicum of dignity. For Marjan, however, this is only a small victory. Her triumph will not be complete until *Khanom jaan,* too, is desperate to leave.

At age thirty-six, Aunt Narges gives birth to a girl she names Meena. Marjan, at age twenty-one, delivers her second child, a girl, named Lidia, and *Khanom jaan* at sixty-three, in poor health and disaffected by her son and his wife, decides to take exile in Phelestine, where she hopes to receive compassion and care in the land where her ancestors had once lived.

Bahman 1333: February 1955
Dear Diary,
By the time I was nine years old, the needle and whip punishment that my earthly father had initiated when I was five finally ended. Perhaps my father had grown weary or I had ceased to misbehave but nonetheless, I was so relieved that I vowed to forget that portion of my childhood and perhaps even all the rest of it. Then at age eleven, a different form of cruelty was exacted upon me... this time by another authority: the one who resides in the heavens and oversees the lives of everything living. He bestowed upon me the curse of womanhood: the budding breasts and the menace of menstruation so dreadful and so excruciatingly painful that I wished to die every time I saw blood on my underwear. I

knew I could not stop the bleeding, but I sewed myself a contraption that flattened my breasts and made them disappear. When the monthly "regle" arrived, I screamed and cried with agonizing pain, pleading with God to strike me dead. But he never heard me or just didn't care. Instead, it was my own father who came to my rescue. He heard my pathetic cry and felt sorry for me. He offered me his poison and I drank it eagerly. It dulled my pain and helped me forgive him.

Yesterday, my parents fought for a long time about where to get money to pay the rent. My sister and brother started crying and I joined them because I was in pain... I had a terrible toothache and my parents couldn't afford to take me to the dentist. I took a shot of Papa's aragh to numb the pain and tried to cheer up my sister and brother. I told them I would ask my parents to pawn me for money so they could pay the bills. They thought it was funny. I would do anything to stop the fighting.

Later, Papa left the house to claim a 500-Toman loan he had given to a charlatan. But he returned with a bloody nose and bruises all over his body. He wanted Maman to go to her brother and borrow money. He always taunts her for not having brought him a dowry.

"Go borrow 200 Toman from your poolparast, money-worshipping brother." Papa roars, "He owes you for stealing all of your father's money."

Maman always says she would kill herself before asking her brother for anything because if he had regarded her worthy, he would not have given her away when she was just thirteen.

"I am going to turn him over to the Military Police and have him arrested." Papa threatens, insisting that Daii jaan Nader had evaded his national duty to serve in the military.

Later, Maman left the house and in a couple of hours, returned with 300 Toman. She had gone to see the man who had beat up my father and, somehow, she had convinced him to give her some money. It was just enough to pay the rent and buy us some groceries. But, our troubles were not over yet. At night, when I went downstairs to put our cheese and milk in our landlord's refrigerator, Mrs. Ebrahimi called me over to talk to me.

"Look, Azadeh joon, there is a notice from the electric company. It's a warning that if you don't pay your bill, they will turn off your electricity."

I knew we had not paid our electric bill in two months. It was now over 200 Toman and I didn't know how we could come up with that kind of money. I was so embarrassed that I wished the earth would open up and swallow me. When I came back upstairs, Papa was into his hand-washing ritual. He washes his hands over and over again as if he is trying to wash away some dirty slime that is stuck to his fingers.

"Papa, we have to pay the electric bill...what are we going to do?"

"Shut up. Don't you see I am busy?" He growled, narrowing his eyes at me.

Later, he asked me to bring him his cigarettes. When I told him that I forgot to buy them, he cursed me and smacked me in the face.

Oh, dear God...who should I turn to for help? My mother bears the entire burden of our family. I feel so sorry for her. I don't know how she survives our endless crises. Yesterday, she had to take my sister to docteur Mohafez because she has been complaining that her heart hurts and keeps her up at night. Fortunately, Dr. Mohafez is Maman's cousin and doesn't charge her a fee. He told Maman that there was nothing wrong with my sister's heart, but I think he is wrong... Just last week, Ruhie threw a brass mortar at my brother that missed his head by two centimeters. It could have killed him instantly. Then later, she tried to set my diary on fire. I asked her why, and she called me stupid. I think her heart is missing something; that is why she is so mean.

My brother, too, is always sick and my mother prays to God every time he has fever. I know that God will not make my brother well but I pray too, because there is nothing else I can do. Then, when my brother's temperature soars at night, I run to the American drugstore on Pahlavi Avenue to buy medicine for him. Sometimes during the night, he gets worse and we rush him to the all-night daroo saaz, pharmacy to get him a shot of penicillin. The doctor has told Maman that Jafar's tonsils have to be removed, but we can't afford it...not until Maman starts teaching again.

I always dream of becoming a doctor someday and saving the lives of children who can't afford to get well.

Bahman 1334: February 1956
Dear Diary,
As soon as my brother turned seven and started school, Maman went back to work and with her first paycheck; she had my

brother's tonsils removed. Then she bought him a pedal car to reward him for getting well. But once Jafar was out of bed, he became a tyrant and I, his devoted subject. Every day, he demands that I take his bulky toy car down thirty-seven steps onto the street so that he can cruise in it and taunt the other kids. Then an hour later, he wants me to take it upstairs, only to bring it back down again. Sometimes he has me going up and down several times in one afternoon. I never say "No" to him... No one ever does, because he is a boy and only boys can grow up to be kings.

Maman teaches algebra and calculus at two high schools and works long days. But, she is glad to be earning an income and being in the company of colleagues and friends who share her passion for education. She hopes to pay our debts and bring home some of our valuables from the pawnshop. She wants to give our barren home some dignity, but Papa is already conjuring up business ventures to invest her money.

Farvardin 1335: April 1956
Dear Diary,
I have an awful secret to tell you. Please be my friend and never let anyone know what I reveal to you.

Last week, we went to Shiraz to spend Noe Rooz with my father's cousin, Mehran. We were so thankful that Maman was earning an income and could treat us to a holiday. But then, something dreadful happened the very first night we were there. I couldn't tell Maman the truth because I knew it would decimate her as it has done me. But since that horrific night, I have not been feeling right. My mind is in disarray and there is this awful panic that makes me shudder all day. I want to believe that what happened was nothing more than a nightmare. But I know it was real. I thought I was going to die. I wanted to die more than anything, but I didn't know how to kill myself. I was afraid that if I didn't do it the right way, then I would be only half-dead and more of a burden for my mother. But even if I succeeded, what would happen to my poor Maman... she would surely be crying and agonizing over my death every day. She has already lost two children. I don't want to cause her any more pain, but I don't know how to end my pain.

I have flashbacks ... images of that woman pacing the floor, the brass bed with me laying under it... those men looking at my naked body...who were they and why did I remember them suddenly after that horrific night in Shiraz? I can't understand any of it. I am so scared ... so afraid that I will lose my mind and become divaneh. At night, I am restless and can't fall asleep; and if I do, I wake up so terrified that I can't stand myself and want to run away.

Tir 1335: September 1956
Dear Diary,
Ever since Maman started to teach, her name has become synonymous with fame. She is one of the most respected teachers in Vezarat-e Farhang, the Ministry of Higher Education. She has received praise and recognition in the academic community not only for her excellence in teaching, but also for her uncompromising sense of ethics, extraordinary wisdom, and her effervescent personality. Since the earlier days, when her teaching career began in Rasht, Maman has retained her maiden name in all her professional endeavors. For this reason, teachers at my school don't know that I am her daughter. I am so intensely in awe and proud of my mother that I wish we shared the same last name so that I could brag being her daughter when people praise her. I have even asked her if I could assume her maiden name as my own when I am an adult and don't need my father's

consent.

At the end of ninth grade, however, for the first time, I wished that I was not known as the daughter of my illustrious mother. That was the day I received my final report card and saw that I had a failing grade in all my subjects. I let out a scream so loud that my eardrums fluttered and my head began to spin. There had to be a gross error...some absurd mistake. How could I have failed all of my core subjects: chemistry, physics, calculus, and even literature. These were all prerequisites for my entry to medical college, and I had always received excellent scores in all these subjects. This was a matter so grave that I felt I might as well have been assassinated. Academic success has always been the only source of pride within my reach and the only reliable pillar of my security. Had it not been for my intense focus on my studies, I could not have saved my sanity in the months that followed the Shiraz nightmare. It was my determination to maintain my scholastic standing that helped me restrain the chaos in my mind and postpone the demise of my spirit. But now suddenly, everything that had kept me safe and stable was taken away.

I waited for Maman to come home but by then, I had cried myself to exhaustion and could hardly speak. I handed her my report card and waited for her to rescue me. Maman looked at my report card and gasped in disbelief.

"Zan-e bisharaf, that immoral woman."

"Ki Maman? Who? I pleaded with agitated curiosity. It was obvious that she knew something. She was quite livid but apparently not too surprised. She sat on the floor next to me.... where I had succumbed. She lifted my aching head to look at her as she explained everything.

"You see, azizam, the principal of my school, Khanom Ekbatani demanded that I give a passing grade in Algebra to the daughter of a prominent family. Of course, I refused." Maman spoke with a firm voice, proud and confident that she had done the right thing.

"Ekbatani?" I bellowed, "But Maman, that is the name of my principal."

"Yes, they are sisters."

"O.K. I can figure out the rest Maman, but how did she know I was your daughter?"

"I had introduced myself to your principal earlier this year when I registered you." She sighed ruefully.

"So, your principal had her sister change my final grades and fail me in all my subjects."

"Yes, even though my principal has already created a dossier against me, charging me with subordination," Maman shook her head in exasperation, "I suppose punishing me was not enough to satisfy her."

"What are we going to do, Maman?" I felt utterly hopeless and started sobbing again.

"Well, she will not get her way." Maman scoffed. "Don't worry azizam. I will take my case to the Ministry of Education and ask for a neutral party to administer and grade your finals."

"But I have to attend summer school, Maman. That is unbearable."

"I am so sorry, azizam. Sometimes we have to pay a price for doing the right thing, but we can never compromise our integrity."

I was proud of my mother for not yielding to the tyranny of corruption and favoritism, which is unfortunately rampant. Maman would gladly offer free tutoring to a student who needed help but would never take roshveh, bribe to give a passing grade to a student who did not deserve it. Although the corrupt principal had disposed of all my final exams, she had not been able to erase my quarterly grades on my permanent report card, which clearly demonstrated the caliber of my performance throughout the year. This was the document Maman presented to the Ministry of Education to justify her case; that my exams should be administered and graded by an impartial auditor.

I was utterly demoralized by this cruel injustice and hated my life more than ever. But my future was in jeopardy. I could not risk losing the entire year and repeating ninth grade. I attended summer school and studied harder than ever. I even asked Daii jaan to tutor me in subjects I had never studied. Naturally, I had to endure his denigration for "having the inferior mind of a female." However, I was fully prepared not to fail. It was a grueling sentence for believing in justice, but at the end I was victorious. I even managed to secure second place in my class of seventy students.

Lately, Maman has not been feeling well. She works very hard. She wakes up early for work and teaches until late in the afternoon. Then, she stays after school to tutor her underprivileged students. When she comes home, she has to deal with Papa's drinking and abominable behavior.

I have asked my mother to leave all the affairs of the household to me because I know that she endures so much more than anyone can bear.

Every day after school, I do the daily grocery

shopping. When I get home, I go straight to the kitchen to clean up and start preparing our dinner. We have no water coming from the faucet, so I sit on the floor to wash the dishes. My legs hurt and I am infinitely tired. If I cry, I do it quietly. I pretend that I am all right because I don't want Maman to worry about me. Most families have a housekeeper, somebody's orphaned child who works for them in exchange for food and shelter. We can't afford to do that because we have neither the extra room nor the means to feed another hungry belly.

Maman's calculus class: Shahnaz High school:
(Tehran: Circa 1956)

ON A FALL DAY in 1957, a week after our school year
has begun, I walk the three-kilometer trek from school
and just as I turn into Tulu Avenue, I am suddenly
struck with an intense stabbing sensation in the lower
right of my abdomen. Instantly, I am doubled over
with excruciating pain and brought to my knees.

Docteur Mokhtar's chauffeur is locking up the
office and hears my wail of agony. He sees me
hanging onto the wall, unable to walk, and barely
standing.

"Wait, Azadeh Khanom." He implores me, as he
runs inside the house.

Minutes later, *docteur* Mokhtar rushes out with

his entire staff and family behind him. He gives me a quick survey and then gently, he carries me into his Military jeep.

"Get us to the hospital, quickly." *Docteur* Mokhtar commands his chauffeur to get behind the wheel.

"It's her appendix..." he calls out to his wife and children who are looking on fretfully. "She needs surgery immediately."

WHEN I WAKE UP in my hospital bed, Maman is crying and chanting gratitude to her God and to *docteur* Mokhtar for having saved me. My roommate, Shahrzad, a young self-declared comedian is telling jokes to distract Maman from worry. Her comedy is treacherously funny. She is rattling off jokes so fast, I can't catch my breath from laughing and my eyes are tearing up so much that I can hardly see.

"Please Shahrzad *joon*, stop." I plead. "I can feel the stitches popping."

Shahrzad is impervious to my appeals and warning. Relief finally comes only when *docteur* Mokhtar walks in.

"*Shoma chetor hasteed, dokhtaram*? How are you, my daughter?"

Instantly, I feel a sense of wellness. His presence exudes such calm and confidence that I feel safe and worry-free. I have always wished I had a father like him.

I smile. "*Merci, khaili moteshakeram:* Thank you. I am very much indebted to you."

He looks me over and checks my temperature, and then asks Maman to step outside for a moment.

As Shahrzad resumes her comedic endeavor,

Maman returns, and she is beaming. *Docteur* Mokhtar has told her that she does not have to worry about my medical bills. "Azadeh is like my own daughter." He has said to her, thanking her for having tutored his children in mathematics on many occasions.

I am so struck by *docteur* Mokhtar's immense and unsolicited generosity that I burst out crying. He must know that we can't afford anything. He wants to save Maman from the embarrassment of having to borrow money.

Shahrzad finally takes a break from telling jokes. "O.K. Go ahead and weep. You have to cry to make room for laughter." She counsels mercifully.

Farvardin 1337: March 1958
Dear Diary,
Today, on the first day of Noe Rooz, as Shah delivered his New Year Greeting on the radio, he was weeping. Yes, our King was crying as he announced his divorce from Queen Soraya because she has not been able to produce an heir to the Throne. It is a tragic conclusion to a fairy tale life. They always seemed so in love and genuinely happy. I think that Shah had become more generous since Soraya became his Queen. Last year, he donated parcels of land to teachers as a token of his appreciation for their valuable contribution to the society. I know that his benevolence made both

Maman and Aunt Narges very proud and happy. Of course, it may be years before the land will be worth a substantial amount of money, but Shah's good will gave Maman and Narges a sense of dignity- the acknowledgement that they well deserve.

I cried for our Shah but even more for Queen Soraya because I had met her once at the Palace when I was in eighth grade. That year, our school athletes performed in a sports extravaganza, first before Princess Shahnaz and then at the stadium before the Queen. I had ranked first place in Ping Pong, Table Tennis, and was invited along with other athletes to join the Queen for lunch at the Palace of Sa'dabad. We spent over four hours with Soraya and I spoke to her one on one briefly. She is not only one of the most stunning women in the world, but also very gracious, kind, and genuinely empathetic. She shook hands and talked with each of us individually, asked questions, and then joined us at the table where we enjoyed a feast of exquisitely displayed and splendidly delicious cuisine. It was an extraordinary experience that I will cherish for as long as I live.

Today, however, I remember even more mournfully, the loss of my own wellbeing exactly two years ago... that dreadful night in Shiraz of which I cannot speak. I have been silently haunted by what happened that night, and also by the recurring and ghastly flashbacks of that inexplicable and disturbing memory of my infancy. I am so scared and confused. I can't let Maman know about what happened that night. But, I have asked her about the images that have suddenly surfaced to taunt me. She has confirmed the existence of the brass bed, the carpet and the woman who fits the description of the neighbor's maid, but she can't explain any of it and feels very sad and guilty that she can't erase this horrific memory from my brain. She has bought me a Mandolin to play ...something to distract me and give my mind reprieve. I try to occupy myself by learning new songs to play, doing schoolwork, and writing stories. But at night, I feel hopelessly alone and agitated. I can't tell anyone about the shame that I feel because telling someone would make me feel even more ashamed. I feel isolated and defenseless, knowing that I have to carry this burden of injustice alone for the rest of my days.

In eleventh grade, three months after our classes had begun, I decided to challenge the boundaries of justice and my fate, at least once and entirely on my own. Like my mother, I had to choose between loyalty and moral integrity and I chose the latter. It was shortly after the first quarter exams that I decided to subvert an academic coup by defying the wishes of the most popular and powerful girl in our school. Her name is Roshan. Her parents own an impressive private hospital in Tehran and her father is a well-respected physician. Roshan is a pretty girl with fair skin and blonde curly hair. She capitalizes on her parental prestige and on her vague resemblance to the French actress Brigitte Bardot. She is arrogant, spoiled, and quite self-assured. She spends her summers in Paris and London and in the winter, she skis on the slopes of Switzerland or Alborz during the holidays, always nestled amongst friends from high society. She wears European-designed clothing and is the envy of every girl except me. I simply resent her arrogance and her air of superiority.

Roshan was in all of my science classes designed to prepare us for entry to medical school. However, she was not a good student, and when our biology teacher refused to give her a passing grade on her first exam, she decreed that all the seventy students in our biology class should go on strike and demand that the teacher be fired. I refused to go along with her plan and sat in the classroom alone for the entire hour while the teacher taught the curriculum as if everyone was there. My attendance somehow saved him from getting fired. The next day, our class was ordered to resume as usual and everyone attended. Ironically, while every student feared the teacher's reprisal, I was the one who became the subject of his excessive scrutiny. He decisively and persistently treated me harshly all year so that no one would accuse him of estesnaii, favoritism without merit.

Ordibehesht 1337: April 1958
Dear Diary,
We are once again facing eviction. Even though Maman has gone back to work, we still don't have money. Papa demands that she give him her salary, and then lends it to others for their awe and loyalty. We owe our landlord two month's rent, but Papa insists that if we pay only half the rent, we will not be evicted. Now our Landlady claims that her parents are coming from Israel and they have to give them our rooms. I think they are just tired of our delinquency and want us to find shelter elsewhere. I can't blame them but I am sad to be leaving my friends. We have lived in this apartment on Tulu

Avenue for almost a decade and shared many memories with our neighbors. But now, we have to leave it all behind and look for another place.

Today, just as Maman was wondering what she could pawn for our next meal, Marjan came over. She was crying hysterically because she had burnt her husband's pants and did not know what to do. Maman calmed her down and was able to mend the trousers so expertly that Daii jaan would never know the difference. Marjan was full of gratitude when she left. She said Maman was the smartest woman in the world and the best sister-in-law any woman could ever want. In fact, she said that Maman was the sister she always wished she had, and loved her as if they were true sisters. Then she told Maman how she was overwhelmed with the care of her three children and all the housework, even though she had a maid. I wonder if Marjan has the slightest sympathy for my mother. Does she know that Maman teaches all day to support her family, takes care of her children, is ruthlessly abused by her squandering husband and yet, she never complains?

I wish I could find a way to make money and help my mother. She once sold one of my paintings and now I wish I had more to

105

sell. I want to paint but have no paint or canvas. Maman says she can't afford to buy me anything now because she has promised Ruhie to buy her a pair of dancing shoes. My sister feels so triumphant, clearly enjoying my misery. Lately, she has been very abusive towards me. She fights with me and insults me constantly.

"Toe khari, you are a stupid donkey."
She curses me whenever I don't obey her ridiculous and contemptuous commands.

"I don't want you to talk to our cousins because I am mad at them. Do you understand, you idiot?"
Yesterday, she tricked my brother to hit me with an iron rod. When I told Maman, she denied it, and then claimed that I was the one who hit her. She wanted Maman to punish me.

"Azadeh hasood -e-maneh." She said I was jealous of her and hated her.
Maman knows none of this is true. She knows how much I love my siblings and take good care of them, but she always apologizes for me and blames herself for my sister's misery. For a while, she thought Ruhie's nearsighted vision was making her angry, but even after getting her prescription eyeglasses, she is still belligerent, and instigates fights with everybody. She is just like papa; she uses his

foul words and blames everyone else when she does wrong.

Last night, I was cooking some rice for dinner, but I was so absorbed in reading that I forgot to check on it until the smell of burnt rice permeated throughout the apartment. I bolted out of the chair but it was too late. Maman was very upset with me. Her verbal reprimand would require a full volume of my diary, but that was not enough. Once we scooped the un-charred rice from the top of the pot, Maman banned me from eating. I was quite famished but fortunately, my agonizing toothache soon paled the pangs of my hunger. I drank a shot of Papa's aragh and fell asleep.

Tir 1337: June 1958
Dear Diary,
Maman has rented a house with a small yard in a nice neighborhood. We were sad to say goodbye to our friends on Tulu Avenue, but this is the nicest place we have ever lived in. We even have our own phone and a little icebox to store our food. I don't know how Maman managed to rent this house. She has even found an orphan boy who now lives with us. His name is Ali. He is a small boy with a sheepish smile and limited vocabulary. He is here to help us

with household chores, but he is lazy and quite pathetic.

Maman has been working late. She is always tired. When I come home from school, Ali is usually sleeping and snoring away like a fat little bear. He doesn't do much all day so when I come home, I help him with house chores and dinner.

Tonight, Maman came home late again and Papa was prepared to beat her up as soon as she walked in.

"Where have you been, jendeh, whore?" He roared. "You should just stay out and never come home."

Maman left to go to her mother's. This was the first time she let her family know the abuse she had endured all these years...the first time she let them see the bruises her husband had left on her face. Uncle Nader called Papa and they fought for a long time. Daii jaan was concerned not about his siter but about his own reputation.

"Bedarrak, bejahannam; to hell with you and your reputation." Papa told him, "If you were worried about your honor and your name, you shouldn't have sent your sister to me without a dowry."

Papa was screaming and calling Daii jaan names: pool parast, money worshipper, bisharaf, immoral, dowzd, thief...etc.

In a few days, relatives I had not seen in a long time were coming by every day. They sat for hours talking to my parents while I hid in the next room eavesdropping and smoking cigarettes. I couldn't make much sense of anything, but while we had company, we also had peace and quiet.

My father's bad temper and indolence drive me insane. Today, he wanted me to light up a cigarette and bring it to him. Then he told me to set the alarm clock for him. He must have an appointment with another charlatan who will promise him the moon and take his money. I waited to hear the time announcement on the radio before I set the alarm but because I didn't jump up right away, he thought I had disobeyed him. Now that of course, quickly got him out of his chair. He delivered such a hard blow to my chest that I couldn't catch my breath and fell to the ground. I don't know why I always try to be a step ahead of everything. I think of the consequences all at once and want to prevent bad things from happening. But at the end, everything backfires on me...so here I am, being punished for trying to do the right thing.

When I am not busy studying, or reading or doing chores, I am writing stories with happy endings. I don't think our story will ever have a happy ending. I hate my life and truly hope for it to end before I am sixteen. I have lived too many years already. I wish I could talk to the spirit of my deceased Uncle Azad and ask him to stop saving me. I would rather be where he is.

There is little optimism anywhere these days. Today, Shah returned from visiting the areas hit by mudslides and flood. There has been loss of many human lives in Kashan and its vicinity. It is so hot in the South that people are literally dying from heat or going crazy. One policeman was reported to have taken a gun chasing after people on the streets of Abadan. A man stuck his head under a water dam and drowned. The only promising news lately, has come from Ghom and Alborz where an abundant source of oil has been discovered. Iran could become the largest producer of oil in the world and this could bring a lot of wealth to our people or to the foreigners who exploit the resources of our country. We sell our oil so we can buy cars, toys, Coke and Pepsi. Today, we bought a bottle of Coca Cola for ten Rial, and each had a sip. It was a luxury we could hardly afford.

-Tremors of Freedom-

My graduation from high school is only a brief amnesty from the persistent chaos that threatens my sanity. In fact, it has become the spark for an avalanche of disaster, bound to bury us all beneath. Ever since Uncle Abe and my cousin Parviz who live in *Amrika* came to visit last year, Maman and I have concluded that it is best for me to leave Iran and pursue my education in a country where women enjoy equal rights and opportunities. At first, I was puzzled that my mother was willing to let me go away alone to a foreign country because she has always been very protective of me, allowing me only limited freedom to socialize with men and never without chaperoning me. So now, her sudden liberal attitude is totally baffling me. I know that she wants me never to suffer as she did; oppressed and bound to a life that was chosen by others. I know that she wants me to be free to choose my own destiny. I know, too, that the only way I can save myself and rescue my mother and

111

my siblings is to leave behind this stifling oppression and inexorable poverty.

THE DAY after I graduate from high school, Maman announces that she wants to divorce my father. This, of course, should bear no surprise. Indeed, what merits the ultimate level of awe is that she has been able to survive so many years of abuse and brutality without breach. Divorce, however, in our culture, is an entirely different matter. It is a taboo subject that is neither discussed nor pursued by women. It is the exclusive right and prerogative of men to ask for divorce or to grant it. Children belong to their father and must live with him as a matter of preserving his honor. For a woman, however, there shall be a life of dishonor, alienation, and shame. Papa is willing to divorce Maman on one condition; she can never see her children. But Papa can't take care of himself, let alone my two young siblings. His solution is to send them off to a Kibbutz in Israel, where Jewish orphans live and work under the care and supervision of the Israeli government. Maman is going to court to fight the system. She wants to find a judge who will rule against our archaic family law and grant her custody of her children. It is a gargantuan task that no one believes she will win.

I am lost in a quagmire of fear and confusion, oddly relieved that I am not a part of this custody equation but worried about the fate of my mother, my fourteen-year-old sister, and my ten-year-old brother. I know with certainty that once my parents are divorced, there is no chance for me to survive the shame and humiliation of the community. I already

112

carry my own burden of shame; the disgrace that has been slowly and quietly thrashing and obliterating me. Now, my only hope and salvation is to leave and pursue my education so that someday I can take care of my siblings and my mother.

These days, our house is filled with grief and sadness. It resembles a morgue, even though no one is dead.

"Maman, I hate everything about life. I hate living." I confess impassively.

"Don't be weak, *azizam*. You must hold your head high and fight like a man!" She counsels.

"Of course Maman, we must fight like a man," I mutter sardonically, "Which man, Maman *joon*? Surely not a man like my father."

Maman is quiet, and so I explicate: "The only women I know who seem happy are those who let men do all the fighting for them. Women are not supposed to be fighters or hunters, Maman." I protest. "Where did you get that idea?"

Maman looks very surprised. *"Bisharaf, zaboon daravordi;* you rascal...you have grown quite a tongue." She means I am getting too wise for my own good. I know it is my mother's legacy to fight for her life. She will do it, as her mother has done and I, too, will follow her imprint just as a duckling would follow its lead.

Later, while Maman and I are engrossed in a conversation about our future and her chance of getting custody, we hear my brother in the other room screaming and yelping. We rush to find him sprawled on the floor, pale and trembling.

"What happened, Jafar?" We kneel down beside

him, taking his pulse and urging him to tell us what is wrong with him. He scans the floor and points to a nail, then fixes his eyes on an electrical wall outlet that he has apparently tried to dismantle. Things that he can take apart have always fascinated my brother. This time, his curiosity has earned him a sobering jolt that he is not going to forget. We give him hugs, sharbat, elixir, and plead that he would never do anything so stupid again. But, he likes to push the limits and there is no guarantee he will listen.

At night, my parents fight for a very long time. Maman is trying to convince Papa to let her keep my siblings, but he would rather send them away than to let my mother win. It is a sad thing about people without self-esteem...they diminish others to make themselves feel mighty.

As the shouting escalates, I stuff my ears with cotton and begin to read a book to escape my reality. After a while, when I sense that the screaming has stopped, I unplug my ears and hear my mother's wrenching words that make my heart constrict and race with fear.

"I am going to kill myself." Maman shrieks.

I run to the bedroom and see her holding an inkwell to her mouth. I snatch it out of her hand and taste the ink on my lips as it splatters against my face and spills onto the ground.

"Maman *joon*, what is going to happen to us without you?" I beg, as tears flood my face.

"Don't you care what happens to us if you die?" I ask as I prey for my own life to end right here and now.

My heart aches for my mother, but do I have the

right to ask her to live this brutal existence when I, too, want to find a way out?

"You always tell me to be strong, Maman. I promise everything will get better." I say feigning optimism.

I wipe my face, clean the floor, and then bring my mother some *sharbat* and cigarettes. I light up a cigarette for myself and once again, I turn to my books to distract myself. I have already cried over "Les Miserables" more than a dozen times, pretended to be every one of the sisters in Louisa May Alcott's "Little Women," and played the imaginary part of every protagonist in Camus' novels. But today, I am reading the works of Sadegh Hedayat because it is well –suited for me. He talks not about hope but about hopelessness. He guides his readers to solidify their decision to end their lives. Recently, a fifth-year medical student ended his life. He was handsome, wealthy and seemingly strong. His name was Sheeri, the Lion. Even a lion can get tired of fighting. These were his last words:

"I have ended my life in search of eternal Peace."

I think eternal peace is the absence of pain.

I HAVE BEEN working at Banque Melli since I graduated from high school. Today at work, the bank Manager, Mr. Mahboob calls me into his office.

"Please sit down, *Khanom-e- aziz*, dear lady." He pulls over a chair and asks me to sit. I am sure he is going to lecture me on an error I have made on our new fancy cash register machines.

"Azadeh Khanom, one of our customers has come to me asking about you. He wants to send his family for *Khastegari*."

"Who is he Sir?" I pretend ignorance.

"*Agha-e* Naseeri." He pauses to forge an air of portentousness. "I am sure you know of the stellar reputation of his family."

"I believe they have already contacted my elder *Amoo*, my father's brother." I say with indifference.

"I must tell you, this is the best opportunity you will ever have in your life. This young man is the most sought-after bachelor in the Jewish community. He has extraordinary wealth. You will never be in want for anything."

"*Agha-e* Mahboob, money does not guarantee happiness." Although I have never known anything but poverty, I know that all the wealth in the world can't diminish my shame.

Mr. Mahboob is visibly dumbfounded, perhaps even downcast.

"I want the best for you, Azadeh Khanon. You are a beautiful, smart, and graceful young woman. You deserve a good man to take care of you."

I wish I could tell him that I can never trust anyone to take care of me; that I have learned to live without what I need, and that my only ambition in life is to save my mother and my siblings from their life of misery. I wish I could make him understand how allowing someone to take care of my needs is tantamount to abandoning my family... It is like running out of a burning building believing that my exit would extinguish the flames behind me. But instead, I thank him and tell him that I am too young to get married.

Late in the afternoon, I see my *Khastegar,* the man

who has been in my pursuit. Mr. Mahboob told me that he came to the bank regularly, often with the intention to see me. Now that he is standing before me, I realize that he has come to me many times before to render his transactions. He is quite handsome, tall and rather slim. He has kind hazel eyes, a chiseled face, and a delightful smile. He seems to be in his mid-twenties, which may be the reason I have not paid attention to him. After all, I am not entirely blind to men who are attractive... I keep them hidden in my private world of fantasy, along with my collection of love letters and poetry from boys who claim to love me. Older men, however, do not appeal to me and this suitor, handsome as he is, would be too old to partake in my fantasy.

- Bondage To Espionage -

There is suddenly a bizarre mystery threatening us and adding more chaos to our already wretched lives. Two days ago, our houseboy Ali told us that four men had approached him on the street and wanted to know if Maman was home. He says he heard one of the men say something about kidnapping. Maman is terrified. She tries to interrogate Ali for more information but he is evasive and uncooperative.

"I have never seen these men before." He snickers, making us wonder if he is telling the truth. Is this a hoax? Is it some wild story that Ali has conjured up to scare us...but why? Maman and I stay up half the night wondering what we should do. However, without any reliable information, we finally decide to put the whole conundrum and ourselves to sleep.

Yesterday, some evidence came to light but only added more puzzle to the mystery. A tall handsome man wearing black suit and dark glasses came to our door. He did not say his name but asked if my mother had come home yet.

"No..." I said curtly, "And you are...?" I waited for him to introduce himself but he ignored my inquiry.

"Tell her that I must talk to her." He said in a deep and stern voice, and then quickly turned around and walked away.

I stood at the door and watched him disappear around the corner. I was both intrigued and scared by his audacity to demand my attention without introducing himself. Does Maman know him? Maybe he had come on some official business from *Daargostary*, the Ministry of Justice, regarding Maman's appeal for child custody. But later, when I told her about this stranger's visit, she seemed quite agitated and uneasy.

"I know him. His name is Farsheed. He is helping me get custody, but I can't tell you anything else."

Then today, when I came home from work, I found Maman crying and beating herself. *Khanom jaan* who has recently returned from Israel had come over to tell her that Nader Khan was quite upset with her. Someone had seen Maman in a taxi with a young man and reported it to her brother. *Daii jaan* had been livid. He had instructed *Khanom jaan* to interrogate her unruly daughter and demand a *dalleel,* a logical explanation for her dishonorable spectacle. "Why is Esther marring our reputation? How dare she behave in such immoral fashion?" He had exclaimed. "Tell her that she must cast aside both the notion of divorcing her husband and sending her daughter away." Then he had decreed: "Azadeh should be married off immediately to repair the damage."

119

Khanom jaan cries as she relates to Maman her son's stern message. She does not want to deny her daughter the freedom that she has finally coveted after so many years of torment.

Maman is in her mode of self-mutilation. She is digging her nails into her flesh and blood is seeping out from under it.

"How long will it be before I can be liberated from this bondage? Am I not human to want to be free from this hell?"

My heart aches and my stomach is wrenching with pain. I try to stop her from scraping her skin, but she pulls away and strikes her fist against her chest...over and over again.

"Please Maman.... Please stop." I beg, as my silent tears turn into desperate shrieks.

"I don't deserve to live," she wails, "Nader Khan never thought I was a worthy human being..." She resumes cutting into her skin.

"Let them say what they want about you." I plead. "Your brother doesn't own you... No one owns you, Maman... You are free."

Now *Khanom jaan's* throat has closed up from stress and she is gagging. I run to get her a pan in case she needs to vomit.

Maman looks at her mother fretfully and tells her she is sorry.

I am hopeless and dreadfully exhausted. I know my surrender to insanity is just days away. I light a cigarette and pretend to be someone else...a forlorn poet, telling her story in a poem just before she ends her life of misery.

"I wish father that instead of my mother's breath.
You had that night kissed the venom of death"

There is a pair of scissors on the windowsill. I reach for it and think of cutting an artery to end my pain, but who will be here to save my mother?

"Stay strong and busy." I counsel myself. I reach for a box where I keep a collection of love letters. I read them over and over again ...those eloquent and passionate words that set my heart on fire...the tender words from young men.... boys who have bravely and surreptitiously expressed their love for me and I have ignored them...letting them believe that I am heartless and immune to loving them.

I hear Maman and *Khanom jaan* leave the house. I presume they have decided to go and talk to Nader. While they are gone, the mystery man calls several times, and I hang up on him every time. I wonder if he is the man who was seen with Maman in the taxicab. I have asked her several times about this menacing stranger, but she is always gives me vague answers.

"His life is being threatened, too." She had once said glibly.

"What are you saying, Maman?" I shouted fretfully, "Does this mean that your life is in danger?"

"I don't know *azizam.*"

My mind is whirling with fear and frustration. I know with certainty that this man is not trustworthy. He is a liar and a chameleon with a sinister plan. I know that somehow, my mother has become his hostage. Just yesterday, Maman told me that she fears Ali is going to poison us...put something in our food to kill us. I am so terrified. I don't know why anyone would want to kill us. Nonetheless, I have warned Ali to stay out of the kitchen and not touch anything that will touch our mouths. I am driving him and myself crazy. I watch his every move, and his wicked smile scares me out of my mind. At night, I can't sleep because I am deluged by fear and uncertainty. I know I have no choice but to kill myself or run away to *Amrika*. I have already started to pack my suitcase. Tomorrow, I will call my Uncle Moshe and ask him to help me find a discounted plane ticket from *L' Aavant Express*. I will buy my ticket to freedom. I will work and study hard to become a physician. Then I'll be able to save my family from this dreadful cesspool. I know that I am seeing my future in fast-forward motion. I know there will be unforeseeable obstacles, years of dedication, sacrifices and hard work, before I can achieve my goal. But I cannot slow down for a moment because I know I will succumb to despair, otherwise.

The phone rings again. It is Farsheed.

"Where is your mother...when will she be home?" He demands intrepidly.

"I don't know." I say curtly and hang up.

My brother is playing outside in a puddle of water. I am so worried about him because he is often sick and we don't know what is wrong with him. Maman is agonized that rheumatic fever has weakened his heart and will kill him at a young age.

"You have rheumatism. You are not supposed to keep your feet in cold water." I plead, "I've made you lunch...Come eat."

"I am glad I have rheumatism." he says with abandon, "I don't care."

Oh no, I cringe.... This little boy has already

become a martyr. This will always be our legacy.

MAMAN HAS TOLD my sister that whatever she is doing is for my protection. Now Ruhie is mad at me and hates me more than ever. She wants me to explain to her why their lives are being turned upside down because of me. I tell her that I have no answers and now, I am plagued with even more questions to wreck my brain.

Oh, what a confounding tapestry our destiny has woven, and what helpless pawns we are in the grip of its trickery. Soon, my sister and brother will be sent to a Kibbutz in Israel and I, too, will go to a foreign land. We will be homeless once again and this time, far away from our homeland.⸙

I stand amid the roar
Of a surf-tormented shore,
And I hold within my hand
Grains of the golden sand—
How few! Yet how they creep
Through my fingers to the deep,
While I weep–while I weep!
O God! Can I not grasp
Them with a tighter clasp?
O God! Can I not save
One from the pitiless wave?
Is all that we see or seem
But a dream within a dream?
Edgar Allan Poe

- Murky Horizon -

On May 21, 1960, thousands of miles away from my home and birthplace, I step on the land that is to become home for my new birth. This momentous day is the beginning of a new chapter in my life; it is the day of my emancipation from shame and the day that I will begin to take charge of my own fate.

As I approach the airport's waiting area, I see Uncle Abe in the back of the crowd waving: "Azadeh, Azadeh...come here, come this way."

I have not heard anyone call my name in over two days. I hasten my pace to join my uncle. He has brought a young man with him. His name is Bijan, a distant cousin who has graciously offered to pick me up at the airport because Uncle Abe does not own a vehicle. We drive in Bijan's late model car and arrive at my uncle's apartment within twenty minutes.

Abe lives on the second floor of a two –story

garden apartment surrounded by three other homogeneous units, each overlooking a small common courtyard in the center. We walk up twelve steps to a narrow doorway, which opens to the living room, the kitchen, and a small dining room. His wife Henrietta and two children, eight-year old Mike and five-year old Jill, say hello and look me over with curiosity and muddled enthusiasm. I am told that Mike has relinquished his room to accommodate me and will be sharing his sister's bedroom for the duration of what I expect to be a short stay. I thank Mike and give everyone a special gift. I have also brought them an exquisite handcrafted silver vase, a token of my appreciation for their hospitality. I show my uncle the antique signet ring and let him know that I am anxious to get a plane ticket and leave for Berkeley.

"Papa told me that this is a valuable piece of antique. He said you know reputable Persian antique dealers and can sell it for me."

Uncle Abe's eyes open with inspired curiosity and now suddenly, he insists on speaking to me in English, which I find even more difficult to decipher than his Farsi. I am surprised at his illiteracy and heavily accented vocabulary, even though he has lived in America for over twenty years.

"Oh yeah, I know who to see about this...He's Bijan's uncle. I take it to him tomorrow...ve"ll see if it's vorth anything."

"*Amoo jaan*, dear uncle, I am counting on the sale of this antique to help pay for my room and board at Berkley." I remind him.

In the next two days, I help Henrietta with

housekeeping chores and wait eagerly for my uncle to come home with good news. I don't know what my uncle does for a living, but he seems aimless and has an air of superiority that seems totally superfluous. He doesn't seem to have a routine or a work schedule. He leaves at random hours of the day and when her returns, he lectures me incessantly at the dinner table.

"Vatch vat you eat...you don vanna get fat."

Every time I ask Abe about the ring, he tells me that the antique dealer is in Europe.

"You should estop to vorry." He advises, "vhy you vanna go to California? Ve have good college here... Go to Queens College...it's very nearby."

"I have to go where I have been accepted. It is Berkley or UCLA." I explain, "Otherwise, my visa will be forfeited." I insist and explain again and again.

SINCE MY arrival at my uncle's house, I have sensed that this is not the home of "Ozzie and Harriet." Henrietta is at home all day playing the role of the happy housewife, but she seems hardly content. The country is abuzz with the presidential elections and the image of John Fitzgerald Kennedy is the only thing that elicits Henrietta's joy and attention.

"Isn't he so handsome, Azadeh?" She cheers.

Mike and Jill are polite and obedient but don't appear to be carefree and happy. Their father doesn't spend any time with them, but he seems to have ample time on his hand to pay attention to me. He regularly criticizes me, gives me advice, and ultimately insists that I should not leave.

Two weeks have passed since my arrival, and I have become increasingly more anxious about my visa

126

and dreadfully more suspicious of my uncle's intentions. Every time I ask him about the antique, he claims that the dealer has not yet returned from his journey.

There is a lump on my right wrist that has been growing rapidly, radiating pain through my hand and forearm, and limiting my movement and dexterity. The daily housework, washing, ironing, scrubbing and vacuuming exacerbates the pain and brings me to tears.

"Lemme take you to Bikman hospital...ve see vhat dey say." Abe grins haughtily. "See, dat's vhy you should stay here? Who's gonna help you in California?"

I feign a smile. I want him to think that he has prevailed, and I need his help to find relief for my pain.

We take the train to Manhattan. It is my first visit to the city and I am in awe of everything I see: the massive tall buildings rising up into the sky...the shops...the cars, and the busy streets with crowds of well-dressed pedestrians. Everything is novel and riveting... I am overwhelmed, trying to take it all in. The hospital, too, is an impressive spectacle unlike anything I have ever seen. It is vast, welcoming and clean.

Soon, a man in a white coat comes to examine my wrist.

"It is a ganglion," he explains, "It is a sack of fluid and it is sitting on a nerve. It has to be excised to relieve the pain."

In a few hours, I leave the hospital, bandaged and ganglion-free. I am grateful that I'll be excused from doing house chores for a couple of days, but certain that Abe will have me feeling indebted to him for as long as I live.

PAPA'S COUSIN, Mehran, has arrived from Tehran to marry his fiancé, Helen. I am invited to the wedding, but have neither a dress nor the proper shoes to wear to the elegant affair. I have only a few precious dollars left and still no promise from Uncle Abe that the antique relic will bring me the fortune my father had promised.

A neighbor offers me a dress she can no longer wear. It fits me well and is long enough to cover my tattered footwear.

"The dress looks good on you Azadeh." Henrietta approves. "You should put on some make up so you don't look like a teenager."

I don't know why I should look older than my age, but I concede. I feel much older than a teenager, anyway.

THE WEDDING is held at the bride's house- a beautiful palace of exotic gardens and rare treasures. Many of the guests have come from Europe to attend the ceremony. I don't know them, but some of the names sound familiar.

Mehran takes me around to introduce me to his guests.

"This is Azadeh khanom. She is the daughter of Esther khanom-e Lahijani."

"Aah... the legendary teacher of mathematics...the esteemed prodigy from Rasht." A guest comments enthusiastically, "I was honored to know her as a colleague at Shahnaz high school."

"She is a woman of exceptional wisdom and wit." Mehran concurs. "It is always a privilege to be in her company."

Many of the guests know my mother personally or have heard of her. I feel proud listening to their anecdotes and accolades as they recall a meeting or their association with her.

Later, when Mehran introduces me to the bride's father, I ask him if he is the eminent Persian antique dealer.

"Yes, he is the best expert in Persian Antiquities?

"Was he out of town recently? Did he just return from overseas?" I ask anxiously, dreading what I suspect his response would be.

"No, he has been here arranging for his daughter's wedding."

Suddenly, my chest tightens and my skin feels clammy. I am enraged and want to tell Mehran how my uncle has betrayed me, but I know that I must remain calm. I have to wait for the appropriate time and place to confront Abe.

A handsome young man in a well-tailored suit walks over to me and I am grateful to be distracted.

"*Salaam* Azadeh Khanom. My name is Mohsen Madani. You may not know that our families shared a close and enduring relationship."

"Indeed, I recognize the name. *Agha-e* Madani. Maman often spoke fondly of her friendship with your family."

"Please call me Mohsen. Would you like to join me?" He walks me to a table for two and helps me be seated.

Two hostesses appear promptly with champagne and trays of Hors D'oeuvres.

"Here's to our meeting." Mohsen smiles and raises his glass to a toast.

"*Salaamati*...cheers." I smile back, grateful that Henrietta had put makeup on me. I don't want to look like marginal teen drinking champagne amongst such sophisticated adults.

Mohsen flips open a delicate gold cigarette case and hope he offers me one. I know how to smoke cigarettes like a grownup. I was stealing my father's cigarettes since I was thirteen. It all started after he molested me. He would ask me to get him a cigarette and at first, I would light it up for him just to annoy him. But later on, I smoked because it calmed me down.

Mohsen offers me a cigarette and I take it without a second thought. As he reaches over, cupping his hand around mine to light it, I feel a warm sensation rush through my veins. I know that I am blushing, and certain that Mohsen has made note of it. He is smiling and now, I am even more embarrassed. I take a long sip of my champagne and a drag from my cigarette to distract myself.

"May I be so bold to tell you that I had a secret but serious crush on you in Iran?" Mohsen reveals extemporaneously.

I am surprised and bemused by this abrupt and unexpected expression of romance from someone I have just met.

"I don't believe we were ever introduced until tonight... where did you see me...how did you know about me?" I ask with a mixture of curiosity and trepidation.

"We were never formally introduced, but I had seen you at several gatherings. In fact, my family was planning to come for *khastegari* before you left Iran."

I scan my memory for any encounter I may have had with Mohsen and wonder what Maman would have said to a suitor from a family she knew and deeply admired.

"You can imagine my great delight when I found out that you would be here tonight." Mohsen divulges fervently.

I take another sip of my champagne but my heart rate has been escalating out of control. I have to change the subject.

"I am sure you know that I have come here to study. I want nothing more in life than to be a medical scientist." I hasten to sabotage my romantic fantasy, but Mohsen is too clever not to recognize my feeble attempt to camouflage my feelings.

"That is remarkable. I applaud you for your determination...." he pauses with an impish smile, "Passion is a good thing to have...no matter where it may lead."

In a few minutes, the voice of Nat King Cole permeates throughout the ballroom. He is singing ... *"Almost Like Being in Love."*

Mohsen asks me to dance and I lovingly remember Vaheed, the boy who had taught me the joy of dancing with a man. Tonight, away from the watchful eyes of chaperones, I am keenly cognizant of how liberating it is to share a conversation and a dance with a man, without the fear of interrogation and moral execution. I take a sigh of relief, then relax in Mohsen's arms and let him lead me into a world of sweet fantasy.

Once we sit down for dinner, he tells me that he and Mehran are in the process of establishing a business partnership. He will be leaving in a few days to manage their art and antique exhibit in London, while Mehran oversees their New York gallery.

"I will be leaving for Berkeley in a few days, as well." I say without conviction.

"As long as we are both here, perhaps we can have dinner one evening. I will show you the city. I bet you have not had a chance to see the glory of a Manhattan night, yet."

"No, I have not. I am sure it is thrilling. When do you plan to leave?"

"As soon as you agree to have dinner with me." Mohsen flashes a mischievous smile that accents the dimples in his cheeks. Then he looks me in the eyes.

"So, if you want to get rid of me, Azadeh Khanom, I suggest you have dinner with me soon."

"Very clever." I say, amused and flushed with titillating thoughts. I am now on my second glass of champagne and feeling no pain. I know I want to see him again.

"I'll be coming to New York frequently. I'll visit you wherever you are, if you don't keep running, ofcourse." He avows with remeakable insight, as he hands me his phone number. Then we mingle with other guests and dance a few more times before we say farewell.

"I look forward to our dinner Azadeh." Mohsen takes my hand to his lips with a gentle kiss, and the twinkle in his eyes makes my heart flutter with reckless reverie.

"Let's go Azadeh." Abe's grating voice steals my fantasy and turns my elation into fury. I know he has been watching me all night and will have a surplus of warnings to deliver when we get back tonight. But I am going to avoid him until I can formulate a plan.

In the morning, I try to calm and compose myself by rehearsing my words before I approach my uncle.

"*Amoo jaan,* you said the antique signet might not be worth much. Mehran is planning to return to Iran in a few days. I'd like him to take it, and give it back to Papa."

"I don't have it anymore, Azadeh. It's gone...I lost it...somebody took it." He says dispassionately, leaving me stunned.... frozen as if I am dunked in a sea of ice water. My heart is about to burst open, and I know that my hope for a new life has ended before it had even begun. I had not anticipated such despicable betrayal by a man who claims to be my uncle. He has no heart or conscience and I am helpless against him.

I collapse into a wretched cry.

"Go to Queens College... You von't need lot of money for that." He says smugly.

I feel sick...nauseated with disgust and fear. I am a prisoner...a pawn in the hands of my uncle and have nowhere to go.

SATURDAY MORNING, while I am cleaning Jill's room, Abe grabs my arms from behind and pushes me down on his daughter's bed. Before I can utter a sound, he is on top of me, rubbing his genitals against me and kissing me on the mouth so forcefully that I can't catch my breath. I am frozen with shock and terror. I gather all my strength to push him away, long enough to let out a scream.

Henrietta is in the kitchen just on the other side of the wall. She has been chatting on the phone all morning. She rushes in shrieking as she tries to pull away her tall and lanky husband with all the might of her petite stature. Abe releases me and saunters out of the room, mindless and unrepentant, as if his only lapse of judgment has been his bad timing.

Henrietta is shaking uncontrollably.

"Get out of my house." She is yelling at me.... yelling as she frantically grabs my belongings and hurls them to the bottom of the stairs.

I am horrified and speechless. My body is quivering violently and tears are coming down my face in sheets. I cannot breathe and my mind is caught in a dizzying spin. How can this be happening? Had I not just escaped my dreadful life back home, fled my abusive father and the shameful memories that damned my existence every day? Now here I am once again, a victim in the hands of my father's own brother. My Uncle...this monster of a man...this evil...this grunge...this filth, and this blemish on the face of humanity who has recklessly molested me in his own home and in the presence of his own family. But why is Henrietta mad at me? Why am I being punished? Did I cause this horrific thing?

Henrietta is now dragging my suitcase and kicking it down to the bottom of the stairs.

"Get out. Get out of my house this minute." She is pointing to the door and screaming incessantly.

I run down the stairs, my eyes blurry and my feet nearly missing every step. I topple over my suitcase and fall at the bottom of the steps.

The door upstairs shuts behind me and I know that I am on my own...homeless and with pittance for money. Oh, God...please make me die right here, right now!

I stuff everything in the suitcase and in my small valise, and then I stumble out onto the street.

Outside, the kids are playing and two women are quietly chatting. One of them sees me and signals her friend to look at me. Then they both walk towards me.

"Hi, I am Shirley, remember me?" I know she is the kind lady who had donated her dress to me for Mehran's wedding. She introduces her friend.

"This is Carol."

I struggle to speak but words are frozen in my throat. I lower my head to acknowledge the women, and then I burst into tears.

"Did they kick you out?" Shirley asks anxiously.

"It wouldn't surprise me." Carol speculates, "That man gives me the creeps."

I hide my face in my sleeve. I am mortally embarrassed. I cover my mouth to muffle the urge to tell them about the horrific thing that had just happened to me.

"Come inside." Shirley takes my suitcase as she leads me to her apartment.

"Let's see what we can do to help." Carol ponders as she hands me a box of tissues.

"Henrietta said you were going to Berkley...are you?" Shirley asks, glancing at my suitcase.

"No. I can't ..." I murmur, "I can't go to Berkeley... I don't have enough money."

The women look at one another inquisitively and

shake their head. I pray they will not press me for details.

"It is best that I stay in New York." I proclaim.

"Where will you stay?" Shirley asks worriedly.

My head is throbbing so badly I can hardly think.

"I don't know," I mutter, "I have to apply to a university here and look for housing."

Shirley holds my hands in hers to comfort me.

"Look dear, my friend is the housing director for foreign students at Queens College. I'll call her and ask her to find you a room. She can help you apply for admission there, too."

For a brief moment, I think of calling Mehran, but I would be ashamed to tell him the truth. I had learned from my mother that we had to guard our secrets as if they were our private jewels, and then we would have to take them to our grave so they would not be a liability for someone else to endure. I know that I will have to guard this secret right alongside all my other shameful memories. I will have to let it fester inside me and consume my soul until I take my last breath.

I have nowhere else to go. I want to cry out loud and demand justice, but I know that my destiny is irrevocably sealed.

It is about 2 o'clock in the afternoon when Shirley finally reaches her friend. Although it is Saturday, she offers to meet us at her campus office where she can check her rental listings.

Minutes later, we are at the Housing Director's office at Queens College, where Shirley introduces me to her friend, Claire.

"Hello darling, don't' worry. I am going to find you a nice room and then on Monday, I'll help you apply for college admission."

Claire is a stunning woman with a beautiful smile and warm eyes. I wonder what I could say to her if she asks me about my expulsion from my Uncle's home. I pray that the question will never be raised. I must never refer to Abe as my Uncle. He is a pedophile, a disgusting predator in a man's suit. I do not want to see him ever again, and I despise having to share his last name.

Claire takes a long drag from her cigarette and begins to survey her inventories.

"Look," she cheers, "There's a room for $10 a week. Can you afford it, darling?"

"Yes, I can..." I rush to reassure her, "I can afford it." I have sixty dollars left, and know that I will have to find a job before my funds and my resolve are depleted.

"O.K.... Wonderful." Claire is relieved, and goes on to explains:

"This house has six rooms upstairs; five are currently occupied by other students...all boys. You have to share the bathroom in the hallway with the other students. The landlady lives downstairs. You can do light cooking in her kitchen as long as you clean up after yourself. The house is within walking distance to the College so you can save money on transportation."

"Write this down darling, you will need it later."

She hands me a pen and a piece of paper. "This is the house phone number, so people can reach you there.... Flushing 3-7343."

Claire picks up the phone and as dials the number.

"Hello, Mrs. Wagner. I have a very lovely girl from Iran who would like to rent your vacant room. May I bring her right over?" Claire smiles and signals to me the landlord's affirmative answer, as she takes another drag from her cigarette.

"Thank you Mrs. Wagner, we'll be there in fifteen minutes."

Outside, as Shirley and Carol help me place my luggage in Claire's car, I thank them and say goodbye. I can't imagine what would have happened to me without the help and compassion of these two extraordinary strangers.

3   June   1960

My beloved mother,

I hope you are well. I miss you more than you can imagine. I am going insane being away from you. Every day at noon, I sit at the door waiting for the postman as if I were a street beggar waiting for a morsel of food. Your letters are my lifeline and sustenance; they are all I have to ease the pain of my separation from you. I feel as if I die every time the postman passes me by and does not hand me a letter from you.

Maman jaan, my beloved, I left Abe's house last week and feel at peace for this decision. I am staying in New York because I don't have money for the plane ticket to go to California. I have applied to a college nearby. It is a prestigious public university and accepts only ten foreign students each year. I have to pay very little for college and for this, I am grateful. I have started to do chores and babysitting for the families in the neighborhood to support myself.

You wrote that the manager of Banque Melli has delivered a check for the overtime work I had done during the last month of my employment. That is wonderful. I want you to keep the money. I don't want it. I will work and support myself. Please write to me and let me know how you are and what your plans are. What has become of my sister and brother? Where are they? Please ask them to write to

me before I lose my mind. Give my love to the whole family.
Ghorban-e shoma, your sacrifice, Azadeh

15 August 1960
My beautiful sister Ruhie and my precious brother Jafar, I pray that
you are both well. I live to hear from you. Your letter arrived in time;
just before I lost my mind from worry.
You can't imagine my joy when I received your letter from Israel.
What is it like to be living in a Kibbutz? I try so hard to imagine
where you are, what you eat, where you sleep and how you spend your
days. So, write to me in detail about everything. My darlings, I, too,
ask why...why did we have to be aavareh, homeless. Why have we
suffered so much misfortune and destruction? Can you believe what
destiny had in store for us? Can you believe it? It is a story that
needs to be told some day.
I wish I could be there with you so we could all cry together. But then
I say thank God that we left our miserable life behind. We had
nothing and our life was not going to get any better if we had stayed
there. Now we can look forward to a better future. I know we could
not live in Iran anymore. It is so hard to be away from each other and
from the family but we have to save ourselves.
My sweet Ruhie, what you wrote about mothers and fathers is
absolutely true. Parents are supposed to take care of their children,
but this is our destiny and we have to do all we can to make our lives
better. I hope you both get nurturing and care from the good people in
Israel so you don't feel lonely and abandoned. Please think positive
and be hopeful. I kiss your beautiful faces. Please do not despair. We
all have to be strong. You must focus on your new life and your
studies. I am glad you have each other and you are not alone. It is so
hard to be away from you. I miss you so much it hurts all the time.
Last week, Maman wrote to me and said that she will be joining you
in Israel shortly. Please put the date on your letter so I know when
you wrote it. I left Abe's house, so don't send letters to his address. I
had to run all the way there to pick up your letter. Don't worry about

me. I love you more than my life. Azadeh

25 August 1960

My dearest Maman jaan, I have been waiting for you to get settled so that I can tell you about something that has crushed the core of me in the past few months. Please Maman jaan, please forgive me for telling you about this heavy and horrifying gham – this angst that has consumed me and does not let me sleep at night. Just two weeks after I arrived here and while I was at Abe's house, the world came crashing down on me. The whole time that I was there, I lived the life of a dog... actually dogs are treated much better in this country. I worked like a maid all day and cried myself to sleep every night. Abe did not want me to leave but constantly reminded me of how much sacrifice he was making letting me stay at his house. Whenever we sat down to eat, he told me not to eat this or that because I would get fat. Then he nagged me to do more ironing, cleaning, etc. etc. It was just like the way Papa used to complain about you, no matter how hard you worked. Abe was interrogating me all the time about what happened with you and Papa. He blamed you for it all. I cried and defended you. I told him that everything he had heard about you was a lie. Then, a terrible thing happened and I had to leave. Actually, Abe's wife threw me out. The neighbors felt sorry for me and helped me find a room. Abe doesn't even care about what he has done to me. I have had to go to his house to pick up my mail several times and when he tries to talk to me, I tell him to forget that I even exist. This may not sound serious Maman, but it is much worse than it sounds. I am sorry that I have to burden you, but I need to talk to you before my heart bursts open from anguish. I am only seventeen and already so broken and ruined.

Papa writes to tell me how his family is humiliated because of your divorce. What does he know about shame and humiliation?

I don't understand any of this. Why does Papa write such terrible things about you? It kills me to read it. What does he think I am made of? Is my heart made of stone? I cry all the time...so much that

I lose track of time and forget where I am. I love you so much. I cannot bear hearing people say bad things about you.

Maman jaan, those days before I left, you were in a predicament where you could not pay attention to me. I didn't know why our family was always in chaos and since no one could explain why, I believed that everything was entirely my fault. I was your oldest child, and wanted to fix everything, but when I couldn't, I felt that I was not worthy to be your child at all. I was not good enough. I suffered a lot trying to understand the mysteries and misfortunes of our lives. I was so afraid that I was going to lose my mind and be hopelessly divaneh, crazy. If all this sounds like rubbish, I apologize. But, the truth is that I have been living in a world that scares me to death. I am confused and hopeless and have no one to lean on. I thought once I came here, things would get better because there has to be an end for everything, but my anguish has not ended and has in fact proliferated.

I swear Maman; life is not worth a black dinar. I feel like a robot and even my acceptance to college, which is quite a feat, did not make me happy. I know something is wrong with me and that is why bad things happen to me. I despise everything and everyone, especially myself.

Maman joon, I have told you only a fraction of what happened. I think I am weak and "bizarfiat" worthless because I cannot fix our problems and do not know what to do. Is that right? We can bear losing everything, but once our dignity and pride are gone, there is nothing left to live for. I can't tell you everything now, even though it may give me some peace.

I have met a Persian boy who has undoubtedly saved my life. He tries to cheer me up. He is from a military family and has been here a long time. He has become my father, my mother, brother, sister and friend. He is smart and funny, a poet and philosopher. He wipes my tears and helps me pass my days- just waiting to hear from you. I wish I could find a way to show you how much I love you and miss you. I am sorry if my words are disjointed; it is because my mind is in disarray. I love you, Azadeh

26 August 1960

My mother, my most cherished love, I remember the days that you and I would lose ourselves in such lengthy and delightful conversations that we forgot the time and the place. Now I have read your letter at least ten times and you are still far away.

You must have received my last letter where I told you about Abe and my Persian friend. I don't understand why you want my pledge to discontinue my friendship with the Persian boy, but you asked and said nothing about Abe. I don't know why you try so hard to shield me from men. Is it because you can't distinguish between a good man and a bad one or perhaps you fear that I can't do that either?

Maman joon, I do not sense anything good from your letters and I am truly grieved by what I have read. You write that you are "badbakht," an ill-fated woman? Are you not glad to have left that horrific and abusive life you had with my father? Is your life worse than it was then? How can you say that you are worthless? You are an extraordinary woman: brilliant, beautiful, and wise with a loving heart. Then why do you hate yourself so much?

I heard from Papa's relatives in Israel. They say that the man who was harassing you in Tehran has followed you to Israel. This is shocking and frightening. Let me say that the news was like dynamite that exploded in my head. Is this true? What is he doing there? Has he hurt you? Oh, dear God, I am going insane knowing that you feel so badly about yourself. Why is this happening to us? Are we not God's children? Are you not out of the hell you lived in? How are you supporting yourself? Did you not sell the land that Shah had given you? Tell me Maman; are you in need of financial help? I can work more hours and send you some money. I am so sorry about the letter that I wrote to you about my life at Abe's. I was having a bad day. I am sure I will never have a bad day like that again. You wrote to me that I was weak. You will see that not only am I not weak, but the challenges I face will make me even stronger. School opens in ten days and I have to study hard. Please be confident that I

142

would never compromise the values that you have taught me. I love
you more than anyone in the world, Azadeh

TWO WEEKS after I write to my mother, a letter arrives from Israel that tears to shreds the last fiber of my hope and strength. It is from a relative who has lived in Israel for decades. It gives me the explanation that I have needed to understand my mother's incoherent and self-loathing letter. It is another page from the dreadful chapter of her gruesome fate. I drop to the floor and sob, as I read the letter over and over again.

"The man who had followed your mother to Israel was arrested. No one knows what has happened to him. Your mother, too, was arrested, jailed and tortured. She was injected with Truth Serum and after a few days of interrogation, released to the hospital for reasons that are unclear."

The letter does not mention anything about the status of my sister and my brother except that no one knew where they were. It goes on to berate my mother as *"shahvat parast,"* a lust-seeker and a scorned woman who had been unfaithful to her husband and deserved her doomed end."

My heart races with dread and my body trembles with rage. The tormented tale of my family defies logic and deludes the most macabre of imaginations. We are caught in a cyclone of calamity, an endless barrage of disaster and tragedy from which we cannot ever be free. I feel weak at the knees, my mind is caught in a vortex of agony and my heart begs my lungs to stop breathing. I do not know if my mother and my siblings are alive or what their fate will be. All

143

the years that Papa cheated, degraded, and abused my mother, no one raised his or her voice of protest, and no one rose to help her. Now everyone was calling her the villain.

I am so scared I can't fall sleep at night. I light one cigarette after another and pace the floor hour after hour and day after day. For weeks, I have slept little and eaten even less, waiting and contemplating my end. But if my mother and my siblings are alive, they will need my help and for them, I have to remain strong.

Downstairs, the landlady offers me a cup of coffee, and I smoke cigarettes to keep my stomach from growling. Sometimes, I boil a couple of eggs before I go to work at Woolworth's Five- and -Dime stores, a few blocks away. I have lost a considerable amount of weight and I know this, because my sparse wardrobe has become obsolete. Everything I wear is too big on me, but I don't care. I have no interest in anything but hearing from my family. The longer I wait, the more I am convinced that they are all dead. That's when I think about killing myself. There is a cupboard full of drugs downstairs. I can take them all, but what if I don't die? What if I become sick and disabled? Maybe if I wait...wait and live long enough, things will get better...maybe something will change. Next week, my classes begin. I will get busy with my studies and work, and then I'll wait...maybe tomorrow will be a better day.

I write a letter to Uncle Nader. I wish I could tell him about my life and ask for his advice, but I only ask if he has heard from his sister.

15 December 1960

My dear Maman, my agonizing grief was lifted when I heard your voice on the phone. Although the words that you spoke were not coherent, I was comforted to hear from you, nonetheless. You kept saying you want me to come to Israel. How can I do that, Maman? I have no money. I have come to this country to study so that I can make a better future for you and for my siblings. Medicine is the field that I love, but I have neither the money nor the time to pursue it. Instead, I may have to consider studying something else, maybe nursing or radiography because I can finish my studies in two years. If you could just stay there for two years, then I promise to work hard and make enough money to bring you here. Even if I come to Israel, I want to have an education-a degree so that I can get a good job and take care of you. All I need to know is that you and my siblings are well so that I can concentrate on my studies and work to support myself. I worry about you day and night. Where are the kids, where do they go to school and how are you supporting yourselves? I have told Papa that I don't want him to send me any money and he should send what he can to my siblings.

I have been in shock to know that the man, who was harassing us in Tehran, has followed you to Israel. I am terrified about what he had in mind. Was he a spy on a mission to go to Israel with you? These thoughts are making me insane.

My beloved mother, if the length of this letter extended ten meters, you and I would still have a lot more to say to each other. Do you remember those days when we used to go to the bathhouse? We stayed there for three hours talking about everything. Now I take a bath in ten minutes and I have no one to talk to.

In your last letter, you wrote that your life should be a lesson to me; that I should never become a victim like you. My dear mother, are we not already victims? Our lives have been everything but ordinary. But we have to rise from the ashes of our misery and be victorious.

Maman, my heart breaks to know that you are in pain, and I wish I knew what to do to take it away.

I am sending you a picture that I took in an automatic photo machine. Please send me pictures of you and my siblings. Give them my love and write soon. Ghorban-e shoma, I am your sacrifice, Azadeh

9 January 1961
Ruhie jaan, your letter was very strange. I do not understand how or why someone in the Sokhonoot would want to arrange for your emigration to Amrika. Is Israel trying to apologize for what they did to Maman? Are they trying to rectify their mistake and reconcile the damage they have caused? Is that why they want to help you emigrate here to join me? Oh, my God…all this mystery is making me insane. Every day, there is a new twist and a new puzzle in our lives. Please write the whole truth to me. Please, investigate everything and write in detail about what is going on and what they are planning to help you with, so I know what to do and how to proceed. Once you are here, I will get you student visas and change your tourist status so you can study. Oh, God…. wouldn't that be wonderful?
Please write soon and give Maman and Jafar a thousand kisses for me. Ghorbanat, your sister Azadeh

15 January 1961
Maman Jaan, your letter has grieved me beyond limit, but you did well to write me a few words, after a very long time, and before sorrow choked and destroyed me. I have no clue or insight about the mysteries that surround you, and I do not have a moment of peace. Ruhie wrote me a couple of days ago to say that you were all in Haifa in a luxury hotel; and that someone in the Sokhonoot has contacted you to arrange for your emigration to Amrika. Is this true? But now you tell me that you have been ill. Which one of your words should I believe? Were you recuperating from your illness when you stayed at the hotel? Are you feeling better now? I have written to you several times begging you to tell me the truth, but it appears that you have thrown my letters into the trash bin or you think that keeping the truth from me saves me from suffering. Every time I hear from anyone, it is a contradiction

of what I have heard from someone else. I don't know what to believe, so I am deluged with my own speculations and dreadful summaries. I swear my Maman, I am not normal anymore. Can you imagine what it is like for me to be alone with my most horrific fears and conjectures? I don't know what to do anymore.

Papa wrote to me that he is not feeling well. Uncle Moshe and Aunt Atefeh wrote that he has lost weight; aged due to the grief of separation from the kids. I have not taken a cent from him since I left. I have asked him to send money only to his other two children.

I love you always, Azadeh

- Solitary Eighteen -

Today is my eighteenth birthday, and I am utterly besieged and beleaguered by the burden of my own existence. At eighteen, I feel as if I have lived a life of despair for eighty years... eighty years and nine months, if I count the time I felt my mother's angst sweltering through her womb.

This is the first birthday that I am alone and away from my family, alone to cry for a past that is replete with grief and a future that promises no more than the same legacy. Will I ever be able to experience joy and happiness? Will this new page in my life bear a different fate? Tonight, I shall pray to the God of Moses, Jesus, and Muhammad and tomorrow, on the Shabbat, I will go to the temple and pray with those who speak of Him with reverence and seem to know His language... I will pray aloud as they do, and perhaps God will hear me. Perhaps eighteen years of agony will be behind me and I can begin a new day of hope and wellbeing.

Today, eighteen inches of snow shut down all the

roads, but did not prevent the postman from delivering to me a chilling letter.

My sister writes: *"I fear that I have become a shell of a human without feelings."* She has lost all hope because *Daii jaan* Nader has banned Maman from ever returning to Iran, and is also vehemently against her move to Amrika.

True to his implacable character, *Daii jaan* has extrapolated a *"formule,"* a firm and logical plan to avoid tending to the deep wounds that smolder beneath. He wants to send his frail old mother to Israel and relieve himself of her care and custody, leaving the two devastated women alone to tend to each other's wounds in a foreign country.

15 March 1961

Maman jaan, I am incensed to hear that your brother has forbidden you from returning to Iran and has instructed you not to come to Amrika. How dare he treat you as if you were his slave with no rights or freedom to make your own decision? Who is he to tell you how to live your life? He does not own you and does not take care of you. You do not owe him anything, so why do you let him take charge of your life? I know that you always listen to him. I don't understand why. I am sure that you would like for Khanoom jaan to be with you, but she is frail and needs medical care. Are you able to take care of her, and the kids, and yourself? How will you ever support yourself? Papa wrote to me that he has been sending my siblings money. He thinks it is best for Ruhie and Jafar to join me here. I have asked him not to press charges against you and not to interfere or disagree with your departure from Israel, in case you want to come with them. I am sure that he will concede. I beg you to make a decision that is best for you... what makes you happy. I beg you to give me back the voice of the mother I once knew. Return to me the fortune I had in a mother who was wise, pragmatic and insightful. Let's plan together for our

future. I need to know that you have regained your health and you are back to being your brilliant self. I need to know that you can help me with our plans. I know with certainty that we must and will be together. You are everything to me and to achieve that goal, I will do anything and everything. Despite my loneliness and hardship here in Amrika, I feel that this is the only place in the world I can make a life for myself. It is the separation from you that makes life most unbearable. Let's wait to see how you feel once your beloved mother joins you. If you decide not to stay in Israel, I will do everything to bring you all here. There are no other options.
Ghorban-e shoma, Azadeh

9 April 1961
My beloved Maman, you cannot imagine how your last two letters have given me hope and warmed my heart. I don't feel so desperately alone now, because your letters speak to me in a voice I am familiar with. I feel I have found you again and can trust your decisions.
It is 2 p.m. and since I received your letter just a few minutes ago, I have read it six times. You said you were concerned that I was sick. Please do not worry. I am feeling much better. Maman, imagine how much you say you miss me, and imagine how it is for me to miss all of you. But Azizam, my beloved, I know that somehow we will soon be together. We need to take care of ourselves so that when that time comes, we will have the health to enjoy it.
The status of my education is not clear and at this point, the chance of continuing my studies in microbiology or medicine is nearing zero. I have many hours of study and laboratory. I cannot work full time to support myself and study medicine simultaneously. I have no choice but to take another career path that is not as demanding. I am not sure what to do about school, but I will figure it out. I promise you, I will not allow myself to fail. I will not give up and I will prevail. I know that our triumph will help us forget all the loss and failures that we have experienced. I promise that soon all this will be behind us. As for my work, please don't worry. I am proud that I can work and

150

take care of myself. For now, I am working two days a week and hope to work all summer to save money for you. I work behind the food counter at a very large store. I make ice cream in big jugs and when I see little kids eat them with such delight, I think about my Jafar jaan and my Ruhie jaan, and wish I could give them some ice cream and watch them enjoy it. Work keeps my mind occupied, so I don't think and worry as much. Please be strong. I tell myself that every day, because I know otherwise I will not be able to get through the day. Maman jaan, being alone and away from you has devastated me. I was sick all of last week and the whole time, I imagined you being here, taking care of me and watching over me.
I love you, Azadeh

IT HAS BEEN over a year since I left Iran. Summer is approaching, and I am exhausted trying to find a way to unite my family. I will have to turn every stone and knock on every door to bring them to America. I have no other option and they have no place else to go. Last week, I fell ill again and missed a week of classes. It is very challenging to compete with students whose native language is English. I am doing well in all my science courses because I studied them in high school, but I have to work at least twice as hard in every course that requires extensive reading. Now I am far behind and have to double up my efforts to catch up on the work that I have missed. Amidst all this, my own visa is under investigation. I am sure it is because I am not attending Berkley. Now I have to go to the Immigration Office and appeal to them to issue me a new visa.

In the past year, I have ignored men who have paid attention to me and wanted to date me, but I was feeling so lonely that I decided to join a youth group,

Hillel, at a nearby temple. Unlike the modest houses of worship in Iran, here in America, they are elaborate and costly to join. The Prayers and Services are conducted in Yiddish, a vernacular that is vastly different and unfamiliar to me. I miss the days when we gathered at our local synagogue in Tehran and heard the melodic Hebrew songs and prayers. Jewish holidays were a festive and fun event for kids. No one cared that we had no money and no one ever asked for it. Jewish Holidays were the perfect time to believe in God because everyone was treated equally and we all felt as if we were members of the same family. The Hillel group has welcomed me like one of its own and without a membership fee. They know that I have no money and no family.

"Why would you ever leave your country and come here alone?" Everyone has asked the question at least once.

The girls always want to know why I don't wear any make-up.

"Eventually, you'll have to become Americanized and do things like everyone else does." Julie advises.

I want to tell her that I will never be like them or anyone else. But I decide to be silent.

The boys are surprised or rather intrigued by my shyness.

"Why are you so polite and quiet?" One boy wants to know.

"Just give her a couple of months and she'll be a chatterbox like the rest of them." Another boy forecasts and everyone laughs.

In spite of a dreadful year of emotional upheaval and frequent illnesses and absences, my final grades are surprisingly good. Somehow, my audacious resolve to succeed has managed to circumvent the sabotage of my eroding grief. Perhaps my chaotic mind had quietly and surreptitiously set out to save me in spite of myself. I feel proud and happy. This is the best I have felt since ... well, I do not know when...But for now, I can say that I feel proud, and that makes me happy. So, when a boy from Hillel asks me to go out with him, I say yes. His name is Marvin. He is cute but overweight. Somehow I think that his handicap makes him trustworthy and safe.

When Marvin takes me out, we meet with his friends and their dates. At the end of the night, we end up at Jan's Ice Cream Parlor on Queens Boulevard. Marvin always orders a large "Banana Split" ... three huge scoops of ice cream, loaded on a bed of bananas, topped with whipped cream and dripping hot melted chocolate. It is a colossal cargo of calories and I wonder if he will be able to finish it. He always does and never surprises me. I think about my days of dearth and deprivation in Iran. How I watched other children gloat eating ice cream, and I wished for just a teaspoonful taste of it. Now I watch Marvin consume a tray full of ice cream and I want none of it.

When Marvin drops me off, all I want to do is smoke and cry. I desperately miss my family and my friends. My throat hurts and the room is filled with a dark cloud of smoke from the cigarettes. I open the window to let in some fresh air. Cold wind blows inside and gives me a chill. The ashtray is filled with ashes and with cigarette butts. My books and papers reek from the stench of cigarette smoke. I look at the pile of letters I have received from my family since I

153

left home. They, too, reek from smoke and ashes of despair. I light another cigarette to numb the pain. I blow the smoke out into the cold air and wish someone would walk through the door and take my pain   away.

MARVIN HAS asked me to join his family for dinner Friday night. It is the evening of Sabbath and they never miss the tradition of lighting candles and praying together at the dinner table. The thought of having a family dinner saddens me and warms my heart at the same time. I know that I need to make peace with my pain and leave it behind for at least one night.

Marvin's mother, Anne is a round woman with thinning hair and a big smile. She is delighted to meet me.

"Marvin has told us so much about you. I can see why he is so smitten." She cheers.

Marvin's father, Jack, a diminutive, round-bellied man is a successful pharmacist and drug store owner. He approaches me with cautious curiosity. His questions are so precise and methodical, I wonder if he has been rehearsing them all day.

Marvin and his twin younger brothers, Arthur and Teddy, are all big and boisterous and tower over both their parents by at least one foot. They all attend the School of Pharmacy at Columbia University and have no interest in discussing anything but sports and their demanding curriculum of study. The dinner table is clogged with a massive and extensive assortment of food, a testament to the portly dimensions that each family member has accrued.

"You don't eat much." Anne remarks, "Please try the brisket. It's my specialty... It's delicious... The kids love it."

"Leave her alone, Anne. She probably doesn't like American food." Jack offers.

Marvin's family loves to eat. On weekends, they always invite me to join them at their favorite restaurant on Long Island, Patricia Murphy's... It is renowned for its tasty, flaky, and all-you-can-eat popovers...delivered straight from the oven. After eating a popover and a salad or soup, I am usually full. My stomach has shrunk and my menses has mercifully ceased due to a ration of two eggs that has long been the mainstay of my daily meals. Marvin is happy to clean up my plate. He orders my main course to suit his palette because he knows he will be the one to consume it entirely.

- The Reunion -

It is a balmy day in August 1961. For nearly two hours, I have been anxiously pacing the street in front of my one- room apartment in Queens, anticipating the arrival of three people I cherish more than my life. Two weeks earlier, I had received a brief letter from Maman, informing me that an Israeli agency had arranged for their visit to America. Now on this day, the day that I thought would never come, I stand here with overwhelming excitement, waiting for their embrace.

A yellow cab turns in from Horace Harding Boulevard and as it slows down to a stop, I see three faces stretching eagerly to see me. I am breathless. The surge of indescribable elation has suffused my body and is about to burst my heart. Tears are coursing down my face like sheets of rain and I can't wait another moment. Before the cab comes to a full stop, I run to grab the door handle as if my dream may slip away. The doors open on both sides of the cab as everyone rushes to exit. We huddle together and hold each other tight so no one would go weak at the knees and fall.

The cab driver is watching us with tears in his eyes.... He must know about the pain of loss and the bliss of reuniting with family. I give him his fare, plus a generous tip.

My one-room apartment, a converted garage, is on the first floor of a three-story house. My landlord lives above me, and a family of three occupies the third floor. This single room serves as my bedroom, living room, kitchen and dining room; and with the exception of the bathroom, there are no walls to delineate its boundaries. The floor covering is entirely of old and discolored linoleum. A frayed mattress sits against the wall adjacent to the bathroom, and on the opposite side of it stands an old oven with an overhead shelf that contains three plastic plates, two coffee mugs, and two stained plastic drinking glasses. Two folding chairs around a dilapidated metal table provide the only seating above the ground.

We bring in the three tattered suitcases that hold my family's entire assets and instantly, my room feels like a castle full of treasures. The shabby space in which I had merely existed is suddenly transformed into a home in which I can live and behold the love of my family.

We spend the next few hours reminiscing, hugging and commenting on how each of us had changed.

After a while, my mother surveys the room and wonders where we will all sleep.

"I am so sorry, Maman *joon.* I didn't want to get a larger place until you got here. I was never sure that

157

you would actually make it. But now that you are here, I promise to move us to a larger apartment in the next few days."

"O.K. *azizam*, all that matters is that we are together." She forces a smile on her tired face.

"Why are you so thin?" She asks warily.

"I am not sick, Maman *joon*." I light up a cigarette and offer her one to distract her but she persists.

"You haven't been eating well. I'll make you your favorite *Ghormeh Sabzi*."

"Aah...that would be wonderful, Maman *joon*. But here, most people eat food that is already prepared." I show her the cans of Chef Boyardee Spaghetti and Meatballs that I have bought for our dinner.

Maman looks aghast. She wants me to give her the can for a closer inspection.

"Let me see."

As she reaches over, I notice a large and unsightly scar on her left arm. It is wide and deep. It extends from inside of her elbow all the way to her wrist. My heart jumps a beat. I feel sad and horrified. I shut my eyes and take a long drag on my cigarette to deflect my feelings but it is too late. She knows that I have seen it because she is agitated. It is clear that the scar bears the mystery of her tumultuous and obscure stay in Israel; something she is not willing or prepared to share.

"This is how it is in America, Maman *joon*... People eat sandwiches and hamburgers." I realize she has never heard of the latter, so I explain:

"Hamburger.... It is like *Kabab Koobideh* but flat like *nalbeki*, a saucer. They put it between two pieces of bread...something like a kabob sandwich."

Everyone chuckles, but they are neither amused nor impressed.

"I am sorry. I'll buy some pots and pans and we'll cook Persian meals, as soon as we move." I promise, then empty the cans of Chef-Boyardee in a pan that doubles as a kettle to boil water. I take out the plates and dole out the meal in three equal portions.

I pledge to my mother that I will find the ingredients she needs to make our favorite meals. We need herbs and red beans, which should be easy to find. But, I don't know where to find Persian rice and *limoo*, dried lemon. I know Maman will be harvesting her own rice and growing lemon trees before she would ever succumb to serving her children food from cans in the pantry.

I hand everyone a plate of Spaghetti and meatballs, and watch their expression as they eat their first American meal.

"It is good." Jafar and Ruhie concur.

"How about you, Azadeh *joon*? Aren't you eating?" Maman wants to know.

"Oh...I am not hungry. I am so excited. I just want to sit here and look at you to make sure I am not dreaming."

After they unpack and I clean up, we sit around to talk about our future.

"There is one thing I must ask of you to do." I appeal to my exhausted audience.... all eyes now fixed at me with apprehension.

"What is it *azizam*?" Maman asks to end the suspense.

"The most important tool that you need to survive in this country is to learn English." I look to gauge everyone's puzzled reaction. They are likely to think of survival as having food to eat.

"Of course, azizam. We must do everything that is necessary to guarantee our success and survival here." Maman hastens to confirm.

"Learning English is a priority because no one speaks Farsi here," I say firmly, "So, I am going to speak to you in English and translate it only if you don't understand me."

"O.K." I hear a unanimous sigh of relief.

"Can you believe that my dreams are now in English? It is not because I don't love my heritage, but I think my brain is telling me that I have to adjust to my new life here." I profess.

After dinner, we all sit on the mattress and talk the night away until everyone is ready to sleep, each taking up a corner of the mattress that had just doubled as our dining table.

I kiss everyone good night, and then stay awake to make plans for our future. First, I have to find my family an apartment. Then I have to contact the Immigration office and apply for the change of their visa status. They can stay here on a student visa as long as they attend school, but on their current tourist visas, they will have to leave the country once their visas expire. I have already located the schools where my siblings will attend, but first I must have their transcripts translated to English, before I submit them to the Board of Education.

On the weekend, I find a furnished two-bedroom apartment on the first floor of a private family house across the street. It is not an adequate dwelling, but it is far better than where we are living; it is all that I can afford. Fortunately in the past year, Papa has been able to maintain consistent employment for the first time in his life, and has promised to send money every month to support my siblings.

IN THE NEXT FEW WEEKS, I make several trips to the Board of Education and the Immigration Office, and by mid-September, my siblings are registered at school and granted student visas. They are happy to resume their education, and are quickly acclimating to their new home and school environment. Ruhie is excelling in Mathematics, learning English and catching up with her classmates. Jafar is adapting well, enjoying the attention of his curious teachers and his new friends. Maman has to enroll in the English Language Program, which is a costly endeavor. But she needs to have a student visa to stay with us here.
I am entering my second year of college, and although doubtful that I can financially afford the pursuit of a medical degree, I continue to declare my major as Pre-Med/Biology. I am not willing to give up hope or abandon my dream.

Last week, we learned that our neighbors from Iran, *docteur* Mokhtar and his family have been living in New York City. We contacted them and they invited us to visit. It was a delightful reunion, and we reminisced for hours about our lives and adventures on *Kouchech* Tulu. They told us about a small shop in Manhattan that imports Persian goods and delicacies, and Maman is delighted that she will not have to appeal to India for rice, or grow her own lemon trees to make *Ghormeh Sabzi.*

IN MAY 1962, a college friend tells me about a great opportunity to work as a camp counselor on a ranch in upstate New York. The pay is good and the position seems challenging and exciting. I will have free room and board, and I can earn three hundred dollars during the two summer months... much more than I can make at the Five-and -Dime store. I don't want to be away from my family, but it would be foolish to pass up this chance to make a decent amount of money. Although Papa has been sending most of his income for the support of my siblings, we need to pay Maman's tuition, so she can maintain her student visa status and stay here.

IN JUNE 1962, as I prepare to go to my summer job at the Indian Trail Camp, Marvin asks me to marry him. For weeks, he has been saying that he is in love with me and wants me to 'get pinned.' But, wearing a boy's fraternity pin as a symbol of commitment seems quite ridiculous to me. Besides, I do not really know how I feel about him. I know with certainty that the thrill and excitement that I used to feel about Vaheed or even the other boys is missing, but that was when I was a naïve and romantic teen.

One night, when Marvin picks me up to join his parents for dinner, he pledges his abiding love for me, then takes a velvet blue box out of his pocket and presents me with a diamond engagement ring.

"I want to know that you'll marry me before you go away."

I stare at the sparkling stone and wonder what Marvin would do if I said "no." But he does not wait for my answer. He takes my hand and slips the ring on my finger.

"My mother was right. It fits perfectly." He cheers.

I don't know how I should feel or what I should say. I know that even with my family here, there is a void in my life that is not filled. Perhaps I need to trust a man and depend on him...a man who will build a life with me, so that I can feel at home with him. Marvin's mother is very fond of me, and I know that she will be good to me. Most importantly, Marvin comes from a hardworking and educated family. They have high regard for academic achievement. I will be proud to have them as my family and they will take pride in me, as I succeed in my own pursuit of education and respectability.

WHEN I RETURN home from camp in August, I learn that Anne has been busy arranging for our wedding. She has already planned the bridal shower, and chosen the venues for the wedding and our honeymoon. She is happy to do it all with delight, because she never had a daughter and always wanted one. I have told her that in the Iranian tradition, the groom pays for the wedding. She knows that we have no money and has offered to pay for everything, including the gown I'll be wearing. She feels justified taking full charge, and I don't mind. All she wants in return is that I change my name to Faye and have Uncle Abe, the man I despise vehemently, walk me down the aisle, in lieu of my father who is not here to give me away. I can forfeit my dislike for my new name, but my repulsion at the prospect of having Abe walk me down the aisle is a feeling I cannot contain. But how will I explain this to Anne?

I pray that Abe and Henrietta decline the invitation. However, to my dismay and surprise, they have accepted to come, and watch me carry the mantle of our secret shame alone.

THE WEDDING is at a ballroom on Long Island. There are one hundred guests and only seven of them are related to me. With the exception of Maman and my siblings, Abe, Henrietta, Mehran and Helen, no one I know, including my friends, have been invited.

Throughout the affair, I feel as if I am playing a part in a movie- a brief escape into a world of fantasy that would end as soon as everyone leaves. What I don't anticipate, however, is that the fantasy will not just end...it will become a shocking nightmare.

Once the guests leave and the wedding party is concluded, Marvin and I are instructed by his mother to stay at a designated hotel suite for the night and leave for our honeymoon destination in the morning.

"You're going to Miami, " Anne announces gleefully, "I have booked a beautiful suite and a seven-day stay for you at the Clarion Hotel."

Anne has already packed our bags.... and there is not much for us to do but to say goodbye.

IN OUR HOTEL ROOM, Marvin looks glib and bewildered. I ask him what is wrong, but he says nothing. My wedding gown is hampering me, and I need to remove it. There are at least twenty miniature buttons on the back of the gown, hugging me from the neck to the end of my spine.

"Would you help me take off this gown, Marvin?"

There is a moment of foreboding silence, and then

I hear words that will echo in my mind for the rest of my life.

"I wish my parents were here." Marvin blurts.

"What did you say, Marvin?" I ask, convinced that my cochlear receptors had temporarily failed me.

"I said I wish my parents were here. I don't know what to do." He mutters.

I am shocked and incensed, as Marvin's words linger and resonate in my head. Then I stretch my arms around and across my back to rip open the gown that has sealed my new fate. I glance at a slothful Marvin sitting in a chair and then, I quickly put on a dress, grab my cigarettes, and leave for the bar downstairs. I want to believe that this is just a bad dream, but the gold wedding band tightly wrapped around my finger is a reminder that a daunting nightmare is about to begin.

WHEN WE RETURN to New York a few days later, Anne has refurbished the basement of her house, which will be our living quarters for an indefinite length of time.

"I hope you like the way I've fixed it." She greets me cheerfully.

"Of course...thank you." I oblige her. I have far more pressing matters of survival to fix; my family's welfare and my education are at great risk.

Marvin has a full-time schedule of classes during the day and works at his father's store two evenings and on weekends. His parents are happy that as a married man, he can now commit to more hours at the drugstore and allow them the leisure they so well deserve. When he comes home, Marvin is tired and hungry. If his brothers are not around, he eats and watches TV. When he is away, I look forward to my quiet time to study, but that is precisely when Anne wants my company. She follows me downstairs as soon as I come home from school and wants to chat with me while she does her laundry.

"The boys are so active, they need their clothes done every day," she explains, "I love them, but I am glad that now I have a daughter."

The washer and dryer are just five feet away, and Anne is loading them up as she tells me about what meals I should cook for Marvin. I have my textbook open at the small kitchen table, where I plan to study. Today, I have to cram for a botany exam. Botany is my least favorite subject, and I have to try hard to concentrate.

"You should not study so much, sweetheart. Your husband will graduate and make a good living. You won't have to work."

"I want to study medicine, Anne. I have dreamed of becoming a physician all my life."

I light a cigarette to disguise my displeasure. I am growing tired of Anne's interventions. Her affection for me has become her own self-serving pleasure.

Soon, pandemonium erupts upstairs, as the twins come home bringing their friends and running up and down the stairs like wild monkeys. I close all the doors and windows to muffle the noise, but it is to no avail. My head hurts from smoking in the windowless kitchen and my future looks as gloomy as a sunless day.

The Friday night ritual, dining upstairs with the family, has also become a dread. Anne invariably

166

reminds me of the importance of keeping a Kosher home, but the hypocrisy of having a kosher household and eating non-Kosher food outside totally confounds me.

"Did you keep a Kosher home in your country?" Anne wants to know.

"We ate meat and poultry only if the animal was slaughtered under the Rabbi's supervision. I knew no one who kept separate dishes for meat and dairy," I explain, "and the consumption of pig and shellfish is forbidden by Muslims as well as by Jews."

"You didn't keep a Kosher home?" The twin brothers scowl as they inquire in tandem.

"No, we didn't. No one did." I say dismissively, hoping to end the interrogation.

The twins always seem to know what is on the other's mind and naturally, my answer is not satisfactory to either one.

"You are very fortunate, Faye, that we have taken you into our home." Arthur exclaims haughtily, and I pretend not to have heard his condescending remark.

"You have to keep a Kosher home for my parents. That is what we do in our family." Teddy argues.

"Yes, my parents have been very generous to you. It would be nice to let them know you appreciate them." Marvin chimes in, not to be out-shined by his twin brothers.

Lately, the twins have been blatantly hostile towards me. They treat me like a guest who has overstayed her welcome. I am sure they are displeased to have lost some of their mother's doting attention, ever since she has claimed me as her 'lost and now found' daughter. She has made it clear to everyone that she is going to raise me all over again, in her own image.

Marvin's father, Jack, always seems to be on the verge of saying something of a profound nature, but instead, he hastily fills up his mouth with food to silence himself. His oversized head wobbles over his small neck, as he restrains himself and avoids my stare. I am watching him because I know he will soon relieve himself; his dam of silence will be unleashed, and his sentiments will run off like a flood of serrated teeth.

"You are wasting your time going to school. This is America. In this country, you have to do what we do. Women work to pay their husband's tuition." Jack's head is quivering furiously, and I know there is much more that he wants to say to me.

"Forget going to school. You are not going to amount to anything. Get a job." He blurts out.

I run downstairs, tripping as I lose my balance, blinded by the haze of my tears. I want to lock myself somewhere, and never come out again. I have come so far and tried so hard to get away from oppression and shame, but it has found me, yet again. I might as well be sitting at *Daii jaan* Nader's dinner table to hear him exalt the merits of good housekeeping and a life of self-denial to please a man.

It is clear that the tragic tenor of my fate has not changed...it has followed me thousands of miles to find a new cast of perpetrators and players.

- Evils and Assassins -

It is approximately 1 p.m., November 22, 1963, when I leave the Queens College campus and walk towards the bus stop on the corner of Kissena Boulevard and Horace Harding Expressway. I have spent the entire morning in the microbiology lab, peering through the microscope, and charting data for my next report. I am feeling weak and malaise, but to feel well on any day would be not the rule...but the exception.

As I cross the street, I sense a foreboding blanket of silence hovering around me. Three students are standing by, pale and petrified, as if air had suddenly vacated their lungs.

"The President is dead...Kennedy was shot...he is dead." Someone howls from the corner gas station and instantly, pandemonium breaks out. People are running around aimlessly...some shrieking with agony, others weeping in their hands... eyes covered to suspend the reality that is too shocking to comprehend. A voice in my head is blaring in my ear.

"No.... please, God... this cannot be happening here...not in America...not in this country." Then

169

suddenly, a blast of cold air rushes to chill my veins ... my legs buckle under me and everything fades away.

AT THE NEW YORK Medical College: The Flower and Fifth Hospital in Manhattan, I wake up to the sound of a respirator and a voice that is soothing and familiar. It is Dr. Simon, my mother-in-law's brother. He is a teaching professor at the College. He wants to know how I feel.

"Quite awful. ..." I mutter.

"You had a fever of 105 when they brought you in," he explains sympathetically, "I admitted you here to keep a close watch on you."

I nod my head in appreciation. Dr. Simon is my favorite member of Marvin's family. He has always been kind to me and unlike his sister, has encouraged me to pursue my studies.

In a few minutes, Anne rushes in.

"What is wrong with her, Harry?" She asks fretfully.

"She has bacterial pneumonia and pleurisy. We'll have to keep her here for a while...at least for a week."

"Oh my God," Anne squeals, "How did she get so sick?"

"We don't know. She may have picked something up in the laboratory."

"I've been telling her she should quit school." Anne grumbles, then demands to stay by my side all night but thankfully, her brother insists she does not.

FOR THE NEXT nine days, Dr. Simon comes to see me every day and assures me that I am making steady progress. Maman and Anne come to the hospital regularly, but no one else has come to visit. It is just as well, because most days I am tired and often sleeping. I have flashbacks of standing at the bus stop and hearing the chilling announcement of President Kennedy's assassination. I hope and pray that I had been delirious.... hallucinating due to high fever. But then, I see and hear the shockwaves of the gruesome truth everywhere... the devastating remainders that America, and perhaps our world, will never be the same.

ON THE DAY that I am released from the hospital, Marvin and his father don't waste a moment to discharge their hostility at me.

"Do you know how much your hospital stay cost?" Marvin sneers.

"Where is your family? Why aren't they paying for your medical bills?" Jack demands.

My illness and medical expenses have provided more than enough fodder for Marvin's family to bolster their contention that I should quit school and get a job. I have missed two weeks of school and have no choice but to take a leave of absence.

I find a part-time job at a dental office in Brooklyn. It is an hour drive but I don't mind. My employer, Dr. Greene is a brilliant and compassionate man who wants to teach me all I can learn to assist him with surgery. During our breaks, we talk about life, philosophy, politics, and science. He challenges me with complex puzzles and abstract riddles, and always compliments my intellect and problem solving skills.

"You are very bright and intuitive. Don't ever give up on your dream of pursuing science."

171

At home, I live a life of despair in the basement of my in-laws, flooded with a barrage of innuendos and harassments. At night, I can't fall asleep and have to resort to taking sleeping pills.

"We need to get our own place." I appeal to Marvin, hoping that living away from his family would bring us intimacy and save our marriage.

"I don't know what your problem is…" Marvin sneers, "I am happy here… you weren't living any better when I married you."

When I cry and tell him how heartbreaking it is to hear him speak to me with such flagrant disrespect, he offers me a bottle of sleeping pills and pushes me away.

"Here, take these…. if you are so unhappy, why don't you go ahead and kill yourself. Just make sure you don't do it in my house."

I know that Anne is the only one who has influence over her sons and her husband. I try to convince her that Marvin and I need to move out of her basement and live on our own.

"You can't afford to get your own place. "Anne protests.

IN FEBRUARY of 1964, two months after the assassination of John F. Kennedy, the Beatles come to the United States to mesmerize the youth, and distract Americans from wallowing in their woe. It is a well-timed diversion for those who extol stoicism and eulogize the disguise of sadness and grief. Jackie Kennedy has earned high praise for her strength and ability to conceal her pain. But today, on my twenty-first birthday, I am mourning not only for JFK, but also for the loss of my faith in the 'free world' that allows men to carry weapons and kill one another. I have come to America to free myself from the evil of abuse and ignorance, but evil thrives everywhere. I have seen evil in the eyes of men who murder others. I have seen evil cloaked as my kin, and I see it in the man I have trusted and married.

I remember the colorful books that I used to borrow from the American Library in Tehran. Those books that depicted kind and peaceful Americans living in immaculate and safe neighborhoods...the happy families ... the friends and neighbors... all waving and smiling at one another... happy children playing in their yards ... dogs chasing them and wagging their tails.

"This is Spot... Spot can run.... See Spot run."

I tell myself that America still holds the promise. It is up to me to work hard and undo the legacy that has followed me here. Perhaps I can change not only my own fate, but make a difference in the lives of others. This is a nation of hope. It will not fail me because America does not tolerate injustice.

IN THE FALL of 1964, after an emotional goodbye, I leave Dr. Greene to begin my full-time job at an employment agency. I find a studio apartment with a reasonable rent on Elder Avenue in Flushing, and hope to build a new life for Marvin and me. I furnish our apartment with secondhand furniture, and cover the floors with remnants of carpeting donated by neighbors most of whom are newly weds. None of the women in our building work; they are either pregnant or caring for their newborn babies. Weekend nights,

Marvin works, and I baby-sit for my neighbors. They want to know why I am always alone and why we never socialize with them. Marvin has not made any friends. He is discourteous to my family and to everyone else. Neighbors often comment about his unprofessional wardrobe and demeanor. I have bought him white shirts and stylish trousers, but he refuses to wear them. He likes wearing his jeans and T-shirts.

These days, I feel very much like a failure. It was four years ago that I started college and now, all my friends have graduated. Academic success has always been a consistent and reliable source of pride and security for me but now, I feel entirely defeated and vanquished in so many ways. Still, I am determined not to give up. Marvin is graduating next summer, and once he begins to work full-time, I hope to resume my studies. I work long days at the employment agency, but our budget is still tight. Marvin is not working because this is his last year of pharmacy school and he needs more time to study. He keeps track of every dollar that I make and every cent that I spend. Nonetheless, I have managed to squirrel away some money from my weekly allowance to help pay for a larger apartment for my family.

My sister is eager to graduate from high school and find a job. However, she can't work full-time on her current student visa. The cost of living and full-time enrollment for Maman, my sister, and my brother is prohibitive, but they all have to attend school full-time to avoid deportation. It is a quagmire that keeps me awake at night. The only salvation is to apply for their permanent residency status, but I can't initiate that process until I become a citizen - an option that will not be available for another two years. I am desperate for a solution.

I reach out to several organizations and finally make contact with Mrs. Blum, the director of the National Council of Jewish Women in New York City. She is a kind woman, deeply devoted to helping displaced and needy families. She is moved by our austere circumstances, but believes that my only option is to appeal to the Congress of the United States. It is an audacious hope, but I must gather all my courage and optimism to pursue it.

I compose an earnest letter to the Honorable Congressman Benjamin Rosenthal, and subsequently appeal to him in person during a lengthy conference. I apprise him of our tenuous circumstances and the dire consequences of my siblings' deportation. Then I wait for the miracle that could save my family from irreparable and ultimate devastation.

- A Private Bill -

On March 11, 1965, the Congress of the United States of America passes a Private Bill on my behalf, granting my family legal permanent residency. This is the brightest ray of hope that has risen to illuminate the darkness of our days. This generous and monumental sanction will allow my family the freedom to work honorably and maintain its dignity.

In June, Ruhie graduates from high school and finds employment at a bank in New York City. Maman's vigilant search for a job, however, ends at a sewing factory far from where she lives. For months, she had tried to find a position that would utilize her expertise in mathematics, but her lack of proficiency in English disqualifies her from such undertakings. She is disappointed but is willing to do whatever it takes to support herself. Throughout our childhood, Maman knitted our winter clothes and created magnificent fashions for us with remnants of fabrics salvaged from the garments she made for others. She is a talented seamstress and now, she is glad that this skill will enable her to earn a living.

The factory is in Manhattan's Garment District. It requires a ninety-minute commute: an early morning bus ride from Ash Avenue to the Main Street subway station, and then a forty-five minute train ride with multiple transfers to west 35th Street.

In a few days, Maman reluctantly admits that her workplace is not the refined sewing facility that she had imagined. Instead, it is a dark and grim dungeon of a sweatshop with harsh rules and no leniency. She stands on her feet on an assembly line, eight hours a day, five days a week, where her value is measured not by the keenness of her mind, but by the swiftness of her hands and feet.

- A Separate Universe -

In Iran, *Daii jaan* Nader continues to expand his gargantuan wealth. He has recently returned from a tour of the Far East and is celebrating the birth of a fourth child, his third male offspring. He has named this son Cyrus, in the image of the King.

Once again, this is an occasion for my mother to indulge her brother with kindness and generosity in the hope that he will acknowledge her worth and validate her right to live. She wants to spend her entire week's earnings to buy gifts, not only for the newborn baby, but also for all of her brother's children so no one would feel neglected or dismissed.

"I want him to remember me." She sighs as her eyes well up with tears. It is as if a simple word of praise and tribute from her brother could magically erase all the injustice and devastation that he has brought upon her.

SHORTLY AFTER the birth of Cyrus, we learn that our beloved *Khanom jaan* has passed away. When I arrive at my mother's apartment, I find her wrapped deeply in her grief. She is staring into the space, weeping and rocking back and forth to soothe herself. She has suffered so many losses in her life but now without her mother, she is an orphan - lost in a sea of angst and loneliness.

We are our mother's child until she dies... We come from her womb and through her we are borne into the infinite universe to endure... nurtured by her love, and sheltered by her invisible shield. But when she dies, our existential bond is broken and our cradle of safety is lost. We need our own child to reconnect us to the universal purpose... the desire to live and to endure. We need our children to cradle us in their love and help us feel safe and vital again.

I hold my mother in a long embrace and let her know that she is not alone. I kiss her face and tell her that she will always have my love and my protection.

It is past midnight when we are empty of tears and out of cigarettes. I put my mother to bed and go home to my own private hell.

IN A FEW DAYS, my father arrives in New York with a colossal cargo of disaster. For months, he had been writing me about his sorrowful state, complaining that he was lonely and missed his children. He was going to resign from the only stable employment he had ever held and come to America, where he was certain to find the means to support himself and his children.

Today, true to his legacy of hollow insight and

bungled management, my father has shipped from Iran crates of handmade pottery, anticipating a great market and a lucrative profit.

Maman is terrified that she is going to be displaced, and that she would have to leave to make room for my father. I assure her that she needs not to worry because I have found my father a place at a rooming house not far away. He shares a kitchen and bathroom with an Iranian man who is about the same age, and has a distant kinship with him. It is a perfect setting for my father who can now spend his days playing backgammon, drinking tea and reminiscing with his friend.

I, however, stand alone once again to carry the burden of my father's mistake. After a ten-hour workday at the employment agency, I go to the storage house to manage my father's ludicrous investment. I unwrap, dust, and catalogue each piece of pottery and transport it carefully, often on foot, to each and every conceivable market. I visit gift shops and consignment stores, and appeal to every potential buyer across the country. But everywhere I go, I hear the same sardonic comment about the absurdity of importing painted clay from a country that is known for its prized carpets.

In a few months, my family is penniless and on the brink of being evicted. Even our combined income does not meet the growing household expenses. Now that my father is unemployed, he needs to be supported, as well.

Lately, Maman has become increasingly more melancholy. I know she is trying to be strong, but the sadness in her eyes worry me. The loss of *Khanom jaan* has broken her spirit and left her with unrelenting sorrow. My father's arrival has added to her anxiety and self-loathing, as she feels destined to re-live the memories of her marriage. Worst of all, the daily commute to the city and standing on her feet all day on an assembly line, is taking a visible toll on her.... She looks haggard and hopeless. The humiliation and the physical demand of her factory job are demoralizing, exhausting, and no longer sustainable.

My dream of pursuing my education, too, has turned into dust, as has my father's delusion that his cargo of sand would turn into a goldmine. I have no choice but to forsake my aspiration to study medicine. However, the commitment to save my mother's life is one pledge that I cannot forsake.

- Saving My Mother -

When I arrive at Mehran's gallery, I find it oddly quiet. There is no one at the reception desk, and there is no visible sign of activity. However, it is a Friday afternoon, and I presume that everyone is away at lunch or has ended the day early.

Mohsen is jubilant when he comes out to greet me.

"I have sent everyone home. I have given them a holiday in honor of your visit."

I am not sure if he is fibbing or flirting with me, but I am glad to see him, nonetheless. Our last encounter, six months earlier, had been unexpected and brief. We had found each other at a crowded New Year celebration at Mehran and Helen's penthouse, where my attendance was typically rare, despite repeated invitations. The couple frequently held lavish dinner parties at their beautiful home and served generous and scrumptious authentic Persian cuisine, prepared by their private chef. Of course, we were always invited to join them but alas, we forfeited the opportunity often, because we could not afford to dress up appropriately. Papa, however, courtesy of

Mehran's generosity, owned several suites that he wore regularly and without scrutiny.

Last week, Mohsen had called to tell me that Mehran was in London en route to Tehran to explore the expansion of their gallery; and that he would be coming to manage the New York office, while Mehran was away. He said he had been waiting to have dinner with me since our first meeting, and wanted to know if I would finally join him for our past due dinner rendez-vous.

I had told him that since I was still in a state of quasi matrimony, albeit loveless and perfunctory, I could not spend the evening with him. We had decided to meet at the gallery and go to lunch on a Friday afternoon- the only day of the week that the employment office was not busy and my boss would allow me to leave early. Now after a forty-five minute ride on the subway, I have arrived a few minutes late, but far more elated than I had anticipated.

Mohsen leads me to a tastefully decorated office, where an ornate sofa and two chairs accent the periphery of an exquisite Persian rug, and fragrant roses adorn a delicately etched glass table in the center of the room. Nostalgic sound of soft Sitar fills the room to add a romantic flare to the ambiance.

"This is a magical place, Mohsen... Do you entertain here?" I ask with nervous curiosity and furtive cheer, "Are you expecting the Queen?"

"Yes, in fact, she has just arrived." Mohsen smiles, as he holds my arm and walks me to the posh sofa.

"Welcome, my queen. I am delighted that you are here."

My heart flutters as I remember our first dance,

183

the unspoken intimacy and the promise of a divine and everlasting love that I had casually squandered. Where was I now, and how far away from my dream?

Mohsen sits in a chair across from me, watching me with delight and adoration, as I try to subdue my own excitement.

"You look more beautiful than ever...." His smile softens momentarily, "I bet you get tired of hearing that all the time."

"*Merci*, Mohsen *jaan*. But I am afraid I feel neither well, nor beautiful." I confess, surprised by my unsolicited and uncensored deposition.

"Ah...Azadeh *jaan*, what is troubling you? What is wrong?" Mohsen looks startled.

"There is so much, Mohsen *jaan*." I mutter, trying to suppress my tears.

Mohsen flips open his cigarette case and reaches over to offer me one.

"It is Gauloise, non-filter... be careful with it." He warns as he lights my cigarette.

There is a soft knock on the door.

"Excuse me, azizam." Mohsen walks away, as I try to recover from the choking sensation in my throat. He was wise to caution me about the cigarettes.

"I have ordered lunch for us," he announces, "We'll have privacy here, and the whole afternoon to talk."

Mohsen ushers in two men in black bow ties and black suits. One man brings in two covered plates, which he sets up on an elegantly draped table. The other man places a platter of iced caviar and two flute glasses on the table, then pops open a bottle of champagne.

"Dom Perignon, Sir, as you requested."

Mohsen gives his nod of approval and the man fills both our glasses.

"Here's to our long awaited meeting." He raises his glass to a toast.

I feel euphoric ... amazed and exhilarated by Mohsen's indubitable desire to please me.

"I am happy to be here." I admit, as my heartbeat speeds out of control and blood rushes to color my face.

"*Azizam*, tell me why a woman as beautiful and smart as you, could ever be unhappy."

I know that once Mohsen knows about my wretched life, he will never again regard me as a desirable and beautiful woman.

"Mohsen *jaan*, happiness has little to do with beauty; it has everything to do with context and kinship... with one's circumstances and family relationships."

Mohsen ponders.... perhaps about the validity of what I have just said.

"Tell me Azadeh, why did you get married, instead of pursuing your dream of studying medicine?"

I can't tell you everything, Mohsen *jaan*. My life is inexplicable and convoluted. I can only tell you that my most compelling concern right now is to save my mother from impending devastation."

Mohsen listens attentively, as I tell him about my father's recent ruinous investment. This is a safe segue to explain why my mother is working in a factory. I am too embarrassed to reveal the truth.

"I am lost for words. It is incomprehensible that a brilliant woman and a distinguished educator would be left with no choice but to do menial work to make a

185

living."

"I know it's shocking but sadly, this is the reality and I must find a way to support my mother so she does not have to do such grueling work."

Mohsen brings me a box of tissues to wipe the flood of tears that have soaked my face, and then lights me another cigarette.

"*Azizam*, how do you expect to take care of your family? It is a daunting responsibility and you can't do it alone."

"I have been obsessed with saving my family since I was a little girl...." I pause with consternation, realizing that I have inadvertently volunteered too much information.

"Since when ...your childhood, you say?" Mohsen raises his brows...his voice resonates with sadness and surprise.

"Do you mean to say that you have lived with such turmoil since you were a little girl?"

"Yes, Mohsen ... but I can't talk about it."

"You have to trust someone...someone to comfort you and share your burden."

"That was the reason I got married, but it was a doomed decision."

"It is not too late to let me take care of you, Azadeh."

Mohsen moves close to me and gently cuddles my face. I snuggle next to him and feel the warmth of his breath. I am safe in the benevolence of his embrace and the generosity of his compassion. My body shudders with exhilaration as his hands caress my skin. He kisses me and I feel our hearts throbbing with anticipation. Every cell in my body is pulsating with excitement, craving to be naked with him and to feel the thrust of his passion coalesce with mine. I close my eyes and soften my breath to let the rapture of the moment saturate my veins. I surrender to him with heart and mind, and we both surrender to a euphoric celebration of covetous passion. I feel free and disconnected from all that has ever pained me; everything that has ever pushed me to the edge of annihilation is now thrusting me closer to him and to my ecstasy; a sensation unlike any other I have ever known... an awakening so inimitable that it makes me feel alive amidst all that is dead and void.

I lay in his embrace for a long time, wishing that this day would not end in eternity.

"Come to England and marry me."

Mohsen's eyes are full of hope and promise, but my heart is sinking with grief... just as it had once before; the day I said good-bye to Vaheed. I knew then and I know now, that I couldn't stay for long. Anything that promises me stability frightens me just the same. All I have ever known in my life has been uncertainty, and the only thing stable in my life has been instability. I feel unhinged when I imagine living a life that is unfamiliar to me.

"I can't abandon my family.... they need me." Tears are flooding my face again. I know there is an inherent cognitive dissonance in my statement, but the belief is far too embedded in my mind to be dismissed.

"I'll wait Azadeh... Someday you will be ready to let go of the chains that bind you, and you will let your heart heal."

Downstairs, Mohsen summons a cab.

"Take the lady to Queens, please." He reaches over to the taxi driver and hands him his tariff.

We kiss goodbye, and I hasten to get in the cab before I change my mind. I can't bear the aching ambivalence that is cleaving my heart.

"We shall see each other again." Mohsen echoes my hope, as he helps me into the seat.

Once we drive away, tears of self-pity flood my eyes. I am leaving a man who has offered me indubitable care, guileless passion, and the promise of a joyful life. He wants to give me everything I need and yet, I am running away mindlessly and steadfastly to escape.

I reach into my purse to take out a cigarette and find a sealed envelope tucked inside. There is a note and a check for two thousand dollars.

"Azizam, forgive me for the audacity to assume that I can ease your pain with an act so insignificant and mundane. Please don't be offended...trust that I care about you deeply and will never give up hope to see you in my arms again. Yours, Mohsen"

I burst into a pathetic cry. I am intensely ashamed and delighted at the same time.

"Are you O.K., lady?" The cab driver glances at me through his mirror. I thank him and tell him that I am all right.

By the time we reach Queens Boulevard, my tears have given way to comforting thoughts... I have been imagining the smile of relief on my mother's face when I tell her that the rent will be paid, and she will not have to work in that dreadful sweatshop.

IT IS APPROXIMATELY 7:30 p.m., when I arrive at my

mother's apartment and discover that she is not home. It is Friday and there may have been delays. But by eight o'clock, I begin to pace the floor imagining every scenario that would explain why she is late.

In another hour, the doorbell rings and I rush to embrace my mother... and tell her how she had me worried.

"Let's go help her," I summon my brother, "She must have bags of groceries in her hands."

As I open the door, my heart drops to the floor, and I stand frozen with panic.

"I am Officer Murphy." A tall husky policeman scans the room from the doorway, and then takes out a laminated card from his pocket.

"What is wrong, officer?" I manage to ask, as fear settles in my throat to choke my breath.

He looks me over and glances at the card.

"I'm looking for this woman's next of kin." Now he holds up the laminated card for me to see, and I recognize Maman's ID card from the English Language Institute. Instantly, I feel the air sucked out of my lungs and my knees are about to collapse under me.

"My God.... What happened to her?" I shriek.

"She is alive." The officer hastens to assure me.

"What happened? Where is she?"

"Are you related to her?"

"She is my mother...please tell me... where is she?"

"She was taken to Creedmoor Hospital. She tried to jump in front of an incoming train."

"Oh God... No, please..." I know Creedmoor is a State Mental Institution, not equipped to treat accident victims.

189

"Was she taken to the emergency room first?" I hasten to ask.

"Fortunately, she had no physical injuries. A couple of people noticed she was behaving oddly, and suspected that she was up to something. They held her down and called the police."

"She was not physically hurt, right?" I plead for reassurance.

"It was your lucky day that two Good Samaritans were standing by and saved her. That doesn't happen too often these days."

"A lucky day indeed, officer."

I turn around to go to the kitchen and call for a cab. But as I pick up the receiver, I remember that the phone had been disconnected because of non-payment. I get my purse and head for the door where the officer still stands, blocking my exit.

"Excuse me, I have to walk to Main Street and look for a cab. The phone is out of order, and I have no transportation."

"You can ride with me. I have to go back that way, anyway."

AT CREEDMOOR State Hospital, I find Maman sitting in a chair cold and catatonic. She is pale and remote, staring into a space I can't see. I am not sure whether or not she has noticed me. She has not moved, nor acknowledged my presence. I reach over to hug her but she doesn't respond.

I had suspected for some time that Maman was not feeling well. I attributed it mainly to the daily commute and the exhausting work at the factory. Now today, on the very same day that I was about to end her burden, she had decided to end her life.

"Maman *joon,* Please talk to me. What happened today? I promise you will never have to set foot in that factory again."

I watch my mother through the blur of my tears and wish I could make her pain go away. I am thankful that she is alive but wherever she is, I can't reach her. I kiss her face and tell her that I love her. Then I pray to her God. Would He make her well because she is pious, or will He keep her ill to punish me for not believing in him?

Thirty minutes later, I sit across from a man who believes he is God; his eyes are cold and his words are empty and unkind. Had he not been introduced to me as Dr. Boulder, I would have mistaken him for a patient who was play-acting the role.
He wants to know how many times my mother has tried to kill herself. He needs this information not because he cares about her, but because he wants to know where on his diagnostic nomenclature he can plug her illness to justify the treatment he has already determined appropriate.

"We have to give her ECT, Electro Convulsive Therapy. It's quick and effective." He explains.

"No..." I object, "I can't allow that. Please don't subject her to shock treatment. I am afraid she'll get worse."

"She can't get any worse," he exclaims, "She is already there."

"No, worse would be if she succeeds at killing herself." I snap, irritated by his insensitivity. "I know she'll feel better once I take her home."

"We can't release her until she has made adequate

progress. If you don't sign a statement for us to give her ECT, there is no telling when she'll be discharged."

I try to convince Dr. Boulder that what my mother needs is affection and compassion, not bolts of electricity to jolt her brain.

"She has lost her dignity, her pride, her home, her mother, and perhaps every hope that she has tried to behold to give her *raison d'être*," I explain, "She wants to die because she has no reason to live. She will have reason to live, if she knows that she will no longer have to work at the assembly line in a factory."

Dr. Boulder is unaffected by my optimism.

"Can you try another form of treatment?" I plead.

"We'll put her on a combination of drugs and see if she responds favorably."

On the way home, I stop at my mother's apartment to tell my siblings what has happened. They are aloof and dismissive of the details.... Living through so many traumas has shielded them from compassion. I, however, am lost to despair. I walk in the shoes of everyone in pain, and I cry for every child who has been neglected, abused, or abandoned. Now, bound by a commanding code of commitment to do right, I am trying to negotiate a balance between being a wife, a student, a full-time wage earner, the guardian of my broken mother, the caregiver to my pathetic father, and a surrogate parent to my siblings who rely on me and resent me, all in the same breath. For so long, I have drawn from my mother's strength and tried to be like her but on this day, just like her, I am defeated and exhausted.

At home, Marvin is waiting to ruthlessly ambush me with denigration and shame.

"Why should I care that you are stressed. Your father is a bum, and your mother is a psycho. Your family is your problem, not mine... you can all go to hell."

I break down and cry.

Marvin grabs a bag of potato chips and blasts the TV so he can expunge me from his world.

"Please lower the sound, Marvin. I need to get some sleep." I plead.

He takes a bag full of pills out of his pocket and hands me three.

"Here, take these pills. Take all of them. They'll knock you out, so you won't hear the TV."

I know Marvin will be watching TV until early hours of the morning. I take all three pills and go to sleep.

WHEN THE PHONE wakes me up the next day, it is six o'clock in the evening. I have slept nearly twenty hours.

"I am at my parents'." Marvin spurts, as soon as I say hello. "I'll come by tomorrow to pack my stuff."

"Where are you going?" I ask, stammering.

"I am going to Boot Camp. I joined the Navy."

"You never mentioned anything."

"I talk to my parents, not you. It is not any of your business what I do."

I remember the pills he had given me the night before. I wonder if he had intended to kill me. As a pharmacist, he has both knowledge and access to every drug. He knows what cocktail of sedatives to use to put me out of my misery and set himself free. He'll tell everyone that I committed suicide; that I overdosed on drugs. He'll say that everything was my fault, and that I was simply too unstable and far-gone.

WHILE Marvin is at Boot Camp, I decide it is time to for me to end the charade of our marriage and get a divorce. He'll be in boot camp all summer, and by the time our lease expires in July; I'll be able to move out. I call Marvin's mother to tell her about my decision. She wants to come over and talk to me and I reluctantly oblige her.

"Faye, my dear," she says fondly, sitting in the living room of our scantly furnished apartment, "Have you thought about having a baby? It would help save your marriage."

I feel sad and livid at the same time. I know it is time to dispel Anne's delusion and tell her the truth about her son.

"Marvin and I don't have a sexual relationship. Our marriage has been a sham, couldn't you see that Anne?"

Anne's jaw drops. Her face has turned blazing red and is shimmering with sweat. I don't know what has overwhelmed her more... the knowledge that her son and I have not consummated our marriage, or my indiscretion to divulge such intimate information.

I light up a cigarette and wait for her to compose herself. Her large head is wobbling and I can see the tiny beads of sweat emerging from the bed of her thin hair that is coiffed with excessive hair spray. I want to offer her a drink or a cigarette, but she is not the kind of woman who indulges in bad habits.

"Maybe you should get help with your problem." She finally speaks.

194

"I don't have a problem, Anne." I sit back and inhale a deep ration of smoke. Then I tell her about her son's comment on the night of our wedding.

She gasps, and I fear that she may suffer a stroke or a heart attack. I hold her hand and tell her how sorry I am.

IN A FEW DAYS, I consult with an attorney and move out of the apartment that I have shared with Marvin for nearly two years. I take with me my meager personal belongings, and a new supply of dismal memories to collate with those from my past. While my mother is in the hospital, I stay with my siblings and continue to work at the employment agency. I give my sister a check to pay the delinquent rent, and deposit Mohsen's generous charity in an account for my mother. I am determined to return to college and resume my studies. I will have to apply for student loans and for work-study stipends to support myself. I know that once I return to school full-time, I will not be able to subsidize my family's expenses. But my sister's income will not be sufficient to support their household, and with my brother entering college full-time, they will not be able to survive. It is time for my father to relinquish his idle days and earn a living. I have to find him a suitable job.

On my way to the registrar's office, I stop to see Claire at the Foreign Student Office. She greets me lovingly and is pleased to know that I am planning to resume my studies.

"Let me know when you need a room. The demand for housing has increased and we are in short supply." She cautions.

"Unfortunately, I can't quit my job and return to school unless I first secure a job for my father."

Claire lights a cigarette and ponders for a moment.

"Darling, I think I may have just the right job for your dad."

I can't imagine my father actually qualifying for any job, but I know that Claire always has first-hand information about the goings-on in and around the campus. Within minute, she is on the phone dialing a number.

"Hello, Frank. How are you, my dear... and how is your lovely family?" Claire exudes congeniality and her sincerity is never questioned. She genuinely cares about people. She is listening to Frank as he gives her an update on the status of his family and then, she explains why she has called him.

"I have a good man for that gate security job. I know his daughter very well and I can vouch for him. Would you do me a favor and interview him?"

I am filled with optimism. Claire knew intuitively that this job would be simple enough for my father to handle.

She writes down something on her pad, and then says goodbye to Frank.

"O.K. darling, it is done. This job is perfect for your dad. Write down this number: Flushing 7-3572. Call Frank and let him know when you can bring your dad over. He has to fill out some forms and pick up his uniform. He can start work on Monday. The pay is good... six dollars an hour, forty hours a week with benefits."

"You are my lucky charm, Claire. Thank you so much. You have saved me, once again." I give Claire a hug and tell her that I love her.

Papa's employment is timely and the best thing that we could have hoped for. He is happy to put on his uniform every day and take a bus to work. He sits in the guardhouse checking IDs and decals of students, and handing out permits to visitors who drive through the gate. His paycheck covers not only his own rent and personal expenses, but he can also absorb the cost of my brother's education.

With their new status as immigrants, both my brother and my sister are eligible for in-state college tuition. Ruhie continues to work full-time at a bank in Manhattan and takes evening classes at Queens College. She is going on dates and wants more than anything to get married and have children.

IN NOVEMBER 1966, I fly to Juarez, Mexico. This is the major destination for Americans who seek a speedy dissolution of their marriage. I have booked a two-day trip during the Thanksgiving break so that I don't miss any of my classes.

Juarez reminds me of towns in the old Western movies. It is dusty, grungy and menacing. At any moment, you expect to see a saloon door suddenly slam open as John Wayne steps out, brandishing his rifle and shooting down half the people in town. Fortunately, the attorneys on both sides of the border have a meticulous and amicable working relationship. All the paperwork is prepared in advance and after a brief meeting with the Juarez attorney, my divorce is finalized.

Anne calls me when I return to New York. She wants me to meet with a Rabbi to obtain a "Get " for her son. She explains that this is an official document that the Rabbi will sign to testify that Marvin, as the righteous spouse, has requested the annulment of our marriage.

I meet with the Rabbi the next day, and sign the appropriate papers. I am glad to be free and not surprised that Anne wants to document her son's virginity.

SOON AFTER Maman comes home and just before my classes begin, she calls to tell me that Aunt Narge's husband, Peymaan, is coming to New York for medical treatment. He has been diagnosed with stomach cancer and wants to consult with specialists in the United States.

Once Peymaan arrives, we realize that he is too frail to travel on the subway. We have to take a cab to and from the city every time we visit a specialist, and Maman insists on paying for his daily care and his cab fare.

"We are Irani, *azizam*.... We treat our guests with kindness...with utmost care and generosity." Maman proudly declares.

Peymaan's prognosis is poor and as he prepares to return home, we have news from Tehran that Aunt Narges has attempted suicide by setting herself on fire. She had been severely depressed after *Khanom jaan*'s death and now, the grim prognosis of her husband's illness has pushed her over the edge. She can't fathom raising her children by herself. They both have special needs: her daughter Meena is mildly retarded and her son, Maher, a Savant, needs daily supervision. Setting herself on fire may have been my aunt's ultimate cry for help but in the end, she has become more helpless...left to endure even more shame and desolation.

For those who do not know Aunt Narges' life story, or have conveniently elected to deny and dismiss it, her dreadful act has become further silage to contend that she is a genetic misfit, a divaneh... a demented woman who has always been her brother's overwhelming burden. But Maman knows well why her sister doesn't want to live. She knows about the angst of betrayal and loss of dignity. She knows all too well, why death is the only end to their suffering.

Shortly after Peymaan returns to Tehran, he succumbs to his illness and dies. Aunt Narge's failed attempt at suicide has left her with ugly physical scars, which oddly elicit sympathy not towards her, but for her brother and his wife.

"Pity my husband Nader Khan," Marjan reports to everyone, "His liability for his sister has now multiplied and the *aaramesh*, peace in our family is all but gone."

In a few months, Aunt Narges will be coming to the United States in search of doctors who may be able to restore her face. It is an unrealistic goal, but perhaps spending some time with us will mend the disgraced woman's heart.

The two-bedroom apartment where Maman lives with my siblings already lacks adequate space and privacy for our small family. Nonetheless, Maman will give up her bed and utilize all her resources to accommodate her sister.

In two weeks, Narges is ready to return home without surgery. She has taken a cursory survey of the multiple procedures that may provide her with a reasonable degree of satisfaction, and has decided that she has no choice but to bear the shame of her grotesque destiny.

Up from Earth's Centre through the Seventh Gate
I rose, and on the Throne of Saturn sate,
And many Knots unravel'd by the Road;
But not the Master-Knot of Human Fate.
Omar Khayyam

- The Abyss -

For months, I have been quietly suffering with a debilitating malady. Suddenly and without warning, my heart begins to race. I feel as if I am caught in a vortex of fear and instability, pulled in all directions simultaneously. I am clammy, seized by terror, and immobilized. I tremble and hyperventilate. The space around me closes in, and I feel the urge to run away... I must run to breathe and to get away from the cyclone that is about to swallow me. I am certain that at any moment I will collapse and die, but I don't want anyone to see my humiliation when I pass out. This is not a nightmare from which I can wake up. This is an inexplicable event that I experience often and with increasing intensity now. It strikes me like an avalanche and leaves me tattered and exhausted in its aftermath. I struggle to get through the day, always hopeful that tomorrow my 'disease' will simply go away.

In my Abnormal Psychology class, I am intrigued

by the analysis of human behavior and wonder if the mystery of my bizarre condition lies somewhere in the recesses of my subconscious. Our professor, Dr. Teiman, is a tall, dark-haired man in his late thirties. He is cheerful, handsome, and always impeccably dressed in a suit and tie. He reminds me of *docteur* Mokhtar, the compassionate neighbor who had once saved my life.

Today, as Dr. Teiman lectures on the subject of panic and anxiety disorders, I realize that he is describing my malady. Suddenly, I feel the urge to flee. My heart is racing so violently, I am certain that the thumping sound of my fighting heart is audible to everyone around me. I try desperately to stay in my seat and suppress the impulse to scream.... Help me...help me, I don't want to pass out here... let me get out.

I'm mortified... wondering if the professor can see right through me. He is undoubtedly feeling sorry for me...and that thought, too, intensifies my anxiety. I tighten my grip on the chair, and pray that I don't pass out before the class ends.

As soon as the bell rings, I jump out of my seat and rush to leave, but the professor is standing at the door waiting for me.

"Wait," He commands gently, "Are you alright?" He motions me to move away from the door and walk over to his desk.

"I saw you fidgeting in your seat." He says calmly and with genuine sympathy.

I stand trembling and speechless.... vulnerable and weak ... all I want to do is run and get away from my panic...but who better to trust with my humiliating secret than him?

"I think I am having an anxiety attack." I confess, feeling entirely defenseless and naked before him. "I had to hold myself down and fight the urge to run out of the classroom." I disclose tearfully and then oddly, my anxiety begins to diminish, as I admit my sin.

"I can help you." He removes a card from his briefcase and hands it to me. "Call me. I have office hours in the evening. We'll set up an appointment for you to come and see me.

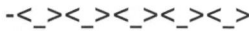

IT IS A COLD winter day and I can see the snow - covered ground from the barred window of the psychiatric ward at Elmhurst General Hospital where I have spent the last thirty days. Today, I anticipate my discharge. I will be released to go home, even though I do not know where I belong and where my home is.

I pace the floor waiting to see Dr. Pasteur. He is the psychiatrist who has been my confidante and shaman ever since he admitted me here. He has pulled me up from the abyss and rescued me from the dismal state of physical and mental ruin that had nearly annihilated me.

My mother had brought me here one month ago, when every effort to save me had failed. She had told Dr. Pasteur that after my first visit with Dr. Teiman, I had come home dazed and disoriented and had slept until the next evening. She had told him how every evening, after receiving a phone call, I had left the house in a hypnotic stupor and returned when everyone had already gone to sleep. I had missed my classes since the first week of school and had refused to eat or to speak to anyone during the brief hours that I was awake.

I have a fragmented recollection of the timeline of the events that proceeded the day I walked out of my psychology class with Dr. Teiman's card in my hand. What I do recall, however, is a consistent theme with vivid images that reappear in my mind clearly and unfailingly. I remember Teiman calling me late in the evening to remind me that it is time for me to leave. I borrow my sister's car and drive to Hillsborough Boulevard to meet him at his office. As soon as I arrive, he offers me a cup of coffee. I sit in the waiting room until his last patient leaves. Then he comes out to take me into his private office and locks the door behind him. I am cognizant of his commands and follow his cues attentively, but I have no control over what is happening to me. I feel as if I am in a dream state, where everything is set into motion without my influence or authority.

Teiman sits in a large leather chair and holds me on his lap. He asks me questions, mostly about my father, sometimes about other men. He says that I have to learn to trust...know what it is like to be truly loved by a man. He kisses me and masturbates me but I don't feel anything. He pledges his love and I hear his words, but mine are frozen inside. He shows me photos of his wife and his children, posing together happily in a frame prominently displayed on his massive mahogany desk. He picks it up and brings it close for me to see. He says he loves his children and that is the reason he can't leave his wife and marry me. He says he will always love me and take care of me.

"Promise you'll never leave me, Azadeh." He pleads, as he undresses me. He kisses me and caresses my body.... tells me how much he loves touching my skin...how much he wants to make love to me but fears burdening me with an untimely pregnancy. He then sits me down under his desk and at his feet. He guides my hands to fondle his engorged penis and move it through my lips. He wants me to thrust his penis in and out of my mouth... to bathe it in my saliva and titillate it with carnal want. He tells me he loves me, as he squirms and quivers with lustful cries. He calls my name again and again with lascivious anticipation, until his ejaculate explodes and his penis is limp.

"I love you Azadeh... Promise that you'll never leave me." He pleads again, and I am silent still.

I come home in the dark of the night when no one is awake, and I go to sleep. After a while... I don't know how long... I am too weak to leave the house. I sleep all the time and open my eyes languidly, only to the prodding cries of my mother. She is begging me to wake up and eat. She carries me into the kitchen and tries to feed me, but I refuse to eat. She is certain that I am dying.

Teiman calls the house everyday and night, often imploring, sometimes demanding that Maman take me to him. When she refuses to let me see him, he threatens her, but then he pleads with her again. "Please let me come and see her. I want to help her. I love her. I can make her well."

Maman doesn't know what to do to save me, but Teiman is the last person she wants to have near me.

ONE MORNING, as the sun rises above the cold winter horizon, my mother puts me in a cab and takes me to a neurologist's office for my first dose of Electro-Convulsive Therapy.   Someone has told her that this is my only hope to regain my sanity.

In a frigid and sterile room, equipped with massive and menacing machines, a nurse lays me down on a cold metal table, camouflaged by an inhospitable pad that reeks from torture and burnt skin. My wrists and ankles are tied to the corners of the table with thick straps of leather. I voice no objection while the nurse plasters on my temples the icy slime at the end of the electrodes, and I show no resistance when she shoves a rubber guard into my mouth without a flinch.

"It is going to prevent you from swallowing your tongue and choking when you convulse".

Another nurse injects me with an anesthetic and I drift into darkness. Then suddenly, a jolt of electricity shocks my brain, jars my body, and awakens me to the gruesome reality of my sentence. My body shudders violently to turn my limbs loose, and my arms and legs pull away from their bowl to rip through the straps that leave my skin bruised. I sink into the dark oblivion again, where I see nothing and no one sees me.

When I wake up, I am vacant and disoriented. A nurse walks me out of the chamber of terror, and ushers me to the cashier's desk. Maman hands me my checkbook. I pause to remember my name, and then scribble it on the check. The cashier will fill in the rest... $500.00 for thirty-minutes of mind- altering, induced convulsions. And, there would be four more sessions before my savings are exhausted, my college loan is spent, and the brutal treatment has pushed me over the edge.

"Maman *joon*, don't worry about me... I am dead. You don't have to take care of me anymore." I announce to my mother, shortly after my last ECT session, wishing to end her suffering by declaring myself dead. But Maman is inconsolable. She knows that I am in a deep and dark place from which I may never return. She has asked everyone for help and been advised to take me to the Emergency Room at Elmhurst General Hospital.

"Please help my daughter... She is dying."

Dr. Pasteur, a young psychiatrist with warm eyes and a gentle demeanor, spends a long time talking to my mother.

"You've come to the right place." He assures her, putting his arm around her shoulder to comfort her.

"Go home. We'll take care of her."

Maman kisses me goodbye. She knows that she has lost the daughter she once knew, but she has done all that she could. Now, she has to go home and trust that God and Dr. Pasteur will save her child.

"*Ghorbanatberam* Azadeh *jaan*, please get well." Tears have soaked my mother's bosom but have given her no comfort.

"Hello, I am Miss Jackson." A large woman announces as she approaches me. She looks harsh and intimidating.

"I'm going to take you upstairs." She says firmly to let me know she is in charge. Then she takes me by the arm and we walk through a cold and barren corridor, which leads to a solid metal door. She unlocks the door to let us through, and then locks it behind us. We walk down the hall and to the nurse's station, where two women quickly scan me with their eyes. The women exchange some words to which I pay no attention. Then, Miss Jackson leads me past a dining hall with barred windows and rows of rectangular wooden tables.

"This here is where you get your meals...it's the only place you're allowed to smoke... you a smoker?" I am not sure, but I say yes. Now we walk through a long hall with doors on each side. "These here are the bedrooms." She explains, then opens the door to a room with barred windows and two small beds. "This here is your room...that's your bed." She points to the narrow bed against the wall. "You got a roommate. Her name's Holly and she don't like talkin' to nobody. So don't bother her. ...less she wants talk to you."

I ask Miss Jackson if I can stay in the room and sleep.

"No, honey... First, I'm gonna make sure you don't got any razors or pins or matches on you." Miss Jackson's voice has softened. Perhaps she has determined that I am not violently insane. Now she gives me a full-body search, as she explains the rules for my safety. She pulls down my underwear, takes off my bra and checks my hair and my pockets, where she finds a pack of cigarettes.

"We keep your cigarettes at the nurse's station. You can't smoke here in your room."

"O.K. She's clean." Miss Jackson announces to a woman who has just walked in.

"I am Nurse Wilson." The newcomer introduces herself, as Miss Jackson leaves the room. She has brought me my ration of medication. "The doctor wants you to take this three times a day. He is going to see you every day in his office downstairs. Somebody will escort you there and bring you back here."

In a few minutes, Miss Jackson is back to fill me in on the ward's rules and regulations:

"Now listen to me good. You can read and you can talk to other patients all day long but you must be in bed by nine." She feigns a smile and continues to recite the ward's copious amendments.

"You can use the shower down the hall, but you have to get in line. Tomorrow, the doctor's goin' to see you and decide if he wants to transfer you to a lower floor where you have more privileges but here on this floor, you're not allowed to smoke in your room or leave the ward. Your family can see you during the visitin' hours. You're not allowed to take anything from them. We're goin' to check you every time you come back from the visitin' room. So don't you get smart. You eat and drink only what we give you. You take only the medicine that the doctor prescribes; and only what the nurse gives you." She pauses briefly to catch her breath. "Make sure your bed is made in the morning before you go eat. We announce the mealtime and expect you to get to the dining room when you hear the bell ring. Breakfast is at eight, lunch is at noon and supper is at six. Did you get all that right?"

"Yes, Thank you."

"O.K... now, I'll show you the bathroom and the

shower. We give you plenty of soap to keep yourself clean."

As we walk through the corridor, I look into other rooms and wonder if I am the only resident of this morbid insane asylum, but every room appears to be occupied. I see the shadow-like bodies of patients sprawled over their beds. There is no sound except for the whimpering of a few patients. I am in the world of the living dead.

At night I see my roommate, Holy. She does not speak to me but I learn later that she had lost her newborn baby and soon after, her own brilliant mind. She was a gifted pediatrician who couldn't save the life of her own child and had tried to commit suicide.

For the next thirty days, I meet with Dr. Pasteur and take my dose of Thorazine three times a day. Slowly, I learn to trust this gentle man whose compassion is surpassed only by his fierce dedication to his patients. Now that I have pulled out of the abyss and reconnected with the world, I have to make sure I can trust it and thrive in it.

BY THE TIME I am released from the hospital, I have lost another semester of college, forfeited my student loan, and depleted all of my savings. Now I have to submit a request to be reinstated and then, apply for another Student Loan to get me through the upcoming semester. I am determined to study psychology and have declared it as my academic major. But first, I must find myself a job, a room, and enough funds to register for the fall classes.

As I walk across the campus from the Admission's building, a young man passes by and seconds later calls out to me.

"Wait...wait. I'd like to talk to you."

I turn around wondering if I know him, but he does not at all look familiar to me.

"I am Alex Taylor, a freelance photographer for an Art magazine. Would you be interested in modeling?'

"Excuse me?" I say with obvious shock and mild curiosity.

"It is legit...I promise you. I like your look... I'd like to photograph you. I'll pay you nine hundred dollars for twelve shots and give you all the negatives that I don't use." He hands me a card with a Manhattan address and phone number.

"You can call the magazine publisher and check me out." He pulls out a magazine from the large bag on his shoulder and I notice the long lens of a camera dangling from it.

I hesitate for a moment but take the card and the magazine and shove them into my handbag. I need money for school and can't pass up this opportunity.

"My name is Azadeh. I'll think about it and let you know."

The next day, I call the magazine and confirm that Alex Taylor is a bona fide photographer. I call and make an appointment to meet him at 10 a.m. on Friday. I am penniless and nine hundred dollars can help pay for an apartment, my books, and my tuition.

The studio is on the top floor of an old two-story building in Greenwich Village. I anxiously walk up the stairs and ponder briefly whether or not I should turn around and leave.

Inside, Alex gives me a warm welcome and makes me feel at ease. He introduces me to his staff, and then he hands me a contract to read.

"It is simple. You agree to let me do twelve shots. I'll use only three to publish, and give the rest to you. I'll pay you nine hundred dollars after we finish the shoot.... count on being here all day. We'll take a lunch break at 12:30."

I read the contract, sign it, and hand it back to him.

"O.K. Let's get to work." Alex summons his assistant, Laura.

"Put her in red satin. It'll be a nice contrast against her black hair and pale skin. No makeup.... I want her natural. I'll work on the hair angle myself."

Laura takes me to the dressing room and hands me a neatly folded satin shawl. She asks me to take everything off.

For a moment, I feel a twinge of embarrassment but dismiss it promptly... My communal bathing as a teenager had made nakedness a natural byproduct of being poor. I drape myself in the shawl, and then walk to the camera room where Alex is waiting for me.

"Perfect." Alex smiles as he leads me to an over sized chaise chair.

"Lie down on your side and relax so that I can position you for the shoot. I 'd like to do a shot that accents your million dollar tush." He smiles, and I blush as if to coddle a secret thrill.

I sit on the chair and slowly lower my body to a reclining position. Alex positions me on my stomach and to my side to expose my back at a revealing angle - careful not to offend my modesty. He circles around me...occasionally repositioning me, and taking the nude photos that will rescue me from naked poverty.

By late afternoon I am on the subway, and then on

board a bus to deposit my earnings. I pick up the paper and call several apartments that are near the college. One in particular seems most appealing and the landlady is willing to have me look at it this evening. The studio apartment is on the first floor of a two-story townhouse on Booth Memorial Avenue. It is in a quiet neighborhood of Queens-just a short bus ride from college and a few yards from a serene park across the street. The landlady is an attractive young woman with blond hair that is visibly bleached. She does not work, lives with her two white French Poodles, and does not appear to be terribly in need of money. She is charging a very reasonable fee for the clean and semi-furnished apartment that is just perfect for me. I give her a check for $240.00 to cover one month's rent and a month's security deposit. I tell her that I don't have much packing to do and would like to move in the next day.

Later at my mother's, I pack my belongings, and write a check to my sister for $300.00. I feel badly that I used her car when I was sick. She has been cold and apathetic towards me. She never asks how I feel or where I have been. I believe she is holding me responsible for everything bad that has happened to our family.

I HAVE TO REGISTER for my classes and find a job before I run out of money. I look in the classified section of the local newspaper and find that The Grolier Publishing Company is looking for sales representatives. The sales office is located on Hillsborough Boulevard, not far from Teiman's office. I recoil as I think of him but quickly dismiss the memory. I have no time to waste ruminating my tragedies.

I take two buses and climb a three-story stairwell to reach the Grolier office, anxious but confidant that this line of employment would be easy and suitable for me. Inside, there are four men. Three are on the phone talking to prospective clients. The fourth, a short, round bellied, redheaded middle-aged man is smoking a fat cigar and reeking profusely of tobacco and indiscretion.

"I am Henry." He speaks with a voice that aims to impress. "I am the District Manager."

I introduce myself, noting Henry's roaming eyes that have been scanning me ever since I walked in. He is a drooling fool with a voracious appetite for food and money.

"I have trained all these guys and they are all making good money. I've been doing this for ten years." He boasts languorously. "You can make a lot of money in this business if you are willing to work hard."

"I am good at working hard." I say sternly.

"When can you start?"

"As soon as I can find a car for two hundred and fifty dollars; it is all that I have and all that I can afford." I expect to hear a roar of laughter from everyone in the room. The truth is that I don't know if I can buy even a motor scooter with my small stash of money.

"Hey boys..." Henry addresses the guys who are quietly chatting. They all turn around in unison to hear what their boss has to say.

"Boys...do you know where we can find this young

lady a car for two hundred and fifty bucks?" Henry snickers and I feel embarrassed. I wait for the men to make some insolent comment, but they are quiet. Then one of them comes over to shake my hand.

"Hi, my name is Shelly."

I used to know a girl whose name was Shelly. I wonder why a handsome man would be called by that name. Then I hear another guy call out, "It's Sheldon... call him Sheldon." I shake his hand and tell him I am pleased to meet him.

"Maybe we can give her an advance, boss." Shelly addresses Henry with stern authority, and I see the other guys nodding and gesturing their approval. Henry looks surprised...perhaps even intimidated. Surely, this was not the reaction he had expected from the boys he had trained for implacable loyalty.

"O.K. Shelly, watch the shop for a couple of hours. I am going to take this young lady to my friend's dealership and see what we can do for her."

"Sounds good, boss." Shelly is pleased, but a hint of uncertainty betrays his smile.

"Come on, let's go." Henry motions me to follow him. Then, as we are leaving the office, with Henry walking a few steps ahead of me, Shelly inches up close and whispers to me. "Don't let him touch you."

I look up and give him a nod of appreciation, relieved to know that he is a trustworthy ally. I am the only woman working in this den of wolves, and I know that I can easily become their prey.

Minutes after we are in the car, Henry's hand is on my thigh. I pick his hand off my lap and toss it onto his, nearly knocking his dangling cigar off his slobbering grip.

"Let me out of the car at the next light." I scream.

He takes the cigar out of his foaming mouth and puts both hands firmly on the steering wheel to regain his mindless mettle.

"Come on.... I know you need this job, and you need money. I'll buy you a car if you spend a couple of hours with me."

I grab the door handle and threaten to leave.

"Pull over, Henry. You can let me off right here. I'll go back to the office and let the guys know what you have offered me."

"No, no...." Henry's red face has turned pale and flaccid, giving more burden of disparity to his bright orange hair.

"Look, I am a married man. If my wife finds out, I'll be a dead man. Let's forget this ever happened."

"Smart move, Henry. Now let's go find me a car. If I can't afford to pay for it, I'll have to find myself another job."

At the dealership, Henry convinces his friend that I am a member of his family and if he sells me a bad car, he'll live to regret it.

Within an hour, I am driving my very first automobile down the street and I am thrilled. It is a massive and magical machine; a white Chrysler Convertible with features I never knew could exist: power locks, power windows, and power seats. I can't believe that I paid $250.00 for all this luxury. Now, I have to get to work and make a few sales before I run out of money.

"Congratulations." Shelly cheers when we return. He is pleased that I have survived the induction training without any obvious injury.

"Thank you Shelly." I say gratefully, smiling to let him know that all is well.

"You can come on my appointments tomorrow night." He offers. "I'll train you so you can make your own calls and start selling."

The next evening, Shelly gives me a copy of "Siddhartha" ... a gesture of peace to overcome the odds. He takes me along on his appointments, and I watch him sell encyclopedias with great confidence and ease. By the end of the day, I have learned the trade well enough to mix it with genuine care and make my sales.

On my first official day as the lone saleswoman at Grolier, I come in early to make my "Cold Calls" for the evening. The three salesmen I had met yesterday are in the room talking to a young man I have never seen. He is strikingly handsome and rugged; his face rivals Paul Newman's, and his stature could have been poured out the cast of Michael Angelo's David. He is a marvel of creation and has my immediate obsequious attention.

Shelly makes the introductions.

"This is John Pollack. He is from Ohio. He is going to join our team."

John shakes my hand and instantly lights up my heart with his warmth and his coy seduction. I see the twinkle in his eyes and know that he has noticed mine. We sit together side by side to make phone calls between our talks. I tell him about the car that I had purchased a few days earlier, and he tells me about the motorcycle that is his main tool of transportation.

"Shelly, I suppose I can go to my appointments on my motorcycle, right?" John asks casually.

"I don't know anything about motorcycles John," Shelly admits, "But if you think you can pull it off, more power to you."

I am charmed, both by John's naiveté and by his adventurous spirit.

"What if it rains?" I ask with apprehension.

"I drive in the rain all the time...not a problem." John says cavalierly.

"Not with a twelve volume set of encyclopedias." I challenge him.

"Good point." He smiles, amused by my grit.

IN A FEW DAYS, John and I have become inseparable. He is fascinated with my life story, the abridged version of it, of course. I have not told him much about my childhood.... not the abuse, poverty, and molestation. I know if I ever told him my secrets, he would run. John's life is not complicated; it is not tainted with mystery and trauma. He had recently graduated from college with a Fine Arts degree only to find that both his hometown and his college education were woefully obsolete. Now at twenty-five, he had decided to come to New York to search for adventure and employment, most likely in that order, in the big city. He has no money and believes that Grolier can offer him flexibility and a convenient choice to earn a living.

During the day, John and I make our calls and make sure to schedule our appointments in the same neighborhood so that we can ride together in my car. We knock on the doors of strangers and potential customers in the evening, and preach to the families their critical and urgent obligation to offer their children the superb educational advantages that our fine books and encyclopedias deliver. John always drives me to my appointments and waits for me in the car. He worries about me going to the home of strangers alone. He always makes sure that the homeowner knows he will be waiting for me outside.

IN THE FALL, I return to college full-time and discover that my demanding schedule leaves little time to sell encyclopedias.

I apply for another student loan and with John's contribution we are able to pay our bills and afford occasional outings.

My family adores John, and he is captivated with both our Persian and Jewish cultures. He wants to speak Farsi and delights Maman infinitely when he compliments her with his charming Farsi vocabulary. My sister is dating an Iranian man and my brother is a junior in college. My parents are civil to one another whenever there is a holiday or a cause to celebrate. On these occasions, Maman never fails to invite people who are alone or away from their home and family. This is a tradition that her parents observed when she was a child and now, she wants it to be the legacy she will be remembered by.

John and I are in love and very happy. We share the bond of poverty, adventure and the genuine desire to take care of each other. We long to be together and make love with passion and tenderness that defies the limits of our fantasies.

Every day, John surprises me with a note or a message he has hidden strategically around the apartment.

"I LOVE YOU AND WANT YOU FOR MY OWN *and forever... I hate to leave. Our evenings should never end. Our talks are invigorating and our lovemaking splendid. You are delightful, sweet, mystifying, hypnotic, and oh...so loving: you are the woman poems and symphonies are written for. Love & kisses, John."*

Some mornings, John and I have to ration off our last dollar and our few remaining cigarettes to get us through the day, but we laugh about it and look forward to the end of the day and being together again.

"Please honey, pace yourself with the cigarettes... only two or three a day...O.K.?" He whispers as we say goodbye.

Later, as I reach into my purse, I find a note tucked inside.

"My sweet love, keep me close to your heart all day because I can't be without you, ever!"

By the end of spring, John is ready to leave Grolier and look for a "real job". He has contacted the Board of Education and has found an opening for an art teacher at Bedford Stuyvesant School in Brooklyn. It is a tough neighborhood... rampant crime and violence define this Brooklyn neighborhood and most teachers avoid working there. It is also a long commute from my apartment, requiring two bus rides and a couple of transfers on the subway trains. John doesn't mind the inconvenience and is not worried about his safety. He is glad that he has found a respectable job that offers him satisfaction and a consistent pay.

"I'll make friends with the kids. They won't be

afraid of me if I am not afraid of them." He assures me.

We realize that since the commute from John's storefront room in Richmond Hills to Brooklyn is considerably shorter and less costly, he may spend some nights there. We agree that a little separation will make our love stronger.

IN NOVEMBER 1968, Maman calls to tell me that Marjan has given birth to a girl. It has been six years since her last pregnancy and five years since the birth of her youngest son, Cyrus. Nonetheless, the delivery of this child has brought new vitality to the family's faith in folklore and psychic premonition. Everyone has determined that the 'accidental' nature of this pregnancy proves only one thing...that the soul of *Khanom* jaan has returned in the body of this angel they have named Arella, the messenger. Maman has proudly announced to her brother that she has indeed had a premonition about the birth of this baby; that *khanom jaan* herself had appeared in a dream forecasting the release of her soul to her son's youngest progeny. Even my Uncle Nader, the resolute atheist, has admitted to a soothing sense of familiarity at the sight of his newborn baby.

The collective conviction by my mother's family that *Khanom jaan*'s soul has returned to live in Arella's body, is as ample a justification for my uncle to feel virtuous, as it is for my mother to forge yet another campaign to appease him. She is going to offer every ounce of her might and money to lavish the baby with boundless gifts.

I take Maman shopping and watch with sad

consternation her excessive expenditure. She has exhausted herself and depleted her savings and still, she does not believe she has done enough. There is yet another gift that she must buy.

"Here, Maman. This is all I have." I give her the thirty dollars that I have saved to buy a winter jacket. I know how desperately my mother needs her brother to acknowledge her worth...the worth that he patently measures not by expressions from the heart but by impressions of gold.

I know that my mother's wish to have her brother's affection is uncompromising ... it is the force of her existence and the source of her vitality. She needs to fill the gaping wound of her childhood abandonment; the existential injury that she has no inherent resource to heal. Her only hope is that the man who abolished her self-worth will restore it for her someday... perhaps when she can prove to him that she is worthy. I know the untenable sequel that keeps my mother hopeful, but I cannot take away her hope. I hug her and tell her that I love her, and then I help her wrap the gifts and ship them to her brother's home. I know he will never call to say that he appreciates her. He will have his wife write a perfunctory letter and Maman will wait for yet another chance to be validated by her brother.

- My Sister's Wedding -

In the spring of 1969, my sister comes home one night, thrilled and triumphant. She flaunts her beautiful engagement ring and announces that she will soon be married. For months she has been dating a young man named Simon and has been telling us about his infinite affection, devotion, and generosity. Simon and his father own a successful garment factory. He is a gentle and congenial man who adores my sister and we have every reason to believe that he will make her happy. Marriage has always been Ruhie's priority, and I hope that having children and a wholesome family will diminish the sadness of her childhood memories.

As the task of making the nuptial arrangements with a meager budget is relegated to me, I have to explore every option available to make my sister a respectable wedding. After days of deliberation and inquiry, I negotiate with the owner of a cozy and elegant Persian restaurant in Manhattan to provide us with entertainment and a feast of delectable Persian cuisine. I am confident that the evening will be festive and everyone will be pleased. To save money for a gift, I sew my own dress and forfeit buying a pair of shoes that I badly need. Then I spend the entire night on my feet, checking every table and tending to each of the seventy guests to make sure they are properly served.

A few days later, while the bride and groom are on their honeymoon, Maman tells me that my sister is upset with me and has vowed never to speak to me again. She had cried to my parents and told them that I embarrassed her by not providing her with a more elaborate wedding.

I am surprised and heartbroken. I had worked so hard during a very busy school year to make this affair a success. Now downcast and overwhelmed, I am having a hard time catching up with my schoolwork.

John is livid when he hears about my sister's complaint. In the past few weeks, while I was consumed with wedding arrangements and unable to type up my reports the night before they were due, he had volunteered to stay up on a couple of occasions and type them for me, so that I could get some sleep. At first, I was reluctant to burden him with it, but he insisted that he was so much more at ease with the typewriter than I was and I couldn't refute that fact.

"Stop crying, baby." John wraps me in his arms to console me. "Your sister is screwed up... she should be thankful for all that you have done for her. Please don't torment yourself."

He is right. I can't afford to brood over Ruhie's discontent. I have to get back to my studies and catch up with all the work that I have neglected.

Later, John brings flowers to cheer me up.

"I am so proud of you, baby. You will be the first woman in your family to graduate from college. I love you forever! John"

- The Missing Link -

Since the normal functioning of my ovaries has ceased due to the prolonged years of malnutrition, I have never been concerned about using contraception and never worried about becoming pregnant. In fact, until a few months ago when my menses reappeared with a vengeance, I had celebrated my infertility, if not for any other reason, but for being free of the excruciating pain.

"Baby, aren't you wondering why you are not getting pregnant, now that the curse is back?" John asks apprehensively, "Is there something you haven't told me, honey?"

"I may be infertile, my love," I say glibly, "But think of it as a blessing ... I have no desire to have a baby."

"I hope you are not serious, honey. What if we want to have kids someday?"

"O.K., darling," I say playfully, "Maybe I am not getting pregnant because I am not supposed to have an illegitimate child."

The truth is that I want to get married. I love John

and I want to be his wife, even though I am not ready to undertake the task of motherhood and raising a baby.

"Well, then let's get married, but you have to convince me that you can bear my children."

John's voice resonates with firm determination and it gives me the chills. Will he leave me if I don't give him a baby?

John's Drawing: "Let's have a baby." (C.1969)

JULY 16, 1969, the day that Apollo 11 is launched, seems to be the perfect occasion for us to test our destiny. I am in my mid-cycle and by all accounts fertile to conceive. We lounge on the floor of the living room lustful and naughty. We tease each other and laugh, we hold each other and talk and for the entire day, we float on the wings of ecstasy as we make love. We are over the moon and in an orbit all our own,

227

pulsating with passion and raptured in delight, celebrating with hope and anticipation that our love will seal our union in my womb and give us a child.

"If we have a son, we'll call him Apollo." I say faithfully. I love John more than ordinary words can explain. I want so much to give him a son. He has told me that his father was not good to him. I know he needs to raise his own son to prove that he is a better man than his father could ever be.

We make love until the sun rises on the horizon, but our mission to conceive fails dreadfully. There would be no son to name "Apollo" and no pregnancy to secure the longevity of our commitment to one another.

MY SISTER RUHIE, too, seems to be suffering from a non-yielding ovary and an inhospitable uterus. Three months after her wedding, she is convinced of her alleged infertility and for her, this calamity is unparalleled. Every month that Ruhie menstruates signals days of brutal anguish and grieving that requires the intervention of the entire family. She becomes irate, inconsolable and abusive, sending her husband Simon into a state of sheer panic.

"Please hurry up and come over...you have to calm your frantic daughter. I don't know what to do for her. She is out of control." Simon pleads with Maman, who in turn calls everyone to come and rally around my hysterical sister.

"It is all your fault." She snarls at Maman. "You ruined my life." She squeals.

No one knows what Ruhie is talking about, but Maman needs no justification for self-loathing and self-reprimand...all she needs is a hint of rejection to feel worthless and guilty. She will punish herself because Ruhie is angry with her. It is a scene reminiscent of our childhood except for a profane twist...It is my mother's own child who is tormenting her and fostering her self-hate.

Jafar is holding Maman down.

"*Baseh* Maman, it is enough." But we know that we are in for a long night of misery and distress.

"You have to relax, Ruhie...the more anxious you are the harder it is to conceive." I dare explain.

"Shut up, you fucking bitch," she growls, "Nobody asked for your stupid opinion."

Papa tries to intervene.

"*Baseh bacheh*, enough child. *Bachehdaar mishi*, you will have children, don't worry."

We try hopelessly to calm my sister, but her random tirade and accusations continue amidst her ear-piercing shrieks.

"I'm never going to be a mother. I'll never get pregnant. My poor husband is not going to have a son. I hate all of you. You ruined my life and took everything from me."

Simon cautiously walks towards his wife and holds her hand.

"Come on honey, your family loves you... See they are all here."

"Get out of my house, all of you goddamn bastards. Leave me alone." Ruhie shrieks.

We pull Maman away and lead her outside. Her skin is oozing with blood from the cuts she has mercilessly inflicted on herself.

I know that it won't be long before my mother

suffers a physical or mental breakdown. She needs to get away for a while... perhaps take a trip to Iran to visit her family. I know I can come up with some cash to send her away. Just two weeks ago, I found my engagement ring in a tattered box where I keep small articles of *yadegari*, the mementos that relatives gave me before I left Iran. This diamond ring is the only asset I have retained from my three-year marriage to Marvin. I had removed it from my finger long before I divorced him and never wondered about its worth. But now, I have good reason to dispose of it. I am going to sell it and send Maman to Iran for the summer. I may even be able to buy a ticket for my brother. He'll look after her and undoubtedly; he will enjoy spending time with Javid, his cousin and childhood playmate.

I WATCH WITH angst John's reluctance to commit to me. Ever since he has become convinced of my infertility, our relationship has been deteriorating. There has been increasing criticism, skepticism, and expressions of discontent concerning my family. It is a subject that I avoid and dread vehemently. But John has been asking too many questions about them lately. He wants to know why my parents were divorced and why they couldn't keep their marriage intact as his parents did. He says he admires his own parents for staying together, even though they did not have an ideal marriage and may have even hated one another.

"Are we going to wind up just like your parents, Azadeh?"

"My love, I am working hard to circumvent the

odds that led to my parents' disastrous marriage. I aspire to have a relationship free of all the elements that caused my family's devastation." I say vigorously, hoping that my voice will be a resounding ally in spite of my own uncertainty.

"There is so much discord amongst you." He complains. "Why is it so hard to maintain peace in your family?"

I know John's misgivings are justified. I have not even revealed to him the humiliating details of my childhood, but there is more than enough damaging debris to make him weary. He might as well run away and leave before my past catches up and wrecks him. I wipe my tears and light a cigarette. I wish we could end this conversation, but John is not done yet.

"When you first told me about your breakdown and hospitalization, it didn't bother me. But now that I see how your sister carries on; acting so irrational and fighting with everyone, I have to wonder if mental illness runs in your family." John is deliberately somber and serious. "What if it is passed on to our children?"

I try to stop the flood of more tears. I am heartbroken and humiliated, but I know that John's fear is valid and reasonable. When I was a child, I used to wonder if we had been infected with defective genes ... germs that had made us poor and crazy. I had often heard Marjan refer to her husband's family collectively as "divooneha" the crazy ones, and I was convinced that she was right. After all, if they had everything and we did not, there was something wrong with us.... It must be that my uncle had the 'good luck genes' and we had the 'crazy bad genes.'

"No, my love. No one in my family has inherited the genes for mental illness. The truth is that we are all victims of a tragic fate that burgeoned from the seeds of my uncle's greed, when my mother was just thirteen."

I pause to gauge John's reaction but he is quiet, so I attempt to buttress my case with a more cogent explanation.

"You see, it is quite evident that it is our dreadful circumstances, not our luck or DNA, that has pushed us over the edge."

John is pondering still, and I know that my defense has not been persuasive. After all, we are a damaged family and that is what everyone sees; it matters not who is the culprit and what the cause is... we will be judged just the same.

Now, tired of waiting for John to ratify my plea, I pledge that even if he apologizes, I will tell him it is too late and he should go away. I will never allow him to humiliate me again.

"Goddamn it...I wish you would get pregnant..." John breaks the silence, trying to inject his harsh misgivings with a dose of gallantry.

"Why would you want me to have your baby if you are doubting my sanity, John?" I ask earnestly.

"I love you so much, honey. I know that life is not ever good without you but I am scared, baby... I am really scared."

Now he is crying, but neither his tears nor my own will ever wash away the bane of the words that echo inside my head. I look at him with sadness and resignation. I feel detached and unsteady. My head is congested from crying and my voice is muffled with uncertainty. I know that what John is scared of, I can't fix. All my life I have tried to fix things I had not broken; tried to make right what was wrong; and tried to preserve things that were unsustainable. Now, I am, myself, entirely broken.... exhausted and utterly hopeless. I know that even if I put together the shattered pieces of my own life, I can never be detached from the trauma and dysfunction of my family. It will be easier to deny myself romantic love, than to forge a relentless crusade to explicate the incarnation of my troubled life. I will let John walk away... I will let him go because he deserves someone better. I will distract myself with work, and I will compensate for my loss with the pursuit of my education.

JUST AS THE CHRISTMAS holidays approach, John announces that he plans to spend his vacation alone in the Bahamas. I don't question him and don't object. Then hours after his arrival in the Bahamas, and just as I have concluded that he has permanently walked out of my life, I receive a telegram from him.

"I MISS YOU AND REGRET THAT YOU ARE NOT HERE. ALL MY LOVE, JOHN"

I shed a few tears...feeling bad for him and sorry for myself, but I must refuse to succumb to self -pity and melancholy.

Saturday night, I drive to Manhattan to spend the evening at club Darvish in Greenwich Village. This is a trendy Persian restaurant that has been my refuge whenever I have missed the sound of International

233

music and the taste of Persian cuisine. I have been here on a few occasions with John and my family... when we were all enjoying a rare interlude of festivity and peace. Tonight, I want to be alone. I know the entertainers, the staff, and even some of the regular patrons who share the same ethnic cravings. A popular international singer, Yacov, performs here regularly. He has a dynamic voice and a prolific repertoire of international songs that he plays on his accordion. He is on the stage performing when I arrive, and his handsome face lights up when he sees me. I order a drink and sit nearby to watch him. Yacov flashes a smile every time he turns his head in my direction. He has always done this, even when John and my family have been in my company. Instinctively, I have smiled back, dismissing John's allegation that I flirt with him.

"He smiles at everyone, John," I would retort, "It is natural to smile back and acknowledge him."

Tonight, during his break, Yacov comes over to my table and asks if he can sit with me.

"Where is your boyfriend?"

"He has gone to the Bahamas"

Yacov pulls back his chair and takes a long look at me.

"He's gone to the Bahamas without you?" he laughs nervously, "Why? Did you break up with him?"

"No.... Well, we may be moving in that direction." I tell him that John and I have been hitting some serious turbulence in our relationship, but I would rather talk about him. I'd like to know where he was born and when he began his entertainment career.

"I was born in Algeria and raised in Israel." He says

dismissively.

"You must have a fascinating life story."

"Perhaps...and it is a story that I'd like to tell you one night over dinner."

"How about tonight?" I say playfully.

He smiles. "I'd like to see you when I am not working. I'm off on Mondays. Are you free?"

"I'll be delighted. It's Christmas and we are on holiday. I am off from school."

Yacov summons the waiter to get us drinks.

"What are you drinking, Azaheh?"

"Rob Roy, please." This is a cocktail that John had offered me on our first date, and it has since become my favorite buzz drink. But now, I regret ordering it when I am trying desperately to get him out of my head.

"Excuse me a moment, I'll be right back." Yacov leaves the table and disappears behind the stage. In a few minutes, he is back with a record album in his hand.

"This is my new recording. It is a compilation of popular international songs. I hope you like it."

His handsome face is on the cover. He is wearing a French beret and a sensual smile. He looks stunningly chic in his classic pose.

He takes a felt-tip pen out of his pocket.

"How do you say I am in love with you in Farsi?" He asks eagerly, "I speak five languages, but Farsi is not one of them."

I take a long look at him, startled by his unbridled and surprising sentiment. Yacov and I may have flirted, but I had never thought it was anything more than a fleeting deception. I am not sure what to make

235

of it, but I am not about to question or dismiss the welcome distraction.

"Ashegh-e tu hastam."

Yacov smiles, and then carefully writes the phonetic words on the album cover.

"Azadeh, Asheg-e tu hastam. Yacov "

As he gets up to return to the stage, he gives me a kiss on the cheek, and insists that I order something to eat. We talk and dance between his sets and exchange phone numbers. At the end of the night, he walks me to my car and we kiss good-bye.

"It is 2 a.m., darling...be safe driving."

I assure him that I'll be alright and look forward to our dinner date Monday night.

On the way home, I decide to take Northern Boulevard and avoid the potential hazards of the Long Island Expressway. This is a route John has always preferred, and I have frequently traveled alone.

As I pass an intersection, I notice a police car following me. I slow down wondering if in my state of absent-mindedness, I had sped or gone through a red light. In a few minutes, the police car slowly passes me by and moves in front of me, as the officer in the passenger seat motions me to follow. This is unlike any protocol I have ever seen for the issue of a traffic ticket. I am not at all comfortable with this tactic. I follow the police car cautiously and at a safe distance, prepared to change direction if I need to get away quickly. At this early morning hour, traffic on Northern Boulevard is sparse and the lights are rather dim. We have driven over two miles and passed several locations where I could have been pulled over, but the police car continues on its path, still signaling me to follow. Then suddenly, the driver motions me to enter a dark alley as he inches over to get behind me, leaving me little room to maneuver. I know that I am being lured into a trap from which I will not be able to escape. Instantly and instinctively, I turn the wheel and speed down the main road, shaking and panting as I try to hold on to the steering wheel. I am afraid to look back and terrified that no one will help me, should the cops pursue and catch me. There have been so many publicized incidents where witnesses have ignored a victim's cry for help because they did not want to get involved. Just a month earlier, I was walking up the stairs at Grand Central Station when a man clutched my leg and tried to drag me down. I shudder when I remember my panic, and wonder what the perpetrator had in mind. Had he been able to grab both my legs, I would have lost my balance and tumbled backwards down to the bottom of the stairs, most likely to my death. I had used all of my strength to keep one foot on the ground for leverage and managed to escape. I screamed for help, but no one came to my aid or seemed to care. I know they heard me, but perhaps such pleas have become as commonplace as the inanimate sounds of everyday traffic. They are the fleeting irritations that eventually fade away, as witnesses rush to their destinations with urgency of perceived life or death, never pausing to contemplate the humanity that they have left behind... the compassion that they, too, may need sometime. That day, in the subway station alone and terrified, I managed to get away. But tonight, the odds are against me and I may not have luck.

I look into the rearview mirror and take a deep

sigh of relief. The police car is not visible as far as I can see, but I am nonetheless worried that my ordeal may not be over. These deranged policemen may suddenly reappear, if not to avenge my audacity, but to let me know that I should never speak of their transgression to anyone; never to report it to their superiors, or I would be sorry.

I get home and fall into bed exhausted, pledging not to ever go out alone again. Luck seems to have been with me once again this morning, but it may run out one of these days.

THE NEXT DAY, I am sick with the flu and can't get out of bed. Yacov calls and wants to bring me soup, but I am in no mood for company or for soup. I miss John and all I want to do is sleep and dream that he is here next to me.

Ron calls to find out how I am managing without John during the holidays. He is my lab partner in the Experimental Psychology class and has been following me around like a wounded puppy all semester. I am very fond of him and enjoy his company. His sense of humor makes the long lab hours tolerable and even entertaining. We work well together and both regret not having pursued our ambition to go to medical school. He knows that I am in love with John and that we practically live together. But now that John has gone away, Ron is hopeful that we break up and he will have a chance to replace him. I tell him about my close encounter with the wicked cops and that the flu has made me succumb to melancholy and weakness.

Two hours later, Ron is at my door with food and flowers. He has written me a note:

"Loveliest Azadeh, words are inadequate. The intensity of my feelings defies articulation, but I'll try to summon those words, which will allow me to feebly express myself. I know I can't do justice to your beauty so I won't defile it with pen and paper. Your mind transcends intellect as it pierces the walls of my mind and reaches my core. I am putty before you and yours to do with what you want. Ron M."

Ron is the most trustworthy and dependable man I have ever known. He is smart, funny, and pleasing to the eyes. I know he will never let me down, but John is the one I want to be with today, and for the rest of my life.

On Monday, I receive a letter from the Bahamas. John writes that he is miserable. He regrets having gone away without me, and can't wait to come back. When he returns in a few days, he has brought me a plethora of erotic lingerie, an exquisite ring with my birthstone, and the promise that he will never leave me again.

"You are messing with my head, John." I protest. "I don't understand the mixed messages."

"I am going through some adjustments, honey." John admits. "Please be patient with me. I don't want to ever be without you, baby."

Two days later, I come home to find the entire living room wall covered with a bizarre inscription:

"SHE LOVES ME, SHE LOVES ME NOT, SHE LOVES ME, SHE LOVES ME NOT… "

I am stunned and entirely clueless about the meaning of this odd message. I wonder if John has found the album that Yacov had given me? Did he find out that Ron had come to see me? And, how am I going to get the wall painted before the landlady sees it?

I wait for him to come home, unsure that he ever will. Was this his way of saying good-bye to me? I am riddled with anger, frustration, and fear...but I wait.

When John finally arrives, it is late in the evening...and he is conspicuously stoned.

"What is the meaning of this message, John? Did you pick up some exotic hallucinogenic drug from the Bahamas?" I anxiously inquire.

"I knew you'd find someone else." He stammers.

"What are you talking about?" I ask fretfully, now certain that he got stoned because he was convinced I had cheated on him.

"I saw you on the bus with a guy." He says fumbling.

"O.K. John... now I know for sure that you are either hallucinating or projecting." I infer, because I have not been on a bus with any man, anytime, or anywhere.

"Oh, yes...I saw you, myself..." He stutters.

"You John...you are the one who has been telling me about a girl you talk to on the bus ...every day on your way to work," I remind him, "Do you have a guilty conscience? Do you need to confess?"

John ignores my question.

"I'll paint the wall this weekend. I have already apologized to your landlady and told her I would take care of it." He informs me as he leaves the house.

I am baffled... utterly exasperated by John's bizarre behavior. Then the next evening he comes home with flowers and a note to muddle my head some more.

"Without you, I don't know what is going to become of me. I know I have caused more pain, for both of us, than our love could ever bear. To the best of my ability, I swear I shall avoid causing pain forevermore. Please forgive me. I love you. John"

We make love with the intense desire that has always validated our boundless passion for another.

"Please say you will marry me, baby. " John holds me tight and I know he is fighting feel his tear against touching s see tears in his eyes. "I don't ever want to lose you."

"Are you sure?" I can't conceal my suspicion. "Why now? What is going on, John?"

"Yes, I am sure baby. Let's do it. Let's make the commitment."

I am ecstatic but cautious. I can't quite let down my guard. I wait a few days in case he wants to reverse his decision. Then I announce to my family and friends that John and I are getting married. But first, we need to get our premarital serology test required by the state to obtain our marriage license.

ON THE DAY of our appointment, I wait at the doctor's office for John's arrival, but he doesn't come. I am crushed to my core ...this is the most malicious injury John could have caused me. The man who claims to love me has shattered my world. How can I ever survive this humiliating catastrophe? I know I will not survive this.... I will lose my mind irrevocably. I must call Dr. Pasteur before it is too late... I'll go see him and tell him that I don't want to live. I know he will leap out of his seat, grab my hand and put me back on the top floor of Elmhurst General Hospital... right where all other suicidal patients live.... pacing the floor aimlessly.... or sleeping away their lives on sedatives. There will be more Thorazine, windows of iron shield, and isolation from a world that continues to torment me. This time, I will stay there and never leave. In that asylum, I would be safe from temptation to ever fall in love again.

When John comes home, it is dark outside. I have been feeling morbidly ill, aching and burning with fever. I had curled up in bed all day letting exhaustion sweep me away... and hoping not to ever see the daylight again.

"How are you, honey?" He asks, surprised to find me in bed.

"I am not feeling well. I think I have the flu again." I mutter.

He walks over and kisses me on the cheek. I know he is waiting for me to burst out with fury, but I am not going to yield. I am determined to preserve my dignity by pretending that I had forgotten our treaty.

"I had work to do." He volunteers.

"O.K." I say quietly.

"I was talking to the Assistant Principal. He told me that I should get my Ph.D. and become a Principal, then a Superintendent, and make $40,000 a year."

"It sounds good. I am sure you can do it."

"I would feel a lot better if I could make enough money to support a family."

"I understand." I say earnestly, feeling a measure of relief to know that it may have been John's sense of responsibility that had suspended his urgent desire to get married. But could he not have talked to me instead of humiliating me?

He volunteers the answer without my inquiry.

"I didn't call you intentionally, because I don't want to feel regimented; tied to a time schedule. I don't want you to think that I am going to do what you want. I am timed and scheduled enough during the day."

Now I am not sure about my earlier hypothesis. It is safer to assume that John is simply besieged by so much ambiguity that he can't think straight.

"I understand honey... It is O.K." I summon every ounce of my compassion not to get mad at him. But John looks disappointed. Maybe he wants me to be angry with him; that would mitigate his guilt, I am certain. I wish I had the courage and the confidence to confront him, but I remain impassive.

IN JUNE 1970, after a grueling decade of battling and defeating academic sabotage, my graduation day finally arrives. John is genuinely happy for me. No one has ever been as enthusiastic about my scholastic success, or an advocate of my mission to graduate from college. He attends my graduation with the pride of a parent, and then takes my family out to dinner to celebrate the occasion.

"Congratulations! A million kudos to you; the first woman in your family to make it on your own, and to graduate from college. I only wish I had the world to give to you in order to gauge how proud I am of you. Everlasting Love, John" (inscribed in Farsi)

In a few days, as the school year ends and summer holiday begins, John announces that he wants to travel to Europe.

"I can get us round-trip discount tickets to London. It's through a teacher's group and the price can't be beat. Are you interested?"

It is clear that I would not be John's companion on this journey. He explains that he plans to explore Eastern Europe on a motorcycle and visit Yugoslavia, the home of his ancestors. I would have to plan my own travel itinerary, if I want to go.

This is once again another twist in the conundrum of our relationship, but I know that I can't change its course. I may just as well plan my life independently and without John from here on. The opportunity to travel to Europe is exhilarating and the timing is just right. I have secured a full-time teaching position that begins in the fall, when I will also commence my graduate studies. I have sold my car and my lease on the apartment will expire in a month. I will have the entire summer to wallow in my misery, if John goes away and I stay behind.

ON JULY 15, 1970, John and I fly to London, both looking forward to our individual journeys. He will be roaming through Eastern Europe on a motorcycle. I will be traveling through Southern Europe via rail, air, and water, until I reach my final destination, Tehran, where I plan to join Maman and Jafar who will have already arrived there.

In the London Underground, John and I say goodbye formally and unceremoniously. Perhaps our chilly farewell is a mutual collaboration to ease the pain of our separation. But sad as I am about saying goodbye, I look forward to embarking on this capricious voyage alone. I always need to challenge my ambition and my ability to survive on my own.

I have in my hand a copy of Frommer's "Europe on $5.00 a day", and a budget of $500.00 that would have me backpacking through two continents, using the least costly, albeit less convenient transportation from one destination to the next. My month-long journey through Europe takes me to Greece, then to Israel, and finally to Iran. It is the most extraordinary and exhilarating adventure I could ever have expected or imagined. Every city and every stop presents an amazing opportunity for learning and discovery...and each day is packed with wondrous and indelible memories. I stay at hostels, often with multiple roommates and student travelers from far corners of the world. I visit many museums and historic sites, always taking the less traveled roads to learn about the culture and lives of the local residents. I find new friends - some continue with me on the same path, while others disperse to other cities and continents.

When I arrive in Tehran, I learn that everyone has gone north to the shores of the Caspian Sea. I promptly take a bus and meet them in Bandar Pahlavi. This is the port city close to Rasht, my mother's birthplace. It holds fond chronicles of her youth, and the cherished memories of those rare summers that we vacationed here, once Maman resumed her teaching career. Those days, Bandar Pahlavi was not populated nor considered a trendy vacation spot. People of affluence spent their summers at the luxury resort of Ramsar. But now everywhere, affluence is the common denominator. Even those who lived modestly a decade ago have become owners of beachfront property.

Bandar Pahlavi, however, a decade later, still seems the same to me. It feels as if time, in this precious corner of our country, has stood still waiting for our return visit. The small hotel where we used to stay has maintained its old charm and authenticity. Its congenial proprietors still remember Maman and treat us like family. Everything looks and feels the same: there is the euphoric fragrance of saffron rice wafting from the kitchen, the mouthwatering aroma of Kabob sizzling on a bed of blazing coal, and the unmistakable scent of Chaii Lahijaani tea that simmers atop the brass Russian samavar in the dinning room.

I feel at home here, remembering those rare carefree summer days when Bandar Pahlavi had the magic and the mystique to wash away our pain.

Maman was always happy here. She felt a spiritual connection with the Caspian Sea. This was her home, where she grew up and where she felt alive and free. This is where she found peace nestled in the cocoon of native friends and nostalgic memories. We spent the days frolicking in the Caspian Sea and bathing in the sun as we chatted with the sparse number of visitors on the beach. Then, after a scrumptious dinner, we strolled along *Boulevar-e* Pahlavi, where the delightful evening breeze from the sea would soothe our sunburnt skin, and the street vendors would tease our appetite with the mouth watering waft of balal, coal-roasted corn from the grill. We quenched our thirst with a cold glass of *sharbat-e aalbaaloo*, cherry nectar, or *sharba-e aablimoo*, lemonade, and let the sweet taste of the elixir linger on our breath as we hugged the night goodbye and waited for the sun to rise again. We wished every day that this piece of heaven would remain unchanged and never far away. Now, outside of Bandar Pahlavi, there is very little that has remained the same. In the span of ten years, Iran has embraced an unprecedented transformation. The influence of Western culture is most striking in large cities, where there is extensive modernization of roads, homes, transportation, and commerce. The urbanization and industrialization is so vast that it has made the familiar cities unrecognizable. The literacy rate, too, has increased significantly and many men and women are pursuing college degrees. They dress fashionably and socialize freely without the stigma that was so prevalent when I was a teen.

In Tehran, the dramatic rise in population has lead to an exponential rise in real estate values. The level of affluence has increased visibly across the board. The poor have become rich and the affluent have become wealthier with greed. My Uncle Nader now owns blocks of property and rows of buildings in the center of the capital city. He also has in his custody the parcel of land that the Shah had awarded to Maman and Aunt Narges in the late 1950s.

Jafar and I visit our old residence on *Khiaban* Tulu. We count the stairs to the third floor and I ask if he remembers his tyranny...when he demanded that I carry his luxury toy car up and down the stairs several times a day. It is a nostalgic visit, but passage of time has diminished both the grandeur of the building and the significance of our memories.

Later, I decide to look for the friends I had left behind, a decade earlier. I am certain that they have all married and assumed the names of their husbands. Oddly, the only classmate I can locate is my old high school rival Roshan, the girl who had commandeered seventy students to boycott the teacher in our Biology class. I wonder if she remembers my defiance; sabotaging her scheme to have the teacher fired. I am not sure she will be pleased to hear from me, but I am almost certain that once she hears I have been living in Amrika, she will be intrigued. Living in America holds a prestige that defies any prejudice.

Roshan is surprisingly humble and friendly. I know that my status was instantly elevated when I told her that I had moved to *Amrika* after high school, graduated from college, and now live in New York City.

"I am having a party at our Summer Villa in Shemran Friday night. Come join us and bring a friend." She offers enthusiastically and I accept. I invite my cousin Javid, who is now in medical school to join me.

ROSHAN'S SUMMER VILLA is a fairytale castle atop a lush mountainous terrain with a spectacular view of the capital city; and the party is an extravaganza of exotic cuisines served by uniformed maids and waiters. The international band and the prominent guests, according to my cousin, authenticate Roshan's membership in Iran's most elite society. I am, however, pursued like a celebrity myself, as Roshan and her guests barrage me with questions about *zendegi dar Amrika*, what it is like to live in America...the country that captures the envy and admiration of so many people of other nations. Everyone wants to know about the joy of unrestrained freedom and the infinite access to luxury. No one asks about the civil rights movement or the devastating assassinations of American leaders in the past decade.

"The line between the lure of liberty and the menace of anarchy is often blurred." I proclaim.

In a few days, as my brother and I prepare to return to America, Maman decides to stay in Tehran. She wants to resume her teaching career and regain the respect and dignity that she had once owned and cherished. I worry that our family will be fragmented and the grief of separation will disrupt the small measure of peace we have just recently achieved. However, I cannot deny my mother the right to live a life of dignity. She is like a butterfly whose wings were cut off just as she was ready to soar. She is stifled, wounded, and incomplete. She feels alone and disconnected from her home and her family. She needs to be free to live amongst her friends and colleagues...she needs to be with those who know her grandeur and value her exceptional qualities. It is her right to pursue her own happiness, and the least I can do is to tell her that I respect and support her decision.

ON MY FLIGHT back to New York from London, I am not surprised to discover that John is not on board. For a few fleeting moments I worry that something may have happened to him traveling on a motorcycle through foreign and unfamiliar terrain, but it is more likely that he has decided to extend his stay and restate his fear of being bound to me.

Once in New York, I rent a room in the house where my father lives, while I look for shelter elsewhere. I have been accepted to graduate school with a scholarship, but even with the additional student loans and research grants, I will have to work to save money for a year of full- time clinical internship.

My employer, Harry Blau, is the director of the school for mentally handicapped children. He is a compassionate man who understands the arduous task of working full-time and attending graduate school. He allows me to take time off when I am overwhelmed with assignments. He has surmised that my family's financial resources are limited, so when I tell him that my brother, now in his first year of college is looking for work, he offers him a part- time job on the school campus with flexible hours and generous   pay.

WHEN MAMAN'S letters arrive from Iran, they are replete with heart-wrenching narratives:

"My search for employment has been futile and my brother has made it evident in no uncertain terms that he does not want me to be here. He is renovating his two-story mansion and has asked me to leave. I tried to stay with my sister for a few days, but Aunt Narges became abusive and I could not tolerate it."

Maman writes that she can't stay in the city because of the exorbitant rental fees. She has found a room in the remote town of Ziba on the outskirts of Tehran, where she has no running water and no heat.

"For twenty days, I have lived here alone and hungry. The weather is getting cold and I have to walk a long way to get a meager amount of food and water. After 5 p.m., there is no one on the streets. I am so frightened that I cannot venture out when it gets dark. Everyone is religious in this neighborhood, and they have realized that I am not one of them. I fear for my safety."

I am sick with worry. How can a family forsake their own kin? How can my mother's siblings neglect her and treat her so heartlessly? It appears that as soon as Jafar and I left Iran, Maman was regarded not as family, but as a tourist whose welcome had expired. With all his wealth and real estate holdings, including Maman's own property, her brother has not offered her shelter. He has abandoned her in the cold of winter to survive alone and without food.

I write to Maman and beg her to return to the United States. But she is determined to remain in Tehran and take care of herself.

She writes:

"The main purpose of my return to Iran was to work in the profession that once offered me respect and security. I want to be able to support myself. I do not want to be a burden on my children, nor do I want to stretch the hands of neediness to anyone else. I have sold everything of value that I had brought with me. I have even sold the sentimental gold watch that my uncle had given me, the only material possession that I cherished above all other things. But now that land values have soared, I have asked my brother to sell my Tehran Pars property. I am certain he can get a good price and give me the money."

A month later, while I wait with anticipation and hope that Maman has received the funds from the sale of her property, another letter arrives that speaks of her despair and unfathomable anguish. She writes that her desperate condition in Shahr -e Ziba had become so intolerable that she had no choice but to leave. However, having no place to go, she had reached out to her cousin, docteur Mohafez, who had felt sorry for her but could offer her no more than his cold underground crypt.

"As I write to you, I am shivering from the chilling cold. A while ago, I tried to pile up some bricks underneath the bed that has a broken leg so that I could sleep on it. Soon I heard a strange noise coming through the wall next door. I jumped and the bricks came down crashing and making a horrifying sound in the middle of the night. I have not been able to sleep and it is three o'clock in the morning as I write to you. I cannot sleep most nights because there is a low window that allows passersby to look inside the room. It gets very scary at night. I fear that someone will climb into the room. I believe it is almost two weeks that I have been living this way. Azizam, today I spent my last single toman to go to my sister's house and pick up your letter. I was full of joy and anticipation to read it. I did not spend more than an hour with my sister because she began to talk about all the grief and misery of our lives. Then, of course, I looked for comfort by going to my brother's. I wanted to see little Arella and give her a hug because I missed her, but my brother and his wife were very cruel to me.

Marjan would not talk to me, and Daii jaan was irate. You see, this summer when your brother was here, he took some pictures of Marjan and the children with his camera. Marjan wants those pictures and she wants them today. But I don't think Jafar has mailed them yet. Marjan is mad at me and tells me that this is all because we do not want to spend the money; that we are cheap. Then my brother said that I had embarrassed him in front of his wife. He yelled, "get the pictures today, not tomorrow- but today." I do not know how they expect me to do that. Please, I beg you to get the pictures and send it to them right away.

It is now 4 a.m. The cold is unbearable and I cannot step on the floor as it is like ice. I am sitting close to a small bokhari nafti, a kerosene heater that is giving me an awful headache. My back is hurting terribly from sitting on this broken bed. I think I best finish this letter and step outside this siah chal, black dungeon to catch a breath of air. I will then come back to pile up the bricks for a makeshift bed, and hope that I get some rest. It has been a hard day and I am very tired. PLEASE ASK YOUR BROTHER NOT TO FORGET THE PICTURES (repeated and underlined seven times) Ghorbanat, Maman"

MY MOTHER IS ALONE and destitute. She is a stranger to her family and a foreigner in her homeland. She feels disconnected not only from her kin but also from the *"many Iranians whose warmth and hospitable character has given way to arrogance and greed. The Western influence and capitalism has soiled and destroyed our magnificent culture and tradition. Everyone wants everything. The values that we cherished are now fodder for jokes and ridicule. Iran has lost its soul to the evil of greed, and Iranians have traded their nobility for an ignoble creed."*

My heart is full of angst, as I imagine my mother shivering and hungry in a cold and confined basement imbued with terror, and infused with the noxious fumes of carbon monoxide. I shudder as I envision her slipping away and taking her last breath, succumbed by the deadly gas. Again, I write to her and plead for her return.

"I promise we'll take better care of you, Maman, please come back." I pledge in every letter.

She finally writes that she is ready to return, but now the American Embassy has denied her visa because she has violated the limit of her stay outside the country. Her Iranian passport, too, has been confiscated because she had declared herself a citizen of Israel when she lived there. Now both her Iranian passport and her visa to return to America are null and void, making it impossible for her to leave the country. This is a catastrophe of an epic proportion. How will I ever rescue my mother from the brutal destiny that plagues her at every turn?

Maman writes to the Iranian Passport Agency, pleading for clemency.

"Gentlemen:

With great respect, I bring to your attention that I, yours truly, Esther Lahijani who has been a resident of New York for ten years and in possession of an Iranian Passport, came to Iran last year having been away from home for many years. I came here with an Iranian Passport to visit my loved ones and my relatives. Three months ago I began the proceedings to return to Amrika to join my children. Unfortunately, my passport, due to my brief travel to Israel eleven years ago, is now confiscated, preventing me from traveling abroad. I am informed that

254

they plan to surrender me to Israel. I am neither young, nor a soldier and not an employee of the Israeli government and can do nothing more but to perform my responsibility as the mother of my three children who remain as citizens of the government of the Shahanshahi of Iran but have been studying in America.

I am an Iranian, born in this great country and spent my youth and precious years of my life teaching high schools in Tehran. Now, after many years of longing for my homeland, I am faced with this dreadful ordeal in my own country and my birthplace. I do not know where to go and to whom I should turn. Does humanity allow that a mother be deprived of her children? In a century where the voice of freedom, equality and brotherhood resonates across the borders and continents, in this century that race and religion does not separate but unites all people, how do you justify breaking a mother's heart by refusing her the right to join her children? Are you going to allow the darkness of prejudice and ignorance overcome the light of compassion and love for humankind? Forgive me for allowing myself to cross the line of what may cause my demise. One needs to keep within one's boundaries and not offend anyone whose status and authority can determine one's fate. I beg of you respectfully to release my passport so that I may leave to see my children. I will be forever indebted to you and very grateful.

With the offering of my deepest respect, Esther Lahijani"

I MOVE my father, brother, and myself out of the rooming house and rent a two-bedroom apartment. I give my father and brother their own room, and partition off a corner of the living room for my temporary stay. I believe this is the most practical and economical arrangement until my mother returns.

Ruhie is incensed that she suffered a miscarriage during the summer while everyone was away, and has raised her bar of animosity and cruelty towards me since I returned. She has resented me ever since she was a child and now, her judgment of me conveniently skewed and deliberately hurtful, is putting a wedge in my relationship with every member of the family.

Maman's letters often bear quotations from my sister's letters that attest to her obsession to hurt me.

"Maman, believe me, Azadeh is the most awful person in the world. She is avazi, weird and crooked. She is living with Papa and Jafar comfortably, and taking advantage of them. They have no room for you in their apartment. I am so sick of her that I plan not to ever speak to her again. Ruhie"

I am outraged by my sister's vicious attacks on me. She is determined to sabotage my relationship with Maman, while she torments her with heartbreaking lies and unnecessary worry. Her letters are exacerbating Maman's anxiety about returning to America.

I quickly write back to my mother to nullify her fear.

"Maman Joon, I do not know why Ruhie is telling you lies about me. I am staying in the apartment with Papa and Jafar temporarily. I do not have a room of my own. I sleep on the floor and in a corner of the living room that I have partitioned for privacy. I am working and going to school. I come home only to sleep and do the household chores. Once you are here, we will discuss the details of our living arrangement. Please do not worry.

I am sorry I did not write to you sooner. Three weeks ago, I was very sick. I had to get on the bus alone to go to the hospital. I had pneumonia and they kept me there for three days. No one came to see me. I have been trying to regain my strength to go back to work and resume my studies.

Maman-e aziz, my beloved, please don't worry about what will happen to you when you get here. We will work it out so everyone will live comfortably. I know you have sold everything you own. Please don't waste your money on gifts to give to your family. You can't buy their love... money is the only thing they are capable of loving. Ghorba-e-shoma, I love you, Azadeh"

IN SPITE OF the inhumane treatment that my mother has received from her brother, she remains loyal to him and his family. Amidst all of the chaos that surrounds us, she writes that Lidia, her brother's older daughter, is on her way to New York City, and that we should make sure to tend to her if she needs anything.

Jafar is studying Computer Science and challenges me regularly with his proposal to develop a robotic brain that can respond to human emotions. I find the debate tantalizing.

"First, let's figure out why some human brains are incapable of responding to the emotions of others... Are they simply heartless...are they robots disguised as humans?"

"Well, that is your department. In the meantime, how about helping me with my term paper. It is due tomorrow."

Jafar is always asking me to do his term papers, and often at the last minute. I never say no to him but warn him without consequence.

"This is the last time I am doing it. I have enough of my own schoolwork...and may I mention having to clean up after you and Papa?" I protest, "Now, see if you can invent a robot to write your term papers...and while you are at it, invent one to pick up after you, and clean up your mess every day."

257

- Summer of Reprieve -

In June 1971, I receive an international scholarship for a two-month seminar in global research and internship. Earlier in the spring, I had been nominated by my professors and subsequently awarded this grant as a unique research opportunity to prepare for my doctoral thesis.

The seminar is held on a private campus in Connecticut. The faculty and the student participants are selected from graduate schools in thirty-five countries around the world. The rigorous curriculum will focus on the convergence of Eastern and Western philosophies and the psychosocial influence of the Western World in underdeveloped countries. I am passionate about these issues and look forward to vigorous debates with my fellow international colleagues.

On June 15, as the sun peaks from the horizon, I eagerly board a bus, and then a train to Manhattan where special transportation is provided to take us to our Connecticut campus.

Upon arrival, I am led to my modest but private room with a large window that faces a vast courtyard and the campus entrance. As I watch my international colleagues arrive, I am stirred with excitement and looking forward to this unique odyssey.

The International Seminar of World Affairs:
Salisbury, Connecticut: (Summer 1971)

IN THE SECOND WEEK of the seminar, I receive a letter from John:

"Thank goodness you are listed in the phone book. I have talked to your brother. We are thinking about coming up to see you next weekend."

John goes on to explain how he had missed our scheduled flight back to New York and decided to turn around and extend his stay in Europe. Since his return, however, he has been actively searching for employment and looking for me; and now he is thrilled to have found both rather expeditiously.

The following weekend, John arrives on campus riding his roaring motorcycle. My brother has decided not to risk his life on a bold man's two-wheeler. I introduce John to my new friends. He attends my classes and we spend the weekend reminiscing about our respective adventures in Europe.

Sunday evening, John and I say goodbye...once again without ceremony, just as we had done the summer before. I am not sure if I'll ever see him or hear from him again. But true to his propensity to spin my fantasy, he sends me a letter.

"My love, I miss you in many ways. My weekend there was truly a new and enlightening experience. Not only was I able to see and experience you in a different light and environment but also had the chance to feel even more proud of you: your ideas and your determination in upholding your point of view. I hope that I can be in a little way as important as you are to my intellectual vitality. Write if you find the time. Love, John"

BY JULY 1972, Maman has succeeded in obtaining her passport and is free to leave. The denial of her visa, however, still remains an obstacle with serious corollaries. She is told that she can re-enter the United States only as a visitor, which requires an affidavit of support, an official document to guarantee adequate financial resources so that she will not become a ward of the United States government. I spend sleepless nights wondering how I can secure such a document. I have reached out to my sister for

260

help, but she claims that her husband does not make enough money to qualify as a guarantor. I feel utterly hopeless and exasperated. I don't know if my mother has food and shelter, and how much longer she can survive under such inhospitable circumstances. I am eager to return to New York and turn every stone until I find a way to bring my mother home.

AT THE CONCLUSION of our seminar and our last day on campus, we are scheduled to take a cultural tour of New York City and attend a UN meeting before we depart for our respective destinations.

As the elected seminar representative, my assignment is to deliver a message of goodwill and unity, on behalf of our international community, to a very large church congregation in Harlem. Later in the afternoon, I am expected to meet with several distinguished members of the United Nations and present them with recommendations derived from our discussions and research. This is a momentous day that I know I will cherish for the rest of my life.

Early that morning, in preparation for our visit to New York City, I decide to coif up my hair by installing a few metal curlers to prime it up for better styling. There are a dozen male students outside, playing ball and making a raucous as they say good-bye to one another. I stretch my head out the window to warn them of the threat of a thunderstorm and the urgency to come in and get ready, lest they will be late for our last day's activities.

Within seconds, a bolt of lightning sprouts through my body, tossing me into the air and slamming me across and against the wall on the opposite side of the room. I don't know how much time has lapsed before I realize what has happened, but I am certain that my brain is fried and I will never be able to speak or think coherently again.

I sit on the floor stunned and bemused. Then slowly, as I begin to remember the humbling and honorable assignment that awaits me, I am adequately relieved that my faculties are still intact and that once again I have eluded death.

THE GREAT CHURCH of Harlem is packed with weekend worshippers, and I feel surprisingly calm when I am called to the podium to speak. I wonder if the jolt of electricity that had sent me flying across the room earlier had vaporized my perception of fear and vulnerability in the process.

My hour-long sermon on universal peace and unity for ALL mankind, at a time when segregation still remains a highly explosive issue in the country, appeases the sensibility of the audience and renders their enthusiastic applause.

I sum up my oration with a plea for compassion, for the recognition of our common needs, the hopes and aspirations that bond us collectively as human beings. I reiterate the prescription for civility and urge everyone to follow the dictum of "one for all and all for one"...together and not divided to serve mankind.

The audience rises to a standing ovation and at that moment, I feel as if they have lifted me on their shoulders and raised me to the summit of hope and inspiration.

In the afternoon, at a private meeting with the

United Nations' dignitaries, I present a summary of our research and recommendations and convey our desire to receive their feedback once they return to their respective countries.

"Gentlemen, let's meet for dinner at 1800 hours at the Waldorf." Ambassador Schneider announces, and then directs his attention to me.

"We would be delighted if you could join us, Miss Hamis." He concurs with his colleagues.

I had hoped to take the train home to Queens before dusk, but this is an honor I cannot turn down.

By six o'clock in the evening, I have checked my luggage at the front desk of the Waldorf Astoria, freshened up and ready to join my hosts in the dining room. They are seated at a large round table that is at full capacity with seven men and one seat that is reserved for me. Seated next to the vacant chair is a distinguished gentleman I have never seen.

"Miss Hamis, meet President Gallagher." Mr. Hughes makes the introductions, as the tall gentleman next to me rises to help me into my seat. Then he leans towards me and whispers genially, "I am Joe Gallagher...It's lovely to have you seated next to me." His face is striking and his voice beguiling and soothing.

"I am honored to meet you, President Gallagher."
I blush, failing to conceal the sudden titillating excitement that has tickled my spine. I am intrigued and want to know more about him, but no information is forthcoming from any one.

"I heard about your inspiring sermon at the Harlem church today.... Congratulations." President Gallagher extols.

"Truthfully, I was surprised to have been coherent at all, since I was knocked unconscious by lightening earlier today." I reveal spontaneously, and realize that now suddenly everyone is watching me. They want to know the whole story.

I give an enthusiastic account of my encounter with the bolt of lightning but hope that the attention doesn't remain on me. I am a guest at this dinner gathering and inevitably, I will be asked to tell them my life story... why I came to this country, what are my life-long goals, and what my parents do for a living. I dread being asked questions about my family or my past...it a subject that is least appealing and most terrifying to me. Throughout the years, I have mastered the art of telling a revised version of my life story...careful to avoid the devastating truth without compromising its relevance. Nonetheless, I often have to censor my thoughts and my delivery so that I can elude the flood of emotions that tempt me to expose my misery. I cannot allow anyone to pity me, nor to suspect that there is incongruity between the confident woman on the outside and the broken girl who is relentlessly hounded by her shameful past.

"It was quite courageous of you to leave home alone, in the pursuit of education." Mr. Kapoor, the Indian delegate remarks.

President Gallagher offers me a cigarette, and as he leans forward to light it, he whispers. "Don't be nervous. You are doing fine." Then he motions to the waiter to bring us drinks.

"Two Jack Daniels on the rocks, please."

He takes a drag from his cigarette and asks the German dignitary about his recent visit to the Middle

East. He is clearly trying to take the focus away from me.

I swallow a full gulp of my drink and take a deep sigh of relief, amazed by Joe Gallagher's incisive maneuver to rescue me.

"I was in Tehran just recently... A lovelier land and people you shall never see." The German dignitary speaks from across the table, his words muffled by his heavy accent.

"They are undeniably a very unique and most hospitable people... and the food is scrumptious," he smacks his lips, "Aah...the tedik is divine. No one can duplicate the art." Mr. Hughes expounds.

"Indeed," I concur, "Making the perfect tah deeg, the crunchy rice sizzling on the bottom of the pot, requires a degree of expertise."

By the time dinner arrives, the conversation has shifted to President Gallagher's philanthropic and humanitarian efforts to foster healthcare and promote education in many underdeveloped countries. The approbations expressed by the dignitaries are so effusive, I am certain that he has earned the trust and admiration of even the least affable members of the international community.

At about 8:30, everyone begins to say goodbye. They will be traveling back to their respective countries over the weekend.

"Where do you live, darling?" President Gallagher asks, as he helps me out of my seat.

"I live in Queens.... Flushing to be precise."

"How are you getting home?"

"I was planning to take the train...or perhaps get a cab, since it is quite late."

"I am going to Long Island. You are on my way. I will take you home." He offers decisively.

I have had two Jack Daniels and very little to eat. I feel off balance and unsteady. Joe Gallagher is quick to notice. He takes my arm and helps me lean on him.

In the limousine, I feel honored and exultant for the privilege of riding home in the company of a man of such extraordinary stature. I steal a glance at his handsome chiseled face while he is momentarily engaged in a conversation with his chauffeur. I have known Joe Gallagher for only a few hours and yet I feel an inscrutable bond with him. His charisma and compassion are dangerously alluring and extremely irresistible. I feel my heartbeat rising as I imagine myself nestled in his broad chest, loving him and being loved by him.

He seems once again to have read my mind. He puts his arm around my shoulder and pulls me close to him. We remain silent for a while, each musing perhaps the same perplexing questions. He lights a cigarette and offers it to me, then lights one for himself, still contemplating. Then he turns to me and asks if I am going to tell him my real life story.

"Why, Mr. President?" I ask impishly, hoping that seduction will avert the desire for emotional intimacy.

He looks at me with the tolerance of a merciful deity. He knows the trick I have embarked upon to distract him.

"You can trust me. You don't have to pretend that your life has been ordinary."

I am bewildered and yet relieved. Who is this mysterious man who knows me so well?

"By the way darling, I won't call you Ms. Hamis, if

266

you call me Joe..." He smiles and guides my head to rest on his chest.

"O.K. President Joe." I quip. "How do you know there is more to my life than what I have already revealed?"

"I see the sadness in your eyes, but you are quite good at keeping your head high on the strength of your pride. I admire you for that."

Tears are coursing down my face. Joe has connected with me on such a visceral level that I feel naked to my core and yet profoundly safe. He kisses my forehead gently and squeezes me closer.

"Would you like to spend the night with me, Azadeh? Better yet, spend the weekend, if you are free. I have no commitments until Sunday evening. We'll have time to talk and hear each other's life story.

"I'd like that." I say without hesitation. I have no real home and no one is waiting for me.

As we pass my exit on the Long Island Expressway, Joe tells his driver that he would not need him on the weekend and that once he drops us off, he can go home to his family.

"Should I pick you up at the usual time on Monday, Sir?" The driver asks.

"Yes, I have a meeting scheduled with the African delegation at the UN. Let's leave at 7:30 to avoid the rush-hour   traffic."

WHEN WE ARRIVE at Joe's sprawling estate on Long Island, it begins to pour. The wind is picking up slightly and the rhythmic sound of rain against the expansive windows in the dark of the night feels magical and exhilarating.

"Let's go dance in the rain." Joe bellows with the fervor of a child embarking on an exciting venture.

Before I can respond, he has shed his clothes and is running outside naked, gesturing for me to join him.

I do not waver. I quickly undress and run after him.

We hold hands, bouncing through the rain and making reckless commotion. The cool breeze from the bay feels like the strokes of a thousand soft feathers against our skin, and timid raindrops mingle with tears that flow from the joy of our liberation. We dance, sing and skip in the rain, then chase each other until we trip over our silly selves and fall into the arms of one another. We are naked...free from all restraints and pretenses - merged by our longing and drenched in ecstasy. We tumble in a whirlwind of passion until the rain and darkness end and a new dawn paints the landscape over the lazy bay.

Inside, we share our stories over copious cups of coffee and Winston cigarettes. Joe has just ended a long and unhappy marriage. His wife was cheating on him at their summerhouse in Martha's Vineyard while he was overseas working on a Global Aid project.

"I gave her the house in The Vineyard because I could never set foot in it again. I kept this one because it has been in my family for generations."

I can't imagine why any woman would cheat on a man of such vibrant presence, engaging intellect, and genuine compassion.

"I am so sorry, Joe." I reach over and kiss him.

"What about your children?"

"They live with me and spend time with their mother on some weekends. She feels no remorse to have relinquished their custody."

"It is unfortunate...but perhaps it is for the best."

"We were not suited for one another, darling. She was not suited for motherhood, either. The kids are happier living with me."

" I trust you are in a better place but it must hurt, nonetheless."

"I am too busy to feel sorry for myself. I get great satisfaction from my work and my children." Joe points to photos of his children on the mantle and smiles. "They are doing well."

At night, we sit outside with an ample supply of Jack Daniels and cigarettes. We are scantly dressed and naked with our life stories. I tell only some of mine, fearing that I would burden him. But the fractional version that I have revealed has already sent him into a tailspin.

"Your father tortured you? How does a man get away with such brutality?"

I can see tears pooling in Joe's eyes. He has devoted his life to aiding the helpless, the poor, the sick, and the underprivileged children. I tell him of my mission to help my family; how relentlessly I strive to fix the wrong so that shame will not be the legacy that would define me.

"It is an ambitious goal, darling...but you can't fix your family unless they each share the responsibility."

"You are right, Joe...but even if I abandon the responsibility to fix them, and I still can't abandon them."

"You don't have to abandon them. You need to differentiate between guilt and responsibility?"

"How does one make that distinction, Joe?"

269

"When you relinquish the right to fulfill your own needs in order to satisfy theirs, then you are hostage to your guilt."

"I admit that I am driven by guilt... I know that I cant' be well, unless my family is doing well."

Joe takes my hands and pulls me close to him.

"Who takes care of you, darling?"

"I do...I always rely on myself."

"You have been swimming upstream. What you have done for your family is anything but ordinary. When will you let someone share the responsibility?"

"I have been asked that question...I've heard it from men who have loved me. But to trust someone requires vulnerability, and that to me is inherently deadly."

"Aah...that is because we learn about trust when we are young and most vulnerable. If as a child you were not able to trust the adults in your life, then you can't allow yourself to be vulnerable as an adult."

"I saw my mother's vulnerability.... I watched how she was abused and neglected by those she loved and trusted. The threat of vulnerability has trickled down to my generation. We either will trust no one, or inadvertently trust those who will betray our vulnerability and abuse our trust."

"Yes, fear of vulnerability is paramount when you have been betrayed by your loved ones...it is hard to discriminate who should and who should not be trusted. Ultimately and unfortunately, if you do not trust anyone, you are bound to be isolated, alone, and even more vulnerable."

I tell Joe about how my mother has been betrayed and discarded by her family in Iran... her desperate struggle to survive ... and the Immigration gridlock that has made it impossible for her to return to the United States.

"I have to bring her back soon or else she'll die."

Joe holds me close and wipes my tears.

"What do you need to bring her home, darling." He asks in a pragmatic manner.

"She needs an affidavit of support and a plane ticket, neither of which I can provide."

"This is easy to fix, darling. I'll have my attorney call INS tomorrow. He has dealt with these issues and knows what to do."

"What do you mean, Joe?" I am perplexed but thrilled. I know Joe would not offer hope without commitment.

"We can help you, Azadeh.... Let me do this for you."

I try to articulate words that would have meaning, but instead I am sobbing.

"It is alright, darling. You deserve a respite." Joe reaches over and rests my head on his chest. I hear the strong rhythm of his heart and feel the burden of angst lifted from mine.

"You are truly amazing, Joe."

"I am happy to help. I have more than I need. Wealth does not grant happiness but for some, it offers a false sense of safety- even immortality. Wealth doesn't *make* a man who he is; it *reveals* who he is... what he is made of... goodness or greed. We leave our legacy through our deeds, and I want mine to reflect kindness and generosity...with no regrets and no strings."

Joe is quietly pondering something. Then his face

lights up.

"When I joined the Peace Corps and saw for the first time the smile of children who would not have to go to bed hungry, I knew that I had discovered the ultimate bliss. I realized that the opportunity to make a difference in someone's life is an honor and privilege unlike any. That experience was so prodigious, it transformed me. I find no greater satisfaction than to give to someone who is in need."

Now I understand the outpouring of praise and accolades from the UN dignitaries last night.

"You are a miracle, Joe... you are the paragon saint who gives people hope to believe in wondrous possibilities."

"It would please me immensely to know that your mother has returned home and you no longer have this burden to carry alone."

"Please promise you will never lose touch with me, Joe."

"You'll always know where to find me, darling." He reassures me with a kiss on my cheek.

I know that I will spend the rest of my life loving Joe Gallagher, but I know, too, that he can't belong to any one person or purpose.... He belongs to the world and the world needs him.

SUNDAY AFTERNOON, we have to say goodbye. Joe is going to pick up his children and take them to dinner. I have to go back to Queens and resume my life of chaos and uncertainty.

"I am sorry, darling. I hope you don't mind if I call my taxi service to send you a cab. I have to drive in the opposite direction to pick up the kids."

"Of course I don't mind, Joe. Thank you."

He makes a call to the cab company, then walks over and holds me in a tender embrace.

"I have to run. Make yourself comfortable. Your ride will be here in a few minutes. You need not be concerned about the fare. I have a running tab with the cab company. I will call you tomorrow after I talk to my attorney. He may want to speak to you directly. His name is David Minkin."

"Thank you, Joe...for everything."

"Goodbye, darling. I'll see you soon."

I pace the floor in a daze. My fairytale weekend has just ended and I don't know when I will kiss my prince again. I hear the cab outside and rush to leave. It is as if standing here alone will make everything seem   unreal.

THE NEXT MORNING, I am surprised to receive a large basket of exotic fruits and flowers delivered to my door.

"The weekend went by too soon. Thank you for sharing it with me. Joe"

Early afternoon, Joe's attorney calls. He has checked with the INS and has prepared an Affidavit of Support indicating that Joe will personally take responsibility for my mother's support for one year.

"Where would you like me to mail it?" He inquires.

I am overcome with elation, trying to catch my breath.

"Hello, are you alright?"

"Yes, I am sorry... I am just overwhelmed."

"I understand. Take your time."

"This document is strictly for formality... it's to

273

satisfy the INS requirements." I say apologetically, embarrassed for accepting charity. "We'll take care of my mother once she is here." I hasten to add, trying to deflect any negative judgment.

"I understand…. I just need to know where to send this document." He says cordially, putting my mind at ease.

I give him the address and thank him.

In the evening, Joe calls to tell me that his meeting with the African delegates has raised some concerns, which require his immediate attention. He is leaving tomorrow to attend an emergency meeting in Sudan.

"I'll call you when I return in a couple of weeks. Your mother may have arrived by then, and we will have good cause to celebrate. We can stay in the City for the weekend and catch a show on Broadway. Does that appeal to you, darling?"

My heart has been racing since I picked up the phone and heard Joe's voice. I am certain that he can hear my heartbeat through my trembling voice.

"I am eternally grateful for what you have done. I can't wait to see you again."

"I am delighted that I could help, Azadeh. I will smile every time I think of you and I assure you it will be often. I look forward to our rendezvous when I return. Good luck with bringing your mother home."

"Have a good trip, Joe." I say in a muffled voice. I am choked up…about to burst into tears and embarrass myself.

"Please be safe." I plead.

The next day, I receive the Affidavit of Support by special delivery. Inside the envelope, there is a check for $1000.00, and a letter from the attorney.

"President Gallagher would like you to utilize this fund in any manner you wish, to expedite your mother's return to the United States."

I call Mr. Minkin to acknowledge receiving the check and the Affidavit of Support.

"He is out of town. I'll be speaking to him in the next couple of days. I will tell him that you called."

"Thank you." I say, wondering when I would hear Joe's voice again. I have been in a somber mood since he told me that he was going away.

I need to get busy with my plans to bring my mother home. I mark the calendar estimating the approximate date when Joe will return, and pray that he won't be delayed. It will be a grand day when I can celebrate both his and my mother's return.

If I am ever going to believe in God, this time is prime because he has given me the miracle of Joe. But if I believe in God, I also have to believe that He is a benevolent God and will never take back his gift.

There was the Door to which I found no Key:
There was the Veil through which I could not see:
Some little talk awhile of Me and Thee
There was – and then no more of Thee and Me.
Omar Khayyam

- Black September -

It is exactly two weeks since Joe has left on his mission to Africa. I have been marking the calendar and waiting for this day to arrive, albeit with a moderate degree of caution in case he is delayed or worse yet, forgets to call. Maman has been able to secure her visa and should be arriving in the next few days. I can't wait to give Joe the good news and celebrate our reunion.

It is 4 p.m. Friday afternoon when I stop at the campus cafeteria before going to the library. As I sit down to drink a cup of coffee, my eyes lock with a young man's gaze sitting a few tables across from me. He looks quite young. I am sure he is a freshman or a sophomore. I don't know why he is staring at me but when he smiles, I smile back at him. He is refined and stunning, with wide sensual eyes and jet-black hair, recklessly flowing just below his ears and above the shoulders. His broad smile speaks of confidence and warmth, and there is an air of seductive charm that instantly draws attention to him.

I take a sip of my coffee and reach for the copy of

the New York Times that someone has left behind. I flip through the pages pretending to be occupied but mainly with the intention of avoiding the eyes that are still fixed upon me.

As I turn back to the first page of the paper, an obscure image flashes before my eyes and a gnawing sentience haunts me to plod through the pages again. Within seconds, I recognize what I had subliminally dismissed and instantly, I am crushed to the core of my being. My heart bursts into pieces to lodge in my throat. I can't catch my breath and I am drenched in a cold sweat. What I see through the flood of tears and before me is devastation beyond anything I can ever imagine. There is a column bearing Joe's photo, his name, and his age. It is an ominous inscription that can only mean he is dead.

"If Joe is dead," I pray, "Then let the searing pain that is ripping through my chest end my life, just the same." I put my head down and cry... I don't know for how long. The world outside has gone silent and I have fallen into a deep trance, where I can hear Joe's voice and feel his presence. I want to give him my breath and save him, but I am drowning in a whirlpool of despair. Joe picks me up and cradles me in his arms. He tells me that I shouldn't cry, and I beg him not to die... I know I will lose my mind.

When I lift my head up, it is already dark outside. I have to get up and find a sanctuary where I can hide. I try to rise from the seat, but the ground is slipping from under me and I can't stand up.

"Hello. My name is Joey. Let me help you. I think you need a friend."

I am startled. I recognize the young man who was

staring at me earlier...just before my world had abruptly crashed. I clutch the tear-soaked newspaper in my hand. I can't leave it behind. It is all that I have of Joe...a black and white photo and a dwarfed summary of a magnanimous man whose life had ended much too soon.

I take Joey's arm and let him walk with me. We sit on a bench in a far corner of the campus...away from the ordinary bustle of an ordinary day...where no one can see the depth of my devastation.

I light up a Winston.... Joe and I liked our Winstons. We had shared so much...just two weeks earlier.

"What happened?" Joey asks cautiously. "You had your head buried in your hands for a long time - crying, I presume."

"My best friend is dead." I point to Joe's obituary that covers two full columns of the newspaper. "An unfathomable tragedy has befallen all humanity and me."

Joey takes the newspaper and begins to read, as I continue to cry and chain-smoke my cigarettes.

"I am very sorry. I can see why he meant so much to you.

"He was coming home. I was going to see him this weekend."

"How tragic to die so young in a senseless accident."

I want to scream and say it is not true. I want someone to wake me up from this nightmare before I succumb to deadly despair.

"Is there anything I can do?"

Did you say your name is Joseph?"

"Yes, I am Joey to my friends. Your friend's name was Joseph, too. That is a remarkable coincidence."

No one can ever take Joe's place in my heart or fill the void that he has left behind but, when Joey offers to drive me home, I don't decline. He wants to be my friend and I have just lost mine. I thank him and tell him that he can call me anytime.

When I get home, I pour myself a shot of Jack Daniel's, chain-smoke a pack of Winston cigarettes, and cry... I cry until my tears dry and exhaustion sweeps me into oblivion.

JOEY MAY HAVE come into my life at a time when I needed to be distracted from my crushing grief, but he has become my best friend and my loving companion. Despite his young age, nine years my junior, he is mature and attentive. He takes me on dates that he has planned thoughtfully to surprise and entertain me. We go to Broadway shows, comedy clubs, and concerts. We take weekend trips and try new adventures that keep my mind engaged and help my broken heart mend.

Then late in November, I am stunned to find out that I am pregnant. After years of infertility, I was convinced that I would never conceive and now, I am fraught with a daunting plethora of mixed emotions: everything from intense joy and jubilation to guilt and condemnation is wracking my brain. Why now and why with Joey? I love him but that is the very reason I cannot welcome this pregnancy. He is a junior in college and I am entering the final year of my graduate studies.

Joey wants us to get married. It is a noble thought

and a romantic proposition, but he has much to do before he is encumbered with fatherhood. I, too, have worked so hard and have come too far to quit. When I tell him that I will have to abort the pregnancy, he is displeased. I am afraid I'll lose him, but I can't give into a romantic fantasy.

THE COUNTY HOSPITAL, where the abortion will be performed, requires a pint of blood from the father or a family member in lieu of the payment of fees. Joey is quite upset with me. He will fulfill his obligation and donate blood, but he would rather that I change my mind.

John has been calling me sporadically since I returned from the seminar, but he has never made plans to see me. Today, when I tell him that I am pregnant and planning to have an abortion, he wants to come to the hospital to see me. I am sure it is merely his curiosity to meet the man who has made conception possible for me.

As I am wheeled into the surgical facility, John and Jafar walk in. I have no desire to share my misery, but they insist on staying and talking to Joey who has welcomed their company. It is undoubtedly a bizarre if not macabre gathering of three men estranged from me and yet joined beside me, each with an ambiguous agenda and obscure offering.

IN THE DAYS that follow and for many more to come, I am left all alone...alone with a lingering guilt and an inscrutable void. Since the abortion, Joey has not called me. It is clear that he can't share my grief. After all, I had made the solitary decision to deny him the option of paternity.

In a few weeks, John calls to say that he wants to see me. I make dinner and renew the hope that we can share an honest conversation about what had gone wrong with our relationship. John, however, has come with his own ominous scheme. He has come to tell me that he is getting married.

"I can't see you or talk to you any more... my fiancé knows about you and has forbidden me to ever contact you again."

I am stymied. Somehow, perhaps foolishly, I had thought that John and I would never completely abandon one another; that someday we would return to embrace the intense love and the unmitigated passion that we felt for each other. I had thought that at the very least, we would always remain friends.

"Who is she?" I ask, riddled inside but trying to appear intact.

"She is a teacher with a solid family...and quite affluent, too."

"I suppose you'll never have to worry about getting your Ph.D. to support your family." I infer bitterly.

"They'll help me start a business..." He admits, "and I am going to convert to Judaism. They know that I embraced it when we were together."

"So, they are going to reward you by giving you money to start a business?" I can't contain my cynicism and anger.

"Well no, it is not quite like that..." John objects hesitantly, as if doubting himself.

"O.K. John... I really don't care." I say curtly, pretending calm but quivering and burning inside.

"Why didn't you tell me this over the phone...why did you have to come here to tell me this at all?"

"I had to see you one last time." John mutters.

I can see the haze of tears clouding his eyes, and I wonder how the man I loved so much had easily lost his soul and his pride.

"Are you done? Please be done and leave, now!"

A dry heave is rushing up my chest, and I run to the bathroom to throw up. There is nothing in my stomach, but I want to cleanse myself of everything that hurts inside.

- A Ray of Hope -

My father and his cousin, Mehran have rekindled their old friendship. Mehran's Art and Antique Gallery has become an international success and he has generously offered Papa the opportunity to earn a living working for him.

Now as Maman's arrival approaches, I contemplate appealing to her with the most awkward and unreasonable request.... to have her live with Papa and my brother who is attending college and depends entirely on my father to support him. We can't afford to provide Maman with her own dwelling. There is no option but for all three to live together.

I find a three -bedroom apartment with affordable rent and adequate amenities. Everyone will have comfort and privacy without being isolated and alone.

In a few days, we celebrate Maman's arrival and I am delighted that the cohabitation plan with Papa and Jafar seems to be working fairly well. It is an amicable arrangement mainly due to the fact that Papa often stays in the city, and Maman has ample opportunity to nurture my brother and cater to him. Nonetheless, except for my sister's continued hostility, everyone seems to enjoy an unprecedented level of calm and harmony.

MY NEW HOME is the basement of a two-story house, twenty steps below the ground floor and twenty-dollars a week. It is all that I can afford on student loans, grants, and scholarships, while I attend the last full -time year of graduate school. I am thankful that I finally have my own space and privacy to study.

Ruhie has grown increasingly more bitter and unhappy as her saga of infertility continues and fades her hope of ever becoming a mother. To distract her from her anguish, her in-laws have supplied the down payment for a spacious and beautiful brick house in a highly desirable residential section of Queens and once they move in, Simon surprises my sister with two Yorkshire terrier puppies to keep her busy. However, she is soon distressed that her house does not have a terrace for outdoor seating and once again, her generous father-in-law appeases her by building an extensive porch that overlooks the street.

In the winter, Ruhie and her husband take a ten-day vacation in Bermuda and in spite of her blatant animosity, I agree to take care of her terriers, hoping that she will return from her vacation with less venom and more kindness towards me.

- My Cousin's Wedding -

These days, the home of my Uncle Nader in Tehran has become the hub of celebration and festivities. My cousin Lidia is marrying a handsome medical student who is completing his internship in Germany.

In a short time, my mother receives photos and a full account of the wedding. The lavish ceremony was held in an upscale club in Tehran, rivaling the pomp and pageantry of a royal wedding. Waiters clad in uniforms carried torches, and ladies in waiting displayed the bride's dowry of precious gold, diamonds and jewelry. Contrary to tradition that the groom pays for the wedding, Uncle Nader not only has funded the extravagant affair, but has also rescinded his own long-standing opposition to giving a girl dowry. He has provided the couple with a substantial *jahaz* that consisted of cash, real estate, and precious jewelry to ensure that his daughter would be treated with respect, comfort, and dignity. The groom, of course, was vetted fully and with the guarantee that his solid and lucrative career in medicine would provide Lidia with a life of leisure and prosperity.

FOR SOME TIME, Mehran's generosity has provided Maman with some revenue in exchange for her restoration of some of his art and antique jewelry. Now over the moon with joy, she wants to spend all her savings not only on wedding gifts for her niece, but also for all of her brother's children. This is a tradition that Maman keeps close to her heart. She never sends gifts to one, but to all the children in her family so that none would feel dejected and left out. The fact that my uncle has given his daughter a substantial *jahaz* is a confirmation of my mother's belief that it was indeed her unworthiness that had compelled her brother to give her away without a dowry.

"I don't want to be embarrassed sending a small gift. I want my brother to be proud of me." She insists.

"Maman *joon*, how are you going to pay for all this?" I ask, watching her fill her shopping cart with extravagant gifts.

"I don't want Marjan to say that her husband's family is cheap."

I am baffled by my mother's ability to forgive. I wish I could tell her that her brother will never give her the validation she seeks, but I know that I can't change the conviction that gives her reason to live. I am frustrated and angry but once I see the tears in her eyes, my fury turns to fear. The image of Maman trying to throw herself in the path of an incoming train always warns me to surrender logic and acquiesce to her obsession to please her brother.

"O.K. Maman. I'll put it on my credit card. I will find a way to pay for it."

IN A FEW WEEKS, a letter from Marjan brings my mother the shred of recognition that she needs, however fleeting and cursory it may be. Sadly but not surprisingly, Marjan, who had denied my mother a helping hand when she was in Tehran, now finds it convenient to acknowledge their familial bond.

"The wedding was 'aali ha' spectacular. Thank you so much for the beautiful gifts that arrived on the night of the wedding. I hope that someday we'll be able to return your huge generosity. Thank you also for the birthday presents that you sent. Javid thanks you for the beautiful shirts. Every time Arella puts on her pretty dress, she tells everyone that her Ammeh, Esther Khanom sent it to her from Amrika. There is not a day that she doesn't think about you and ask where you are. Well, I have no more to say. I wish you all well. Marjan Lahijani"

TODAY Maman calls to share her joy, having received Marjan's congenial letter. She also has some rather interesting news to convey to me.

"A man named Mohsen Madani, a friend of Mehran jaan wants to come to us for Khastegari. I know his family from Rasht...I am sure you remember me talking about our long- standing friendship. He lives in England and was divorced recently."

"Whose *Khastegari*, Maman *joon?*" I pretend ignorance, surprised to know that Mohsen is no longer married. I had seen him with his British wife a couple of years earlier at Mehran's gallery.   It was an awkward encounter but we were both calm and civil.

"*Chi shod, azizam*? What happened, my dearest?" Maman is asking why I am silent.

"I am O.K. Maman joon...Just wondering if I know him."

"Mehran *jaan* and Helen want to know if you would like to meet him. They want to invite you both to their house and make the introductions."

"I don't think so, *Maadar joon*, beloved mother, we live in *Amrika*...people don't do *khastegari* here," I try to humor her, "But please thank them on my behalf."

The thought of Mohsen evokes memories of our incredible connection. A rush of nostalgia and longing permeates my body and I feel an aching desire to be with him. But then, I remember the charity that he had extended to me to save my mother...the act of kindness that had oddly foiled my longing to see him because I was so deeply embarrassed. In all those years that had followed our splendid encounter, I had made sure to put the entire experience, alongside many others, in a dark corner of my mind so that my survival would not be hijacked by shame and regrets.

In a few days, Mehran and Helen call to reiterate what Maman had told me earlier.

"He is ideal for you, Azadeh *joon*" Mehran assures me.

"How does he know me?" I ask with trepidation, fearing they may know that we have already met.

"He met you at our wedding and knew about you before you left Iran." Helen explains and I take a sigh of relief, grateful for Mohsen's scrupulous discretion.

"You have a lot in common. He is educated,

modern, and lives in London." Mehran elaborates with notable enthusiasm.

"You wouldn't mind living there, Azadeh... Would you?" Helen asks eagerly. "You know I spend a lot of time in Europe. I promise to visit you often."

Had my circumstances been different, I would have married Mohsen a decade ago. However, the echoes of my dreadful past continue to haunt me and degrade all my relationships, either directly or circuitously... but always and every time with tenacious reliability. I do not want to revisit my past, nor do I want anyone to rescue me from it. I have to come to terms with it on my own. It is only then that I can trust someone. I thank Mehran and Helen and tell them that I am not ready to get married.

LATELY, I have been deluged by horrific nightmares that wake me without mercy and leave me with no insight or memory. I am overwhelmed by obscure emotions that began to surface shortly after the abortion, but have become more intense since. I feel as if there is a crater of grief inside me, something hollow that needs to be filled. I ache with emptiness and want to eat to fill the hole that burrows inside of me. I eat impetuously all the things that I do not like to eat. I fill my abyss of emptiness but even when I am full, I am filled with cravings and with nothingness. I want to get rid of the void that is hurting me. I want it out of me; I want to extract it from me and rid myself of everything that is inside me. I stick my finger down my throat and thrust it in and out until I vomit, hoping that I am cleansed and empty. Then soon, the respite ends and the emptiness will begin to ache, urging me to fill the void again. I gorge on the forbidden food that has no appeal or taste. I stuff my innards with everything that I can find until I am full of disgust and self-loathing. Then once again, I get rid of it all, thrusting it out of my belly until I succumb to exhaustion and fall asleep. I know that my guilt about the abortion is reaping havoc on me, but I don't know how to fix it.

- Promise of A Rose Garden -

There is a small two-story brick house across the street from my sister. The owner is desperate to sell and I am seduced by the temptation to dream again: to make whole a family that has long been broken. I imagine my parents having their own private home and living across the street from their children, just like all Iranian families do. I am filled with jubilation thinking of the possibilities. My brother and sister share a special bond, not only because of the scars they shared in Israel, but also because they have the same birthday, four years apart. I believe that living near my sister will give everyone great comfort and joy.

I have no knowledge or experience in purchasing a house, but the fantasy is fueling my drive to learn all I can and to proceed with a plan. After a quick and cursory tabulation, I assess that with a down payment of $20,000, the monthly mortgage payment would be less than what my father currently pays for rent. I know only of one person who can loan me the money for the down payment. I rush to find a phone booth and call Mehran.

He is surprised but pleased to hear from me. "Aah...Azadeh *joon,* Have you changed your mind about marrying Mohsen?" He asks mischievously.

I wish he had not asked me that question.

"No Mehran *jaan...* I am sorry, this is not about Mohsen." I tell him about the house and my plan to purchase it for my parents.

"It will give my parents a sense of security...a safety net for their future." I explain.

Mehran agrees that the idea is sound. He is willing to provide the down payment, with no strings attached.

"You are *Shahanshahi,* the king of nobility, Mehran *jaan.* I thank you from the bottom of my heart."

"Helen and I are leaving for Paris this evening, and your father has already left the office. Mohsen will be here if you'd like to pick up the check tonight. Otherwise, he'll give it to Papa on Monday."

I hesitate for a moment, reluctant to see Mohsen. But if I wait until Monday, I may lose the house.

"Thank you so much Mehran *Joon.* I'll be there by 6:00 to pick up the check. Would that be too late?"

"I'll ask Mohsen to wait for you. Don't forget to invite us for *shirini khori,* eating sweets to celebrate."

Mehran has a wicked sense of humor and for a moment, I wonder if he hopes that my encounter with Mohsen will change my mind and lead me down the path of matrimonial celebration.

"Of course, Mehran *joon.* We'll celebrate my parents' new home... Maman will be delighted to make your favorite Rashti dishes. Please give my best to Helen *Joon* and enjoy Paris."

I take the train to Manhattan, infused with mixed feelings ...flashbacks of the magical time I had spent with him alternate with flash-forward of my mother's delight as she plants roses in her garden.

When Mohsen comes to greet me, we are instantly in each other's embrace as if time had stood still for the entire decade. Everything looks the same...the spectacular display of fragrant flowers, the tray of iced caviar and the bottle of Dom Perignon Champagne; all to remind us of the tender intimacy that we had shared so long ago and cherish still.

We sip on Champagne, smoke cigarettes, and catch up on our lives in the past ten years. He tells me that after I declined his proposal, he returned to London and married a woman of British descent.

"I was never able to recreate with anyone the special magic that I felt with you. I was longing to be with you but somehow, I filled the void with a woman who was entirely different from you. It was an act of sheer rebellion and desperation."

"For me that magic never faded. It has always been the rousing passion that ignited all others."

Mohsen smiles with a twinkle of pride in his eyes.

"Are you happy to live with just a memory, Azadeh?"

"Happy?" I ask rhetorically, "Happiness means peaceful existence ... that is something that I haven't found, nor do I believe that I ever will. "

"Maybe you'll find it with me, *azizam*. Why don't you concede? Why not let go of your stubborn streak and give us a chance?"

I move close to him and kiss his cheek. I feel I should be apologizing, even though it is my own happiness I am sabotaging.

"Come to London for a visit, and then decide if you want to live there and marry me."

I owe Mohsen the truth. I want him to know that my inability to commit to him is not because of how I feel about him but because of my loyalty to my family.

"You are willing to relinquish your own happiness to tend to your family? Is that a reasonable wish?"

"I don't know how to be any other way, Mohsen. I swear I would do it if I knew how."

"*Azizam*, you are not the parent.... you are the child ...you have to live your own life."

"I am constantly threading between the two. I want so much to be able to depend on someone...at least someone in my family, but being vulnerable paralyzes me. I feel safer being on my own. It is a paradox of incongruities... It is the oxymoron of my existence and it gives me no peace."

Mohsen rests my head on his shoulder and wipes my tears away. His love is soothing and yet incomprehensible to me. I promise to evaluate my options and he pledges to wait for me again.

IN SEPTEMBER of 1973, I sign a mortgage loan with my father and appoint him and my brother as the bona fide owners on the deed. I trust that once Jafar graduates and begins to work, he will take over the mortgage payments and share the responsibility of caring for my parents. However, soon after they move into their new home, my brother accepts a job with RCA in New Jersey and leaves all the financial responsibilities of the house to my father and me.

Ruhie, still nettled by lack of conception and now

disgruntled by jafar's decision to move, seizes every opportunity to purge her frustration and hostility towards my mother and me. I had hoped that both she and Maman would benefit emotionally from each other's support and company, but I now realize that my enthusiasm and optimism were grossly and disastrously misplaced.

Maman calls, often sobbing, because Ruhie has yelled at her: "Why don't you leave me alone? Every time you come over, the dogs run out of the house and I have to chase after them."

I am appalled by Ruhie's callous treatment of my mother. I feel enormous guilt having moved Maman within such unavoidable proximity to be brutalized by her daughter.

"Don't go to her house, Maman. Wait for her to invite you over." I plead.

Papa, too, continues to criticize and berate my mother. He still drinks and smokes excessively at night but in the morning; he is energized and spirited to take a bus and train to Mehran's office. I remind him frequently that he no longer lives in Iran nor married to my mother.

"If you give Maman a hard time, I will have her live with me and you'll have no one to cook, clean, and do your laundry."

For my mother, there are brief periods of peace and tranquility that coincide either with my sister's belief that she is pregnant, or with my father's absence when he stays at Mehran's penthouse in the city.

- The Golden Degree -

The last two years of graduate school have been over-whelming. The long hours of internship, extensive research and exhaustive course work allow little respite or sleep. I am alone and tired and my sins have become my friends and my family again. Coffee and cigarettes are my only reliable and soothing company. I smoke and nurture myself with food that is not nourishing. I have put on weight...that convenient shield of defense that will protect me from men and from the intrusion of feelings that might revive my dormant pain. I can't allow myself to mourn the loss of those I have loved, nor can I wallow in self-pity. I have had to crawl into a cocoon of denial and emotional numbness, lest I would break down and miss my own Golden Graduation ceremony.

IN THE FALL of 1973, I am offered a faculty position at the Brooklyn campus of the City University. It is a prized and rare opportunity to work within the same venerated academic institution that has nurtured and educated me for thirteen years.

I buy my first car with credit and decide to rent an apartment near the college to avoid the daily fifty-minute commute from Queens. I live on the second floor of a four-story building with windows that face the main street on one side and a narrow alley on another. This is my first home with a bedroom, kitchen, and a dining room. It is not someone's basement, a converted garage, or efficiency.

I am quite delighted with my new home, but disappointed that the building appears desolate and sparse with human traffic. With the exception of a single brief encounter with a man in the hallway, I have not seen anyone in or out of the elevator, and don't know if I have a next-door neighbor. Had it not been for the missing articles of my laundry from the dryer downstairs last Saturday, I would have wondered if anyone else inhabited the building. Amongst the stolen items, the only thing of value was the exquisite lingerie that John had given me on our last Valentine's Day. I was sad that it was gone but so was John, and it should no longer matter.

What was far more disturbing than the stolen laundry, was what I found in the in the morning when I opened the window that faced the alley. I was aghast to see right beneath, the naked body of a dead man with a large gash across his torso and beneath his chin. His body looked bloated and no blood was trickling down from his wounds. I thought he must have been murdered elsewhere and dumped here for someone to see. I closed all the windows before calling the police. They assured me that this was a targeted Mafia hit and should not worry me. But now, I am afraid to go out at night and prefer to lock myself in the apartment most of the time in the evening.

A few weeks ago, while I was apartment hunting, I had stopped at a coffee shop and met a young man named Eddie. He owns a private tennis academy. He has called me several times and I finally agreed to have dinner with him. These days, I feel isolated and alone. I rarely drive to Queens to visit my family because the toxic environment drains me. I can't risk going to work feeling depleted and weary.

Eddie is loving and attentive and I am once again in a relationship with a man who is considerably younger than me. I feel safer with younger men because reality will not allow either of us to delude ourselves with long-term commitment fantasies.

ON A COLD November night in 1973, my brother calls me from New Jersey. It is past midnight and I know instinctively that something is wrong.

"Azadeh, I am not feeling well. I need your help." He bawls.

"What do you mean Jafar *joon*, what is the matter?"

"I have bad thoughts…. Whenever I a drive, I have the urge to crash the car."

"You mean you want to kill yourself?" My heart is racing but I manage to keep calm.

"I try to get it out of my head but I can't. I am really scared."

Now I feel my heart slip down to the ground. In my first year of graduate school, I had asked my brother to be my subject for a clinical case study. I had given him an extensive battery of personality tests and looked forward to learning how to interpret the clinical data. When I presented my case to the class, my professor shook his head with chagrin. "Azadeh, I hope this person is not related to you."

I was embarrassed and alarmed but quickly composed myself and denied that I knew my subject. For years, I worried about my brother and feared that our traumatic childhood would someday erupt with its dormant wrath to avenge his life. Now that day was here, but Jafar was miles away and out of my reach.

"How long have you been feeling this way?" I try to collect my nerves.

"Since I came here, but it is getting worse...much worse!"

"Have you considered seeing a psychologist?" I say sympathetically, hoping not to rouse his defenses.

"No, that is why I am calling you. I need you to help me."

"I can't be your therapist, Jafar *joon*, but I'll find someone to help you."

"I have no health insurance." Jafar explains. Our first six months at work is considered probationary and healthcare is not covered. "Please come here. I am really scared. I need you here now!"

"It is a busy time of the year at the college, but let me talk to the Dean tomorrow and see if I can get away for a couple of days."

The next day, I find a commuter flight to New Jersey and drive to Camden where my brother lives. He comes to the door, disheveled and pale. His eyes are bloodshot from lack of sleep and copious tears.

"Have you had anything to eat?"

"No, I am not hungry." He lights up a cigarette and asks me to make him coffee.

"I'll make you some Persian food. What would you like to eat?"

"I don't care, Azadeh. Don't bug me. I told you I am not hungry."

I look in the refrigerator and find some eggs and tomatoes. I know he likes *Nimroo Gojeh*, Tomato Omelet.

I drink coffee and smoke cigarettes as I watch my brother reluctantly feed himself. He has always had a large appetite and his lack of interest in food is abundantly alarming.

In the next two days and through the weekend, we talk for long hours. It is clear that being away from home and family has brought to surface his repressed conflicts and fears. I know he needs hours if not years of psychotherapy but for now, all I can do is to coach him through Primal Therapy techniques to release some of his pent up rage.

"We can't stop here. You have to work with a therapist."

I call several psychologists to assess who would be best suited for him. I give him two names and urge him to call on Monday and make an appointment. Before I leave, I prepare a few Persian meals, clean the apartment, change his sheets and do his laundry.

"O.K. you are all set for at least a weak. You have no excuse to postpone therapy. You also need to find an enjoyable physical hobby to stay healthy."

He gives me his promise.

"You are coming down for the Christmas holidays, right?"

"Yeh, yeh... for sure." He confirms.

I hug him good-bye, reassuring him that I love him

and that he will be all right.

When I return to my office on Monday, I find a pile of folders and a note from the Dean.

"These are the files of students who have been referred to you by other faculty for psychological counseling. We believe that you are better equipped to deal with the unique challenges of these students. Let me know if you have any questions. Thank you and welcome back.... Tony"

I am flattered to know that my colleagues have trusted me with their difficult cases, but my mood is quickly dampened as Newman, my immediate supervisor- a tenured old grump- saunters into my office.

"It's good to see you're back, but don't make a habit of taking time off ... we want you here on time and on schedule every day."

"Of course. It is good to be back." I say coldly, hoping for the conversation to end promptly. But I don't succeed.

"You can't bring your family problems to work. This is your first year here." He growls, "You are not presenting a good impression by taking time off for personal business."

"The Dean did not have an objection to my leave." I assert, not hiding my contempt.

Newman is impervious to my irritation and wants to interrogate me.

"Where are your parents? Couldn't somebody in your family take care of your brother so you wouldn't have to jeopardize your job? Do you know how many candidates were interviewed for your position?" He hammers on.

301

"Dr. Newman," I say confidently, "I am sure I will live up to everyone's expectations." I point to the pile of folders on my desk. "You see, the Dean has asked me to review these cases. So, if you would please excuse me, I 'd like to attend to them immediately."

Newman has had a problem with me since the day I moved into my office. As soon he saw my name on the door, he was fired up and wasted no time to express his views.

"How do you pronounce your name? It is a strange sounding name... Is it Arabic?"

"Perhaps it is. Arabic and Farsi share the same alphabet and there are words that are common to both languages."

"Why would a Jew have an Arabic name? If you move the letters around, it spells 'shaim.' Doesn't it?"

It has been difficult to determine or decipher Newman's agenda because there are occasions when he speaks like a friend. But more often than not, he sounds like an adversary. Whatever the case, I find him obnoxious and repulsive. Unfortunately, I share the same office complex with him, as well as with two other male colleagues. They, too, harass me in some form or another and on a regular basis. The male faculty, the majority of whom are married, rein over women with a 98% majority. In fact, with the exception of a wheelchair -bound counselor, I have not met a single female faculty.

AT OUR CAMPUS Christmas party, I am harassed by my male colleagues and wish I had been able to excuse myself from attending. But this event I have been advised, is just as important as the student orientation and cannot be missed.

As soon as I walk in, Michael Zibrin, the esteemed tenured chairman of the mathematics department commandeers me to dance with him.

"You are a wonderful dancer," he gloats, "Do you notice every man here is watching us?"

I know the old man is flirting with me and I don't know how to get away without being rude to him. I wait until the song ends, and then excuse myself when he asks me to dance with him again.

"I have to take a break... I am feeling quite exhausted." I walk away.

Then, as I pass by Ernie, another faculty member, he shouts enthusiastically for everyone to hear.

"What a lush broad!"

Ernie 's office is adjacent to mine and he has been leaving me love notes ever since I returned from visiting my brother. He even calls me at home so often that I no longer answer the phone. But he always leaves me messages:

"I can't stop thinking about you. I'll leave my wife if you tell me you marry me."

I hate having to listen to these disturbing messages, and often turn off the answering machine, but that makes my mother worry because she can't get a hold of me and can't leave me a message. I have thought about reporting Ernie to the dean, but he is tenured and can get away with anything. Even if he is reprimanded, I'll be the one embarrassed and ostracized at the end.

Now I see Newman walking over to me.

"You know... Dancing with faculty doesn't give our department a good image."

"Excuse me… Was I supposed to refuse dancing with the Chairman?" I bellow, "Why don't you tell him he crossed the line asking me to dance with him? After all he is tenured and should know better about campus policies."

Newman rubs his hugely overhung belly. "You didn't see me asking you to dance."

I am flustered and sick to my stomach. I know that a binging episode is imminent. I feel guilty for getting attention…I feel responsible when men behave this way. It must be my fault, I have concluded.

I leave the party and come home feeling alone and depleted. I am craving food… I need to stuff away the rage and purge my guilt and shame. My obsession with food and vomiting has me in ruins. But it is the only thing that I can control; it is the only thing that I can undo after it is done. As soon as I feel overwhelmed by conflicts… in need of nurturing… confused by its boundaries… and fearful of its consequences, I fill the vacuity of my existence with anything that appears to be soothing. I feed myself until I can't breath…until the weight of shame and the guilt of my indulgence begin to suffocate me. And then, I run to purge myself from the poison of neediness that keeps me forever hostage.

RON CALLS. He still loves me and makes me laugh about our mischief in the 'Rat Laboratory' so many years ago. I tell him I am not well; I am very depressed and need to talk to a shrink.

"If you would let me take you out and show you a good time, you wouldn't need a shrink." He pleads. "You'll feel better, I promise."

"I am sorry, Ron. I would not be good company but thanks for caring."

I wish I could fall in love with Ron and marry him. Or perhaps, I should just run away...leave everything behind and go to London.... marry Mohsen with the promise of happily ever after. But I know that no matter how far I run, my past will follow me everywhere. My burden of shame is too onerous and my vulnerability too deep to allow me to nurture a relationship. I can't let anyone come too close to me because eventually, even those who claim to love me will use my fragility to hurt me. I can neither set myself free from shame, nor can I be free from my bondage to guilt. If I flee, who will take care of my mother and who will watch over my family? Papa's temper has been muffled by age, but he still remains inept, self-centered and abusive. My sister is cruel and unpredictable; often so vindictive that I fear she will send my mother to her grave or an infirmary. My brother, too, is unglued, teetering on the edge of self-destruction or a mental breakdown.

I call Eddie and ask him to come over and spend the night with me.

"I miss you babe.... love to be with you but The Godfather wants to see the family tonight and I won't be able to get away until after midnight. Would that be too late?"

"The Godfather?" I let out a nervous laugh. "That is really funny, Eddie.... the most original B.S. excuse I have ever heard."

"It is not a joke baby. Haven't you noticed a black limousine following you?"

Suddenly, I feel a wave of panic come over me. I

remember a black limo circling the apartment on a couple of occasions but never thought it had anything to do with Eddie and me."

"Are they going to kill me?" I ask, still hoping he is playing with me

"They know who you are and where you live baby, but everyone is cool about it."

"You are scaring me Eddie. You are telling me I have been sleeping with the Mafia?"

"Hey baby... I'm not a bad guy. I was just born to the Family. They know you make me happy and they have no problem with it, unless I decide to marry you or you do something to hurt me."

"Great Eddie. Would I be hurting you if I said we have to quit seeing each other?" I chuckle half seriously. "I don't want your boys following me."

"Don't say that, baby.... of course that'll hurt me. You know I love you. I'll see you later. Do you want me to bring you anything?"

"Yes, write me a promissory note with your own blood that you will never have me killed."

"You are funny baby... That's why I love you so much. Please wait up for me."

At 1:30 a.m., Eddie is buzzing the bell from downstairs and I decide to let him in. Tonight, my fear of the Mafia pales next to my fear of feeling lonely.

The next day, Maman calls to let me know that my brother has come home for the holidays. "He is not looking well," she whimpers, "I wanted you all to come here for dinner tonight but he is going out with his high school friends."

Maman loves her son with the same intensity and adoration that she has loved her brother, Nader. She never expects anything from him, never questions him, and always wants to please him. She has been heartbroken that he has moved away and doesn't live close. I am sure she blames herself for that, too. Now that Jafar is here for a visit, all Maman wants to do is to make him happy. She has prepared her son's favorite dishes and hopes that this family gathering will leave us all with good memories.

"O.K. Maman *Joon*. Let him go have fun. We'll get together tomorrow. Please don't stress about it."

It is a very cold night and the heavy snowfall has left many roads inaccessible. All day, the radio has been broadcasting strong warnings about the dangerous roads and icy conditions, urging people to stay home and refrain from driving. I assume that my brother is going to stay close to home in the old neighborhood with his friends. But when I call Maman later, she tells me that Jafar and his friends, impervious to the repeated weather advisories, have piled up in a small car and headed out to a popular disco out on Long Island where they plan to party the night away.

I talk to Maman for a long time to allay her anxiety about the boys' excursion even though I, myself, am worried. Then I go to bed looking forward to a peaceful visit with Maman and my brother the next day, while Ruhie is away. She has gone on vacation, which is just as well, because she likes to monopolize Jafar's attention and instigate discord and hostility whenever we are together.

At 2 a.m., an ominous nightmare jars me from deep sleep. An armed man is chasing my brother through a winding ally. He is waving a gun and aiming to shoot him. I am running breathlessly to stop the gunman as

I urge my brother to run faster to get away, but it is too late and the man shoots Jafar in the head. I hear the phone ring, but I am not sure if it is in my dream or my phone is actually ringing. I shake myself out of bed and pick up the receiver. I hear my mother's heart-wrenching cry and her muffled voice telling me that Jafar has been in an accident.

"Please Azadeh *jaan*, go to the Long Island Jewish Hospital immediately. We have no transportation."

"O.K. Maman, I'll go right away. I'll call you when I know what has happened." I am shaking inside but trying to compose myself. I have to be strong for my mother. There is no one else.

I run to the street to get my car. The surge of adrenaline has all but erased every ounce of my fear to defy the icy roads and drive to the hospital fifty miles   away.

WHEN I ARRIVE at the Emergency Room, I am told that my brother is in the ICU. I plead for someone to tell me how badly he is hurt. In a few minutes, the ER doctor appears from behind a curtain and leads me to the x-ray projector.

"Here, there is a fine line fracture on his right temple. He has had a concussion. We will monitor him through the night and if he does well, you can take him home in the morning."

I am scared and stunned, but too worried to forge a correlation between the nightmare that I had hours earlier, and the reality that could suddenly turn into a nightmare.

"Can I go up to the ICU to see him?"

"Yes, but only briefly. He is sedated. You won't be

able to speak to him."

In the ICU, my brother is hooked up to an IV and several monitors. He is pale and motionless. I kiss him and tell him that I love him, hoping he can hear me. Then I call my parents from a phone booth in the lobby downstairs. I give them the rundown on Jafar's condition and reassure them that their son is going to live. I wait outside the ICU all night, taking occasional breaks for coffee and cigarettes and praying that the morning will not bear any bad news for my family. By noon, the doctor informs me that my brother has done well overnight and he is going to discharge him.

"The first forty-eight hours are critical, so you need to keep a close watch on him. If he falls asleep, wake him up every twenty minutes to make sure he is alert. If his breathing is labored or there are any signs of stress call 911 immediately."

These instructions sound rather perfunctory and unsettling to me.

"Why can't you keep him here another night-another twenty four hours to make sure he is closely monitored?" I plead for a reasonable explanation.

"He doesn't have insurance. We can't keep him here more than twenty four hours."

As my brother is wheeled out into the hallway, I run to see him and hold his hand to comfort him. He looks pale and not fully alert.

"How do you feel, Jafar *jaan*? I whisper, "You banged up your head rather badly but it could have been worse. You are going to be alright."

Jafar opens his eyes slightly to look at me. He speaks laboriously and slowly. It seems as if he has difficulty remembering or articulating.

"A guy was killed. Gil...he's hurt... badly." He mumbles.

I have known Gil for years. He was my brother's best high school buddy and they have remained close throughout the years. I don't know who else had been in the car and who had perished, but this is a tragedy that will probably haunt my brother for the rest of his life.

"I am so sorry, Jafar. We can check up on Gil later, but now, I have to get you home before the next snowstorm hits."

At home, my parents are waiting anxiously. Maman has been up all night smoking, crying, and praying. Her face is inscribed with new lines of worry that accentuate the many she has earned from her relentless tragedies, but she is grateful to see her son alive. She is chanting all the praises that she can conjure up to thank God for His mercy.

I give my parents instructions to watch Jafar while I take a nap, so that I can stay awake and watch him overnight. Later, while my parents sleep, I sit vigil by my brother's bed and watch the rise and fall of his chest with his every breath. Every twenty minutes, I shake him lightly and call his name to make sure he is alert.

At 3 a.m., Jafar does not respond to my prodding and for the second time in less than forty-eight hours, my heart has dropped to my feet for fear that we have lost him. I call 911 and wake my parents up to tell them that we have to take my brother back to the Emergency Room. The paramedics arrive shortly and administer emergency care. They wheel him into the ambulance and to Jamaica Hospital, a state-subsidized facility that cares for indigent patients. This is where I had come for the abortion and where I received medical care whenever I fell ill. I have come to this facility so often that I know many of the doctors and staff. It was here, too, that the attending internist, a South African doctor recommended Naprosyn for the relief of my excruciating menstrual pain. He said that the medicine was given to female inmates as an experimental drug to relieve their arthritic pain and the women had reported incidental relief from their premenstrual cramps and discomfort. Since I began taking this drug, my menstrual ordeal was no longer a looming threat. I felt as if I had a new lease not on life, but on my gender disability; I could pardon my misfortune of being a menstruating woman. I was truly indebted to this doctor but avoided seeing him when I realized that examining me and touching my body was giving him tainted pleasure.

AT THE EMERGENCY room, doctors are surprised that my brother had been released so quickly after a serious head injury. They decide to keep him under observation for the next two days, assuring me that he will be able to resume his normal activities once he is released. However, having known since childhood to expect bad things to happen surreptitiously, I am instinctively driven to anticipate the worst possible scenario whenever I am faced with a threat. I always try to arm myself with a backup plan so that I can singlehandedly manage the worst consequences. It is an arduous and exhausting compulsion, but it is the only way I can feel safe. Now, uncertain about my brother's diagnosis and worried that the doctors may have missed something, I set out to have a private neurological consultation.

A few weeks ago, I had met William C., a charming young physician who was doing his residency in Neurosurgery at a New York City Hospital. He had given me his card and told me that it was up to me to call him if I wanted to see him.

I dial his number.

"Well, Azadeh.... what a pleasant surprise ... what took you so long?" William cheers.

The night I met William, he was surrounded by attractive young girls- all competing for his attention. Admittedly, he is a very desirable bachelor; a great catch. Notwithstanding his obvious intelligence and good looks, he is humble, caring, and genuine. We had spent hours talking at the party and got along so well that we thought we would see each other again. However, William's flawless eligibility made me feel extremely vulnerable to him. I feel that the more perfect a man is, the more imperfect I become and the more damaged I look standing next to him.

"I have to confess. I am calling because I need your professional help." I say apologetically.

"Well, O.K., I'll accept whatever excuse you can give me...Go ahead."

I tell him about my brother's accident, the unsettling aftermath, and the reason I want to consult with a private neurologist to make sure he'll be alright.

"Can you get his x-rays, labs and the ER notes?"

"I already have them. I have all of it."

"Good work! Hold on a moment." I hear William speak to someone briefly, and then he is back on the phone.

"I am on call at the hospital this weekend. I'll send my driver to pick you up and bring you there."

I knew that William's family was quite affluent but alas, having a personal driver seems extremely vulgar.

"Your driver?" I ask with lucid surprise.

"Parking around here is a monumental hassle. I don't want your car towed away. I'll have Bruce pick you up after he drops me off at the hospital on Friday."

As I hesitate for a moment to ponder a decision, William is quick to remind me that he has not dismissed my concern for my brother.

"There will be a few neurologists here over the weekend. You consult with as many as your heart desires. I'll even take you on my hospital rounds...wouldn't you like that?"

I know William will never know my secrets. So, for this weekend, I can pretend to be someone else, an unblemished child of a fairy godmother. I can let him take my hand, albeit briefly, and sweep me into a whimsical world of dreams where I can forget my sadness and everything that hurts me.

FRIDAY AFTERNOON, I am in the back seat of a late-model Mercedes heading for New York City.

"Dr. C. must like you a lot. He has never had me pick up his date or have her stay over at the hospital."

Bruce is talking to me through his rear view mirror.

"Really?" I smile inquisitively. "Aren't you a good friend...covering up for him?" I tease him.

"I am not putting you on...It is the truth." Bruce

313

reassures me.

Once we arrive at the hospital, Bruce leads me to a room where William is waiting for me.

"This is where the residents stay when they are on call... Not a glamorous life, is it?" William hands me a rose and kisses me gently on the cheek.

"I suppose not...but medicine was never intended to be bed partners with glamour and greed?" I retort candidly.

"Touché, indeed.... But I would have liked a nicer venue for our first date."

He gives me another tender kiss, and then helps me put on a white coat he has just removed from the closet.

"O.K. Now we have to do our rounds for the evening."

"How do I look?" I ask enthusiastically.

"Perfect.... Perfectly beautiful and astute...Let's go."

As soon as we enter the patients' floor, there are smiles and cheers as if a ray of sunshine has beamed into the room.

"This is my colleague, Dr. Cohen." William announces, "She is here to observe me. I hope you don't mind."

The female patients are impervious to me, and not shy to express their zealous adoration for him. They flirt ... praise his handsome face, his curly black hair, the dimples on his cheeks, and the twinkle in his eyes.... all the things that inspire them to live.

Back in the room, Bruce has brought us dinner and wants to know if he can leave.

"What time do you want me to pick the lady up on Sunday, boss?"

"I'll call you...I'll let you know in advance so you won't have to rush."

"By the way, I got the lady a couple of magazines." Bruce says solicitously, as he turns to me. "We don't want you to get bored when the boss has to leave to tend to an emergency."

"You are a good man, Bruce. Now why don't you stay here and eat dinner with us."

"Thanks, boss. I have a date. I'll see you on Sunday."

The next day, William reviews my brother's medical records and consults with a radiologist and another colleague.

"We all concur there is no evidence to indicate that your brother's brain is damaged... at least not anatomically." He says cleverly ... maybe suspicious of why my brother had risked his life, venturing out to party in defiance of an obvious threat.

"Thank you for putting my mind at ease, William."

"Now, quit worrying and let's make love." He beams, as he pulls me close.

A WEEK LATER, my sister is in the hospital for a gynecological procedure. I pick up some flowers and go to see her. Maman is at her bedside holding her hand and consoling her. She gives me a long warm embrace and I feel as if I have been infused with life's true elixir. No one's embrace ever feels like my mother's. So many of our days have been consumed trying to ward off our dysfunction that we have lost the essence of life and being connected. Now for a moment in this hospital room, I feel that the three of us are bonded. Ruhie is uncharacteristically peaceful and calm, perhaps because she is sedated. It is, nonetheless, remarkable that she is pleased to have us near.

A week after her surgery to remove a cyst, Ruhie complains of chest pain and shortness of breath. I take her to a cardiologist who decides to put her on a heart monitor for twenty-four hours.

I worry about my sister and always feel guilty that I didn't keep the baby I had conceived, but she can't conceive the baby that she so badly wants and needs. When I get home, I am riddled with self- recrimination and feel the urge to binge. I know it is time for me to talk to someone and find a remedy for this dreadful disease... this vile disorder that defies logic and torments me daily.

I find a therapist in Manhattan. His uptown office is an hour drive but I don't mind because he has a stellar reputation. However, I soon realize that his laudable credentials offer me no comfort or relief. Within a few minutes after my arrival, my esteemed therapist falls asleep. I wonder if the drama of my life exhausts him, but I know he has not heard any of it to tell me what he thinks. When his buzzer announces the conclusion of my 45-minute session, I ask him if he remembers anything. He is embarrassed and apologetic. He says he works long days teaching graduate students, and then sees patients in the evening. By the time I arrive for my session at 8 p.m., he simply can't resist the lure and luxury of his recliner that summons him to sleep.

I feel as though I am just an addendum on my therapist's busy calendar; one more patient he should have declined but couldn't resist. I pay him his $40 fee and set him free. I tell him I will not be back to see him.

On the way home, I feel angry, disillusioned and alone; these are all the ingredients for a binge to crush my vulnerability and make me feel in control. I stop at a convenience store and buy all the things that I hate to eat - forty dollars worth of waste that I will consume in a dazed fury and then regurgitate into the lavatory. I will have a voracious feast and a manic frenzy to feed the beast that is gnawing inside me, and then I will vomit.

Today would have been a good day for a skillful therapy session. However, I am left with no choice but to be my own therapist. I pour myself a drink and light a cigarette. Then I do what I have always done to comfort myself... I write in my diary and commit my mind to long hours of introspection, self-analysis, potential restoration and recovery.

Over the weekend, I turn down dates. I want to be alone but when Joey calls, I am filled with optimism and want to see him. It has been a long time since I heard from him. He says his heartaches because of what happened, but he still loves me. I wish he had called sooner. I wish he knew how the abortion has made me ill... how I have hated myself every day for killing our baby. I need to hear him say that he has forgiven me... I don't want him to think that he had given his heart to a heartless monster that feels no shame, no regret, and lives free of pain.

We go out to dinner and talk. He says he has forgiven me, but I know that I will spend the rest of my life grieving.

ON A COOL and sunny day in April 1974, Maman calls to tell me that my sister has come home with an infant girl that she has adopted from out-of-state. Ruhie and Simon had gone out of town for a few days, but no one knew of their mission or destination.

I am delighted and call to congratulate them.

"I am so happy for you. I can't wait to see the baby."

"Not now." Ruhie snaps, "Can't you see we just got home? I'll let you know when I am ready."

I send my sister flowers and spend the afternoon buying baby clothes and gifts for my new niece. I want to be ready when my sister tells me I can see the baby.

Maman invites everyone for dinner to celebrate this momentous occasion. My sister is beaming as she holds in her arms the beautiful infant they have named Jocelyn. She does not want to tell us any details about the adoption and we respect her wish. She has much to do and learn about caring for a baby and Maman is happy to be living across the street, available at any time of the day or night to help her.

In a few months, however, echoes of discontent begin to rattle our peace again. Ruhie complains that no one cares about her and that she is not given the sympathy she needs.

"Why didn't any of you ask me where I got the money to adopt a baby?" She demands with enmity. Then she complains that Maman is encroaching on her life by wanting to spend time with Jocelyn.

"I don't want you in my house everyday. Don't come over when you feel like it. I'll tell you when I need your help."

Maman feels guilty and condemned. She resorts to the only salvation she has ever known, wishing for her life to end.

"I want to die," she cries, thrashing her body like a disposable flaw because Ruhie has disapproved of her.

"Don't Maman." I run to stop her from bashing her head against the wall.

"Let me die. I am not a worthy mother. Why does she treat me with such hatred?"

"You have to stop apologizing, Maman? You have done nothing wrong."

I know my words will not comfort my mother. We have been here so many times before. Maman is convinced that there is something wrong with her. She always forgives her abusers.... She can't walk away from them because she believes that she is at fault.... She believes that she can make things right if she tries harder next time; that all she needs is another chance. Tomorrow, she will be back at my sister's doorstep, seeking clemency again, and so the vicious cycle of abuse will continue until someone is dead.

On Mother's Day, my brother is in town and Ruhie has invited him and my parents to her house. Jafar and Papa call wondering why I am not there.

"She didn't ask me to come." I say tearfully. "If it makes her happy that I am not there, it's O.K."

My sister's cruelty is reprehensible. She does not care that she inflicts pain upon everyone. But we all give in to her demands because we don't know what else to do.

IN THE SPRING, Uncle Nader writes that he will be coming to New York to buy accessories for his newly constructed mansion in a Tehran suburb. Earlier this year, his daughter Lidia had given birth to her first baby, a girl named Nadia, and Maman, once again, had found ample excuse to drain her savings to buy the baby exorbitant gifts. She feels especially privileged, believing that Lidia has chosen the name that she had recommended for the baby.

Now, with her brother arriving to stay with her, Maman is infused with elation so intense, as if the Shah himself was coming to pay her a visit. She is proud to cater to her brother's needs and has volunteered my spring vacation to devote to his broad itinerary.

I take my uncle to many exclusive shops and manufacturers for comparison-shopping, and endure his hour-long haggling- the hallmark of his business doctrine to get the best deal. His extensive purchases include luxurious gold accessories, faucets, ornaments and various sundries, which will adorn the glorious mansion none of us will ever see.

As the summer recess begins, I feel isolated and despondent living alone and away from my family. The academic year has ended and I have the entire summer to contemplate my miseries. Maman stays with me for a few days and life seems heavenly, but once I drive her home and return to my empty apartment, depression returns with its smothering claws and generous penalties.

On a July afternoon, I receive a chain letter that is on its tour of travel around the world. It claims to have originated from Venezuela and written by St.

Antoine de Sedi, a missionary from South America. It promises me an abundance of wealth and good luck, only if I make copies and send them to twenty-four people within twenty-four hours. Otherwise, I will suffer bad luck and misery for the rest of my life. But I have already had a wealth of bad luck. Had I missed the first round of messages from the Saints? Did God's disciples forget to set the universal clock, so that all His children could claim their fortune in a timely manner...within twenty-four hours?

I tear up the letter into twenty-four pieces and set it on fire in the ashtray. Then I blow the ashes into the wind ... what better way for a saintly message to swiftly reach God's deserving children?

IN WINTER of 1975, my cousin Javid comes to New York on his way to Chicago, where he will begin his medical residency. I have always had a special bond with Javid and cherished our relationship. I am delighted to see him and hope that we remain close, now that we are on the same continent. We reminisce about the time he used to come to me for art lessons back in the days when he was six and I was thirteen. He, unlike me, has had the luck and the fortune to pursue his ambition to study medicine and I feel vicarious pride in his success.

While Javid is in Chicago, Maman calls him regularly to reassure him that although he is away from home, we are here as his family and never far away from him. He and I talk often on the phone about his work and his relationship with his colleagues. He has a gentle soul, which I adore, and the abrasive personality of his department chief offends him. I can relate to his dilemma first hand, and glad to be a sounding board to comfort him.

IN JULY 1976, my brother marries Diana, his girlfriend of three years. We like her instantly and welcome her to our family.   She is reserved, humble, and caring. She embraces both the Jewish and Persian cultures and enjoys celebrating the holidays with great enthusiasm and appreciation. She is particularly fond of Maman and has confided in her that she feels more affection and tenderness from her than from her own mother.

Earlier in the year, there had been rumors of severe budget cuts at the City University and there is a strong possibility that the untenured faculty will not receive a contract for the next academic year. I am a new member of this elite, competitive league and on the bottom of the totem pole. I like the academic environment and enjoy working with my students, but unlike the faculty at my own Alma Mater, I find most of my current colleagues highly arrogant and non-supportive. I am certain that my contract for next year will not be renewed, and I am simultaneously saddened and relieved.

In midsummer, my aspiration to find a new direction comes to fruition with a call from Claire.

"Azadeh, the Foreign Student Office is looking for a multilingual faculty and advisor for Immigration and Academic Affairs. I have told them that you are the perfect candidate. They are expecting your call, darling. It would be wonderful to have you work next door to me."

I meet with the Dean briefly and he is pleased to

have me on board in his department.

"When can you start?"

"Tomorrow." I offer, knowing that the Foreign Student Office has been without supervision for a several months.

"Excellent!" The Dean rises to shake my hand. "Now, let's go and meet the other members of the department. "

I MOVE OUT of my apartment in Brooklyn and into my parents' basement temporarily, while I look for a place of my own in Queens. I am jubilant and relieved to be near my family, and ecstatic to be working on the campus of my Alma Mater; my second home, where I know many of the faculty and have established extraordinary friendships. The memory of the horrific ordeal that shattered my life and hurled me into the darkest abyss a decade ago has mercifully faded. I have never seen Teiman nor heard anyone mention his name in the Psychology Department or elsewhere. My thoughts about him are fleeting either because they are deeply buried or because the wounds have never stopped bleeding.

A FRIEND from graduate school has introduced me to a handsome and educated man named Wayne. We have been on a few dates and getting along quite well. In a few months, Wayne and I decide to get an apartment and live together. We both enjoy our work and make a comfortable living. My brother and his wife seem happy. My sister Ruhie is finally pregnant, and with the exception of a few outbreaks of hostility, there has been an unprecedented peace in our family.

Now, for the first time in my life, I feel a safe level of trust and stability that allows me to acknowledge a long-denied desire ... I want to have a baby. At age thirty-four, I may be too old to entertain pregnancy and motherhood but the drive that fuels the need to nurture our own child and repair our own childhood injuries, supersedes all fears and anxieties.

- Havoc in Our Homeland -

On January 1, 1977, as Wayne and I celebrate the dawn of the New Year and the first day of our marriage, the seeds of a major revolution are fermenting insidiously in many parts of my homeland country. In recent months, there has been a substantial and visible rise of rebellion uprising against the Shah's regime, evidenced by the disruption of his recent visit to the White House by a large crowd of angry Iranians who do not support America's pro Shah policies.

At a state dinner, President Carter has proclaimed Iran as "an island of stability in one of the more troubled areas of the world." However, while praising the Shah for his brilliant leadership, President Carter has criticized him for his oppressive strategies, imploring him to institute reform to address the sensitive and exploitive issues regarding political freedom and human rights policies.

There is a counter –intuitive phenomenon that some leaders of the free world do not recognize: that there is a direct correlation between the Shah's iron-clad fist and the existence of that "island of stability" that keeps peace in the Middle East. Carter, nonetheless, wants the 2500-year-old Monarchy of Persia to become a democracy and his voice has resonated the message of support and solidarity to the revolutionaries whose leaders have no interest in democracy.

The hallmark of every revolution is the arrest and execution of the men and women who are at the helm of political and financial power. Maman worries that her brother, Nader, a prominent businessman with extensive assets and real estate will be arrested and executed. She is in a state of chronic fear, even though *Daii jaan* has told her that his assets and his family will be safe. No one knows what Aunt Narges's fate will be; now older and more hampered by the ravaging scars of her suicide attempt, she is overwhelmed by the responsibility of caring for her two children amidst the current political unrest. While they are shunned by the community and isolated from the family because of the shame and embarrassment they elicit, Marjan and *Daii jaan* receive praise and sympathy for being linked to such pathetic family members. Maman is sleepless at night, fearful that the fanatic Islamic Revolutionaries will show no mercy to the Jews in the country and will execute them indiscriminately.

"Please Azadeh *jaan*," she weeps, "You know about the Immigration laws...you have contacts at the Immigration Office, please find a way to get my family out of the country and bring them here safely."

"Your brother told you that they would be alright. Please stop the panic.... you'll get yourself sick."

326

Maman suffers from severe hypertension, which is now exacerbated by the overwhelming stress about her family's status. I am worried about her health but unable to calm and comfort her. She has no health insurance and relies on the generosity of a neighborhood physician to provide her with samples of medicine. Recently, when she needed dental care, she took the train to the city several times a week, grateful to receive her free dentures as a study model at the New York University School of Dentistry. The cost of insurance is prohibitive and I dread the day that my parents would need major healthcare.

- Becoming a Mother -

In September 1977, I am delighted to share the news of my pregnancy with my family. I am filled with excitement unlike any, and I know that my world will never be the same.

I celebrate the prospect that both my sister and I will give birth just a few months apart and that our children, similar in age, can enjoy a close bond. I am hopeful that as we watch them grow and prosper, our past will become a fading memory and the dream of having a united and loving family will become a reality.

In the spring of 1978, my sister gives birth to a beautiful girl they name Alicia and three months later, after twenty hours of labor, I give birth to a little girl we name Sophie. She is thin and tiny with big brown eyes that are fixated on me as if to say, "I know you are my Mommy."

It is intuitive and instinctive for a woman to feel a closer bond with her own mother once she, herself, experiences the intractable paradox of motherhood, the bliss and the burden of it; the joy and the daunting responsibility that transforms her life forever. And now, more intensely than ever, I am in awe of my mother for her resilience to have cared for us amidst poverty, abuse, and unfathomable losses. I am grateful that she is here to give me advice and to share her wisdom as I raise my daughter. I know that Sophie will be loved and nurtured by Maman's extraordinary grace and compassion and in turn, as the natural cycle of universe has intended, my child will give my mother's life purpose and immeasurable pleasure.

For my sister Ruhie, however, motherhood has become a new and convenient platform to display her hostility and rage. Her woes have intensified against Maman because of her attention to my daughter and me, which albeit not preferential, fuels her robust antipathy towards me. Motherhood seems to have revived the wrath of the neglected child within her. The joy of motherhood has not diminished her anger; it is diminished by it.

"I am making up for all the years that I was quiet and no one paid attention to me." She proclaims.

Although Ruhie has immediate access to Maman and can summon her help whenever she needs it, she begrudges me for having asked my mother to take care of Sophie one day when I had to work and my part-time nanny was not available. Now, she has taken revenge by banning Maman from seeing her grandchildren.

"You are more excited that Azadeh has a baby. You don't care about me." She complains.

Maman calls me frequently, crying because of altercations she has had with Ruhie or with my father.

Often, both my parents are subjected to my sister's hostility, and they argue about how to placate her and who should apologize to her first. We all walk on eggshells not to unhinge my sister and ultimately, it is always Maman who accepts all the blame and begs Ruhie to forgive.

"Once I die, everyone will get along." Mamam yields. Lately, she has become withdrawn and contemplative. She smokes more and sleeps less.... She is often fatigued and listless.

Amidst my own recovery from childbirth, the sleepless nights, and a nursing schedule that has become challenging due to Sophie's severe colic, I am worried that my mother may be suffering from something she is not willing to admit.

On the day that I am about to cancel a scheduled visit with my internist, I offer my mother my appointment, hopeful that the doctor will determine what is ailing her and give her relief.

"Let him examine you thoroughly, Maman *joon.* Tell him to send me the bill."

When Maman returns from her appointment, she is calm and cheerful.

"The doctor complimented me and said that I was a beautiful lady." She reports bashfully... "He said my blood pressure was fine... that I should throw away all my blood pressure pills."

FOUR WEEKS LATER, Maman invites everyone over for dinner. For days, she had been ill, but today, perhaps she feels well or foolish enough to push her limits.

I come to my mother's house early to help, and find

her distraught and crying. Ruhie has told her that she is not coming to dinner because she believes that Maman waited until Sophie was born to have this celebration. She claims that this gathering is for Sophie and not for her daughter. Although my sister's assessment of reality is often not within anyone's reach, her bizarre allegations, nonetheless and without exception, hurl Maman into a whirlwind of self-loathing and despair. I plead with her not to succumb to my sister's manipulation but once again, she wants to pledge her loyalty and seek forgiveness.

Minutes later, my mother returns wailing and shaking. Her mission to convince Ruhie to join us for dinner has failed.

In an instant, before I can put the baby down and run to stop her, she has thrashed her body against the wall and struck her head against it so violently that I fear her skull has cracked open.

"You are going to kill yourself and leave us motherless." I cry, begging my mother to stop torturing herself. I know that her desire to live had ceased when she was thirteen; the day that her childhood was stolen, but I don't want her life stolen from my baby and me.

I kneel by her side where she has fallen and place a cold cloth on her forehead. I kiss her face and plead with her not to ever hurt herself again, but we both know that our tragedy will never end. We can never build a safe house on the debris of our dysfunction. The essence of our lives has been permanently marred with instability and fear of abandonment...all carved out of the noxious and muddy foundation of my mother's ill-fated marriage.

The Moving Finger writes; and, having writ,
Moves on: nor all thy Piety nor Wit
Shall lure it back to cancel half a Line,
Nor all thy Tears wash out a Word of it.
Omar Khayyam

- Darkest Days: Irrevocable Grief -

August 31, 1978 could have been just another day: another summer day of stifling heat and humidity; another day of discord and disharmony that for us remained commonplace and ordinary. But this day would be far from the ordinary...it would be the worst devastating day to darken the rest of our lives.

In the morning, Maman had called to say that she had made peace with Ruhie and wanted everyone to come over for dinner. It had been a week since she had seen her grandchildren and she missed them.

At 3:30 p.m., as Sophie stretches to wake up for her four o'clock feeding, the phone rings and I pray that it is not my mother calling about another feud and the cancelation of our dinner plans this evening. But it is Ruhie on the phone. She is in panic and her voice is barely audible.

"Hurry up... get here…. Maman doesn't look good… something's wrong with her."

A lump instantly clogs my throat and I can't catch my breath. Sophie is crying...she needs to be changed and has to be fed. But I am in a frenzy and don't know what to do first.

"O.K. I need to feed her...no, I should change her first...but there is no time...I have to go to my mother's right away…. I have to drive. But Sophie is hungry, she is crying... How can I feed her and drive?" I mumble and weep... I weep and I plead…. I repeat my words again and again, hoping for clarity.

"Oh God, please help...please don't let it be bad."

I quickly change Sophie's diaper. I cradle her in one arm under my breast and stuff diapers into a bag with my free hand. I run to the garage and secure Sophie in her car seat. I ask her to forgive me for cutting off her sustenance so abruptly.

My sister's words echo in my head: "Maman doesn't look good."

My mind is scanning through every possible scenario, dissecting every word and speculating what might have happened. I know it is something serious. Ruhie did not say Mom was sick; she said she did not look good. What did that mean? An accident, an injury, a severe cut, fire…? Yes, she must have burnt herself. Maybe she had started the grill to make Kabob and her clothes caught fire. Or maybe it is the scorching heat that got her sick.

My thoughts are fragmenting... I am running out of hope and out of breath. "Oh God, please don't let it be bad," I pray again and again, pledging to become a believer if God makes my mother well.

As I turn into 212th street, I see an ambulance and a crowd of people gathered in front of my parents' house. I grab Sophie and run inside. Two paramedics are hauling my mother out in a wheelchair. Her arms are limp and dangling over the sides. Her eyes are bulging out of their sockets and filled with blood. She looks at me with a blank stare.

I gasp for air. I am paralyzed with fear and the flood of tears has blinded my vision.

"Maman *joon*." I cry out.

She raises her head arduously and looks at me briefly. Her eyes speak of resignation.

I follow the paramedics and watch as they pull her up to place her on the gurney inside the ambulance.

"Can I come with you? I plead.

The medics look at Sophie in my arms and shake their heads.

"Not with the baby."

"*Velam Koneed...bezarid beram*, let go of me...let me go!" Maman's voice cuts through my core and my heart recoils. She wants us to let her die. Even today, as she was preparing for dinner and pretending to be happy, she knew that she would welcome the end of her life.

"Where are you taking her?

"Long Island Jewish Hospital."

"Papa, please go with her... get in the ambulance and stay with her until I get there." I plead, cursing creation's irony. My father is the last person I would want to have near my mother when she is so helpless and ill. I want to be the one in the ambulance to comfort my Maman. I want to tell her how much I love her...tell her how sorry I am to have failed her...tell her that I will be a better daughter and make it all up to her... But I can't be with my mother unless I leave my baby behind.... and my baby needs my breast milk to survive.

Across the street, three-year-old Jocelyn is peering through the glass window wondering about the commotion at her grandma's house. Outside, the neighbors have gathered looking somber and sad; some have tears in their eyes and others are in prayer. I run back to the house to call Wayne. I can't drive the thirty-minute distance to the hospital alone. I need to lean on someone before I break down.

When Ruhie comes in, I ask if she knows what happened. She says that Maman and Papa had gone grocery shopping earlier. When they came home, she started cooking. Suddenly, she screamed *"Saram, Mordad, Saram,* my head, my head..." and then she collapsed.

AT THE EMERGENCY ROOM an hour later, we learn that no one has attended to my mother since the ambulance had brought her in. She has been placed in a "holding room", pending proof of her medical insurance coverage. But Maman has no health insurance. I am stunned...nauseated with grief and disbelief.

"How can you deny lifesaving medical care to a woman who is so critically ill?" I shriek.

"It is our policy. I am sorry." The admission clerk informs me dismissively. "Besides, it is the Labor Day weekend...not many people are working. We are short of doctors and staff."

"Please tell me what we need to do to have her admitted? What do we have to do to have a doctor examine her?" I appeal to everyone who is standing by. I am about to lose my mind.

Someone shouts from behind the desk on the other side of the nursing station.

"We need to get authorization to admit her, but our offices are closed and we can't find a neurologist."

These words cut through my chest like a serrated dagger.... these are the same callous and meaningless words that I had heard earlier from another cold-hearted staff member.

"Are you going to let my mother die here in the waiting room?" I grab onto the sleeve of the ER doctor. "Please... please, don't let my mother die. Please tell me what is wrong."

"We think she has bleeding inside her skull. We have to get a neurologist to evaluate her. She has no insurance and that poses a major problem."

I will offer everything and anything I own...even a limb or an organ...I will do anything to save my mother's life. But none of these terms are negotiable. This is the worst betrayal of humanity that I have ever seen. I am stumbling in a whirlwind of confusion and despair. There is no one to lend a hand ... no one to make a coherent suggestion or offer a solution.

"Are you going to let my mother die here?" I confront the ER physician, as I look him in the eyes, hoping to jar his morality and ethical pledge.

"I'll send her up for a CAT Scan." He summons a man to take Maman upstairs to the Radiology Department.

As I sit in the Emergency Room waiting for an

336

update on my mother's status, I think of her family. It is 3 a.m. in Tehran and everyone is sleeping, but death doesn't know about time...it has its own agenda and schedule. I need to talk to my mother's siblings and let them know of the dire state their sister is in. Most of all, I need to know that they care about her.

I call *Daii jaan* Nader and tell him that Maman is gravely ill; that she may not live.

"Iran is in turmoil right now." He says coldly, "Call Javid. He is in California."

I have not talked to Javid since he moved to Beverly Hills, but Maman has told me that he had recently bought a house there, a few blocks from where his sister Lidia lives.

I pace the floor and wait for the ER doctor. Every minute feels like a lifetime, until he calls me into a room where two images are mounted on an x-ray projector.

"She has had extensive hemorrhaging inside her skull. It is very serious." He points to the CAT scan of my mother's brain drenched in blood.

My body goes cold and I burst into a crippling sob. My poor Maman...my beautiful Maman... I need to see her and hold her hand.

"Can I see her?"

"We are going to keep her in the ICU until we get a neurologist to evaluate her." The ER physician announces as he walks out, "You can see her briefly; one person at a time."

I call Javid and leave him a message about what the CAT scan has revealed.

In the ICU, Maman is strapped to a bed. Her hands and ankles are tied at all four corners. It is a heart-wrenching tableau so symbolic of the life she has lived. Her face is flaccid and void of expression, but it bears all the inscriptions of her life of torment.

"Why is she restrained?" I ask the nurse, recalling my own wretched confinement when bolts of electricity were delivered to my brain.

"She'll be thrashing around. We don't want her to fall out of bed." She says tersely and devoid of compassion.

I think of how only a week ago, Maman was thrashing herself against the wall and beating her head against it. Did she finally get her wish? Did she make her brain bleed?

I hold her hand in mine and tell her that I love her.

"*Ghorbaan -e-shoma beram, Maadar-e Azizam.* I will sacrifice myself for you, my beloved mother."

I ask her to squeeze my hand if she can hear me. She opens her eyes and looks at me. Then she squeezes my hand and I feel her love radiate through me.

"There is hope. There is a God, after all." I console myself, convinced that I have witnessed a miracle. I thank God repeatedly and pledge never to relinquish my trust in him or doubt his authority.

"Maman joon, next week is Rosh Hashanah. You will be home and we will have the biggest celebration ever.... Right?"

She is quiet, and I am embarrassed to have put such an unreasonable burden on her. I kiss her hand and her forehead. I see that her lips are dry and chapped. She is moving her tongue around tentatively and unsuccessfully to moisten them. I walk over to the nurse who is oblivious to my presence and barely raises her head.

"My mother is thirsty. Can I give her some water?"

"No. We 'll have to wait for the doctor to tell us if it is O.K."

"Can I at least wet her lips with a cotton swab?"

"No. You have to leave now. You can't stay in the ICU and get in our way."

My mother is the only patient in the ICU, and I don't know how I can possibly be hampering this woman with my presence. I know I can't trust this nurse. She is remote and inaccessible. I don't know why she has chosen a profession that requires goodwill and compassion. I thank her anyway, just to be polite, but mostly out of fear.

Downstairs, Wayne is with Sophie. She is hungry and needs to be fed. My breast milk has already diminished from the overwhelming tension and I fear that it is saturated with the poison of my stress. I am torn between nursing my child and nurturing my mother. They both need me and I feel cleaved to my core every time I leave one to tend to the other.

LATER, as I sit with my father on a bench outside the ICU, I witness the most bloodcurdling view of my mother. She is convulsing violently; her body is plunging forward to propel her from the bed, then thumping her backward and thrashing her against the mattress. My chest caves in and my heart is crushed with the weight of my anguish, watching my mother die.

"*Joon mikaneh.*" My father declares, "She is fighting for her last breath."

Instantly, I am besieged by irrepressible rage. I

want to reach over and choke my father; I want to silence his malicious mouth with my bare hands. As a child, I had heard this ominously descriptive reference to a flaying chicken whose throat had been cut. The animal leaped around erratically and mindlessly, smashing into walls until it took its last breath and died. My father often used this diabolical expression to curse people he did not like. I had heard him say it to my mother many times. *"Joon bekan,* hurry up and die." Now, his words cut through my heart like a serrated knife. I am sick to my stomach and feel a dry heave coming up. I hate my father, now and forever, for hurting my mother. Why is this sinful man alive and my benevolent mother taking her last breath?

I get up to leave. I need to run to the bathroom and throw up before I kill this evil who does not deserve to live.

As I walk away, I hear his cry.... he is whimpering and weeping like an abandoned child.

WHEN THE SUN RISES to mark the fourteen hours that I have sat vigil outside the ICU, watching my mother's tortuous battle to stay alive, a Resident Neurologist, Dr. Biddle, comes to speak to me of hope. He is kind and compassionate. He tells me that he has examined Maman and although her status is grave, there is a chance she will pull through. He warns, however, that there will be some sensory losses and disability, the extent of which can't be determined until later.

I call my sister who has gone home with Papa. I give the encouraging news to her and to my brother who has just arrived.

Late in the afternoon, Javid arrives from California and speaks to the incoming neurology resident, Dr. Balas who will be covering the night shift. Unlike his predecessor, Dr. Balas is a cold and unapproachable man who is not optimistic about Maman's recovery. He has told Javid that he wants to do an angiogram. I don't know what such procedure entails or what purpose it will serve, but I trust that Javid is here to help us and oversee all critical decisions. I have faith that he will discuss every aspect of Maman's treatment with the doctors and will make sure that she is receiving appropriate care.

As the night approaches, the thirty- hour sleepless vigil has left me physically exhausted, mentally fatigued, and nearly depleted of breast milk. I know that I need to get some rest, and I have to wean my baby from breast milk.

When Javid and Jafar promise that they will stay at the hospital, I feel confident that Maman is in good hands and agree to leave and get a few hour's sleep. On our way home, we stop at the pharmacy to buy formula for Sophie and cigarettes for me. I have not smoked in two years, but I know that the darkest days of my life are about to begin.

When we come home, I nurse Sophie one last time as I weep. I ask her to forgive me for breaking the bond that nourished her and nurtured us both. Her birth has been the most profound event in my entire life. It has given me purpose and vitality; it has stirred in me an intense sense of bonding and belonging...not just with her but also with my mother. Now, as I nurse my baby for the last time, I am agonizingly aware of the looming threat of losing my mother. My long-awaited days of privilege and peace have suddenly turned into grief. It is a cruel and brutal injustice that I could have never foreseen.

My tears have soaked Sophie's blanket and she has fallen asleep. I prepare some feeding bottles for the next day, and then light my first cigarette in two years. Wayne lights up one of his own: those Carlton's with a perforated filter that promise no taste and deliver no toxin. But I need the potent fumes of Winston's nicotine to choke my pain.

I call my sister to tell her about our mother's status. She is aloof and impervious, but her state of mind is of no consequence to me. It was just days earlier that she had driven Maman over the edge.

It is long after midnight when I finally drift into sleep. Then at 2:30 a.m., the phone rings and I know instantly the devastation that will overwhelm my life for as long as I live.

"Your Maman has passed away." Javid reports somberly.

I feel my heart burst into pieces and my blood rush down to my feet. The room is devoid of air and the world has gone dark and still. I try to breathe...but I let out a cry...a cry so thunderous that it knocks me off my feet.

Wayne picks me up and holds me. He lets me lean on him and for a long time, we both weep. I have never seen Wayne's tears, but tonight he's crying.

I have never felt so lost and so diminished.

WE DRIVE TO THE HOSPITAL in shock and disbelief, shedding floods of tears quietly and amidst silence that is deafening. We fear that the exchange of words would confirm the devastating reality.

I am preoccupied with a delusional flight from reality; I am expecting someone to wake me up from this nightmare and tell me that everything is fine. I imagine myself teetering on the threshold of time in another universe ...where I can slither into the past for one split second to grasp my mother's hand and bring her back. I review the events of the past few weeks over and again, trying to revive and re-structure every moment, and searching for that critical opportunity; that moment in time when I could have changed the trajectory that ended my mother's life and forever tainted mine.

"We are here." Wayne's voice jars me out of my fantasy. We are back at the cold and inhospitable place where my mother spent the last day of her life, alone and in agony.

Dr. Biddle, the neurology resident who had offered us hope and compassion yesterday, leads my sister and me to a private room and tells us how sad and sorry he is that we have lost our mother. He says he had done his best to save her, but he had not been the one on duty when she took her last breath.

I have so many questions to ask, but answers don't matter anymore. My mother is forever gone. I will never hear her melodic voice again, and never will I be able to take comfort in the wisdom of her words and in the warmth of her embrace. Maman was gone, as was the rainbow that I had painted with hope and optimism...the promise to spend more time with her, to listen to her life story, and to show her how much I loved her.

The small room where we stand with Dr. Biddle is

filled with cigarette smoke, but the gentle doctor doesn't seem to mind. I have been lighting one cigarette after another because I can't do anything else and everything else hurts. The core of our lives, the luminous center of our universe, the singular bond that holds a family together is extinguished forever.

"What was the cause of death?" I ask with the clear conviction that my mother was left to die or someone killed her.

"We are not sure. We need to do an autopsy... Would you like us to do that?"

The thought of having my mother's body mutilated makes me shudder, but I am not in the right mind to make any decisions. I ask my siblings but none of us knows the answer. We are each in shock, trying to borrow strength from one another. There is no one to help us through this horrific grief.

Maman died on September 3, 1978
Her 55th birthday

My Mother is Dead

They hollowed my Heart
And drowned me in Pain
There's no hope, they said
God, I'll go insane

I kneeled by her bed
I begged her to stay
I wept and I pled
Please show me the way

She lifted her head
Her eyes full of Red
Her fingers were cold
And words weren't said

I prayed to my God
I trusted the Lord
He gave her a moment
Then severed the cord

I stood by her bed
With heart full of dread
I called out her name
But my mother was dead

I am left all alone
My baby just born
There's no one to hold
My Spirit is torn

With grief of her death
Her flowers are bent
Grace, love and wisdom
Was all she'd ever lent.

Her loss is uncanny
Her memories unsung
For my final goodbye
I'll be writing the wrong.

THE WISDOM of the Jewish Law that commands the burial of the deceased within twenty-four hours is remarkably purposeful and astute. It compels the mourners to expediently perform the final act of caring for the deceased so that they can proceed with the ritual of 'sitting Shiva' and mourning. The bereaved cease to perform their daily activities for seven days while family and friends provide them with emotional support and physical comfort. They share memories of the deceased, bring food for nourishment, and offer love and insight to ease the pain of the mourners. The presence of family and friends serves a significant function in both the grieving and the healing process. The bereaved take comfort in knowing that they are not alone and abandoned; that they can begin to heal and resume their lives, embraced by those who share their sorrow and care about their wellbeing.

I am completely alone with the grim responsibility of burying my mother. I have to find a funeral home, a Rabbi, a cemetery, and a burial plot for the young mother I have just lost. Since it is the Labor Day weekend, I endure the agonizing delay, while she is kept in the morgue for two days. The thought of her mutilated body lying on a cold slab churns my stomach with unbearable pain. All weekend, I cry alone and smoke cigarettes. I grieve both for the loss of my mother and the loss of the special bond that I had shared briefly with my newborn daughter.

Early Tuesday, I locate a cemetery on Long Island and arrange for the purchase of two adjoining plots. I want to be buried next to my mother when I die. I contact a funeral home that will pick up my mother's remains and bring her casket to the cemetery. I find a compassionate Rabbi who knows about broken hearts, shattered spirits, and unrelenting tears. He volunteers to read, on my behalf, the eulogy I have written for my mother.

At the funeral home, a handful of my father's family and some friends and acquaintances have come to pay their respect. Maman's generosity, wisdom, and compassion touched everyone who knew her. There is eighteen-year-old Jacque, a nephew of my father's who my mother had kept close to her heart so that he would not feel lonely away from his family. There are several young couples that Maman had befriended because they, too, were alone and away from home.

At the cemetery, as the men fill their shovels with dirt to pour over the casket in the ground, Ruhie lets out a deafening shriek and runs towards the grave.

"I want to be buried, too. I want you to bury me with her."

Jafar and Simon rush to pull her away. Everyone looks on in disbelief. This is the most overt and severe expression of grief that I have seen from my sister in the past two days.

The Rabbi is quick to explain apologetically that this behavior is not uncommon in the culture of people raised in "that" part of the world.

For the next seven days, we sit Shiva at the house where my mother lived, but only briefly. It was not long ago that I had celebrated her new life here...where I had hoped she would find tranquility, planting her vegetables and flowers in the backyard and watching them grow wondrously. She knew well how to nurture her seeds. We watched her garden bloom, enjoyed her succulent vegetables, and basked in her love and bounty. But her peace was short-lived and always remained elusive. She was forever hostage to those who denied her goodwill and abused her generosity.

The news of Maman's sudden and untimely death has shocked and saddened everyone who knew her. There is an outpouring of sympathy and condolences from my father's family. Mehran and Helen call from London and talk to each of us individually. Relatives are calling from Iran to console us with their heartfelt sentiments and loving memories. Everyone speaks of Maman with admiration and deep fondness. They all tell us how much they share our grief and sadness and yet, even in her death, her brother does not acknowledge that she had ever lived. He has not contacted us and we are left to mourn alone and without a word from those we need the most... my mother's family.

IN A FEW DAYS, I receive a letter from my Aunt Narges. I recognize my Uncle's handwriting on the envelope but inside, there is no word from him.
My Aunt Narges writes:
"The news of my sister's death hit me like lightning and I have not stopped crying. My blood pressure has gone up dangerously and I cannot talk to you over the phone. I have had nothing in life but misfortune. She was not only a sister but also my friend and my advocate. Now I have no one left. Her beautiful image is before me constantly and I dream of her every night. Whenever her letters arrived my children Meena and

*Maher were be filled with joy and optimism. They knew
that she genuinely cared about them.*

*I was at Daii jaan's house for Shiva and I cried the
whole time. I remember how she always thought of us
on holidays and sent us gifts. I have her letters in front
of me - all of them. I read them over and over again
and keep them in my chest, next to my heart. I do not
know how this wicked world has so mercilessly buried
the fingers that wrote such beautiful words. One would
need the heart of stone to accept such loss and grief.
The death of my dear sister has renewed the pain of all
my losses including my young husband. I wish I had
died instead of her for how she wanted to see her
grandchildren grow. I am sorry but I cannot stop the
tears as I write and I am soiling the letter.*

*My darling, we have no choice but to surrender to our
fate. This is our Ghaza va Ghadr, our destiny. We have
to try to continue life. I beg of you not to grieve and be
saddened for you have a young baby to care for. I want
so much to see you and kiss each of you, as my sister
would have done. Do you have time if I come there for
20 days to see you? I have such great desire to see you.
Please write to me soon and send me a picture of your
baby and one of Rubie's, too."*

*Meena and Maher are very sad about the sudden death
of their beloved Aunt and pray that God keeps you in his
embrace. I kiss you all from afar.*

"Ghorban-e shoma, your sacrifice, Narges"

A distant cousin on my father's side of the family
writes:

*"I swear to you that my hand cannot hold a pen to write
my condolences for the tragic loss of Esther Khanom.*

350

We are grief stricken and share your sorrow. I hope that God gives you patience and strength to live with this dreadful loss. What can we do but to succumb to our destiny? I hope that her lost years will be added to each of yours. I cannot forget when I was in New York, Esther khanom said next time you come here, I promise to take you everywhere and show you around. I am thankful that she was here for my wedding. I think of her all the time. Your cousin, Rebi"

For a long time, I cannot comprehend why my uncle would 'sit Shiva' for his sister but not call to share his grief with her children. It finally occurs to me that 'sitting Shiva' was merely a formality; it was a liability that he had to endure lest his character would be marred amongst his friends and affluent neighbors.

IN THE NEXT FEW WEEKS, my life is awash with unbearable guilt...why did I not stay with my mother all night to make sure she was not neglected? Why did I not soothe her dry chapped lips? Did the nurse ever tend to her? And what happened that last night at the hospital? Why did I not question the doctors about the angiogram? Why had I surrendered my natural tenacity to ask questions and insist on getting answers?

I pick up my mother's medical records and read them over and over again. For the first time, I learn about aneurysms and subarachnoid hemorrhages. Javid told me that a few weeks ago, Maman had called him after midnight, knowing that it would be early enough on the West Coast for her to talk to him. She had complained that she could not sleep because of

351

severe headaches. I wish I had not encouraged her to see my doctor who told her to throw away her blood pressure pills. Did he not realize that the pills were maintaining her pressure at a normal level? Did the onset of the severe headaches correlate with the discontinuation of her antihypertensive medicine? Did Javid question the physician's judgment? Nothing is making sense and I blame myself for everything...for not taking charge and for trusting others.... for believing that they cared enough to do the right thing. But now, I need answers.... I need to find out what happened to my mother and what transpired that fateful night in the hospital. Where was Javid? He had told us to go home, reassuring me that he would be there to keep an eye on things. He was the last person to have seen my mother alive- the only one who may know what happened in the last few hours of her life. But I know now that he had left the hospital to spend the night with his mother's relatives in New York City.

I study the X-rays, CAT scans, and the chart notes. I read the research and the survival statistics and learn that some patients had survived the aftermath of similar ruptures and intracranial bleeding. My mother had been responsive in the first twenty-four hours and that should have made her a fair candidate for surviving the catastrophic event. So, why did her condition deteriorate? Why was there such a drastic shift in her prognosis earlier by Dr. Biddle who said, "there is a good chance for recovery" and later by Dr. Balas who said, "there is no chance of survival." I was suspicious of Balas from the moment that I met him. He was abrupt and condescending. I am convinced that the sinister doctor neglected my mother or subjected her to a risky procedure that killed her. I wish I had questioned him about the angiogram. Now I know that angiograms bear the risk of rupturing arteries and causing a fatal stroke. My brother, who had stayed behind in the hospital, had heard repeated emergency calls for Dr. Balas to go to the ICU at 1:30 a.m. This was shortly before Maman was pronounced dead. She had suffered cardiac arrest. Did she receive inadequate and minimal care because she did not have health insurance? This was indeed the same hospital that years earlier, had released my brother prematurely after a head injury because he did not have health insurance. It would have cost him his life, had I not sat vigil at his bedside after he was discharged. Was my mother costing the hospital money every hour that she was alive? Is this what happens to patients who are indigent? Did someone decide to play God and let her die? I have heard of nurses who have pulled the plug on patients they believed would never fully recover.

I am so haunted by these thoughts that I can't sleep at night, and my days are plagued with restless quandary and sheer sorrow. I have so many questions and I know that I will not have peace until I find the answers. I had tried all my life to save my mother from her bleak destiny but in the end, I had failed her dismally.

I decide to hire a malpractice attorney. He is impressed that I have done my own research and have brought in copious notes and documentations to ease the task of discovery.

"You know we can't ask for a lot of money."

"This is not about money... I want justice.... I want

what every lawyer claims as the supreme motivation for choosing this profession... the passion to fight for justice."

"We work for money. So, you have to put your sentiments aside and help us win."

When I call my sister to tell her that I have hired a malpractice attorney, she is furious with me.

"Snap out of it. Give people a break. Stop talking about her. Enough! We have to get involved with life and try to forget it." She hollers.

"It has been less than a month since Maman died. How can you snap out of it so quickly, Ruhie?" I ask, distraught and staggered.

"Well, I am selling my house and moving away."

"Oh... no Ruhie, we need to stay together, especially now that Maman is gone. We have to keep our family together." I protest.

"I can't stand looking across the street and not seeing her." She retorts.

I don't know how my sister can reconcile this statement with her brutal treatment of my mother. But I know that I can never hope for an insightful answer from her.

"It is better to work through our feelings and not run away...we need to stay together and be a family for our children."

"You do what you want. I don't need you to be my therapist." She shrieks with contempt.

In a few days, we gather in my Maman's room and for the first time, I question why she had relinquished the large master bedroom to my father, choosing to live in the small room that was suited for a child. She had asked for little and expected even less, because she always felt she was "bizarfiat," unworthy of a better life.

I am reduced to tears as I look around and see how little I knew about my mother. There are dolls and trinkets... old and tattered... most likely rescued from garage sales. These are the precious little possessions of the young girl whose childhood had been stolen. They speak of her profound loss, deep loneliness and intense insecurity. But then, there are the diaries filled with her poetry and prolific writings, the awards and salutations for her professional achievements, and the copious documentations of her fierce desire to live proud and independently. Unbeknownst to us, she had been studying diligently to earn a degree in Architectural Engineering- a solemn testament of her drive and determination to save us from dishonor and poverty. We had taken so much for granted and had done so little to make her life better. We had never asked her to confide in us, to share her fears, and tell us what she needed. We were too consumed fighting for our own survival... too afraid to exhume the dreadful memories; for fear that they would stifle our denial and escape from pain.

"I wish I had talked more about her life and less about my own." I cry, overcome by guilt and remorse.

"Stop your goddamn psychology crap. What is wrong with you... trying to make everybody feel bad for you?" Ruhie growls.

Diana bursts out crying. She is holding the picture of her wedding that Maman had prominently placed on her dresser.

I hold my mother's bed pillow next to my heart and bury me head in it as I weep. Everything in her room is infused with her unmistakable scent... that unique and familiar fragrance that has remained faithful and undiminished in spite of tragedy and time. It is a reminder of my childhood when I nestled in her bosom for comfort and safety. I close my eyes and take a deep breath to inhale her scent. It is eerie to hold her belongings, wondering when she had last touched them. Everything is an extension of her and an intimate part of her life that speaks to me... There is her tattered wallet with a picture of her brother and a folded letter he had written to her a few months earlier. I am hesitant to open it and read what is in it. I fold it and put it back where I had found it. Perhaps I will be able to read it some day.

I hold the hairbrush full of her fine hair, her last pack of True Blue cigarettes, and the transparent plastic change purse with her last dollar bill that she had tucked away inside it. I can't dispose of her belongings...everything bears her imprint and keeps me connected to her. I want to keep safe all her possessions... I want to organize and put them away neatly.... I want to believe that she has just gone away for a while and will soon return.

"O.K.... Let's just throw all this junk out." Ruhie commands.

Jafar has retrieved a ring from Maman's jewelry box and wants his wife to wear it.

"Diana and Maman had a good relationship." he mutters, "She loved Maman a lot... I want Diana to have this ring." He hands the ring over to his wife and tells her to put it on.

"Take whatever you want. I want to get out of this house." Ruhie snaps impatiently.

"I am not ready to get rid of anything." I admit tearfully, "Take anything you want. I'll come back and clean things up a little bit at a time, when I am ready."

FOR A LONG TIME after my mother's death, the lump in my throat dams my every breath and I wonder how life can ever go on without her. Every time the doorbell rings, I instantly think that she has come to visit; that she has walked the three-mile distance from her house to see her granddaughter. Every day, I walk to the phone and habitually dial her number...wanting to share some news or ask her a question. But then, I reluctantly put back the receiver, as my eyes flood with tears to remind me that she is forever gone and I can never speak to her again.

When a loved one dies, we heal by connecting with those they loved. I long to embrace my mother's siblings... I need to share with them our memories and our grief. However, weeks have gone by and except for a couple of letters from my Aunt Narges, there has been no word from *Daii jaan*, the brother that my mother had loved so intensely.

?

- Scrupulous Exodus -

In December of 1978, just four months after my mother's death, as the strikes and the demonstrations against the Shah continue in Iran, my cousin Javid calls to tell me that his mother and his two sisters, Lidia and Arella have safely arrived in Los Angeles.

"*Salaam* Azadeh Khanom, do you believe we are here?" Marjan asks rhetorically.

"Welcome to *Amrika,* Marjan Khanom *jaan.* I am glad you are here."

"But what a nightmare, Azadeh *joon.* Aaah... you don't know what we had to go through. There were so many questions and inspections at the airport we didn't think we'd ever get on the plane."

"How is *Daii jaan?*" How are Aunt Narges and her children? Are they safe?" I inquire with trepidation.
"You know how your *Daii jaan* always bears the burden of watching over your aunt and her children." Marjan laments, and then without pause continues a monologue of lengthy inventory about how Narges' troubles have distracted her husband and deprived

her children of a normal family life. Her voice has been quivering...progressively rising in decibels, as if she is running out of breath, reaching the finale in a grueling marathon. But I know that this is a tactic she uses to accentuate her suffering. She wants me to know that she is far too overwhelmed and anguished to offer me any comfort or sympathy.

IN A FEW WEEKS, Marjan calls to say that she is going back to Iran and wonders whether or not to take her eleven-year-old daughter along. I am baffled. After all, it was just a few weeks ago that she told me at great length how traumatizing it had been to leave Iran.

"I don't understand, Mrjan khanom, why are you going back, anyway?

"We still have our precious art collection, all our rugs and custom made furniture to ship before it is too late."

I know that my uncle is a meticulous businessman and would have left nothing to chance. He has, like many other affluent Iranians, guaranteed the safety of his fortune by securing it in Swiss banks and other sheltered overseas investments. Undoubtedly, he had already sold his extensive real estate holdings to the incoming mass of the revolutionary entrepreneurs, competing to acquire his prime properties.

"There should be no question or doubt, Marjan Khanom. Arella should stay here where she is safe."

"But she is just eleven years old." Marjan protests. "I can't leave her alone."

I have flashbacks of my life at the age of eleven... Loneliness was a reality I could not escape, and living without the fear of abuse, hunger, and eviction was not an option.

"She is not alone. She lives with her older brothers in Beverly Hills... Her sister Lidia lives just a few blocks away... in the safest and most affluent neighborhood in the country...amongst celebrities and movie star royalties and she will go to school with their children. She is safe here with her siblings. Why would you want to take her back to Iran where her welfare may be at risk and her vulnerability will encumber your mission?

"You are so right, Azadeh *joon*. Thank you. You have always been the voice of wisdom and maturity."

"Don't worry, Marjan Khanom. Let Arella register at school right away so that she doesn't fall behind. She will be fine. I promise to call her often and make sure she is all right. *Khoda negahdar*, may God keep you in his embrace. Be safe and give my best regards to the family."

I know Marjan doesn't need my help or my prayers, but I offer them anyway. I am, without a doubt, a woman cast in my mother's image. I can't help but be loyal to those she loved because this is the legacy that she has left me with; and this is how I can remember her and feel her presence with me.

A few days later, Lidia calls. She wants me to send her a picture of Sophie. It is not because she wants to put it on her mantelshelf or in her photo album.

"The school wants a picture of Arella when she was born, but we don't have any. We think Sophie's picture could pass as Arella's because they look alike."

"Of course, "I say, "I will mail it to you right away."

360

- Mother's Day Mourning-

It is my first Mother's Day and there can be no celebration on this day without my mother. I have mourned her loss each and every day and while the universe has not missed a turn since her death, my world has tumbled upside down since then.

Today, I am alone without my mother and the dark cloud of depression is sapping every ounce of my vitality and inspiration.... All I want to do is to curl up in a corner and succumb to my pain.

I remember last Mother's day when I took her out to dinner and surprised her with her favorite bottle of perfume. She was infinitely grateful for this minor treat, wearing her graceful smile and dressed so elegantly as if she were going to meet the Queen. I wanted so much for her to feel like a Queen. I would have treated her like one every day of her life, had I known that our time together would be so brief. But I was naïve... I thought that because she was young and resilient, she would live for decades or for a long time, at least. I was foolish to believe that my love would protect her and keep her safe. But I knew neither the depth of my love, nor the gravity of my foolish faith until it was too late.

That day, as delighted as she seemed, I knew that something was troubling my mother. I pleaded with her to tell me what was wrong, and she finally broke down and cried. She told me about yet another altercation with Ruhie earlier that day and once again, it had ended with a ban on her visits with her grandchildren.

Today, a year later, we are motherless and I cannot celebrate her day without her. Instead, I want to go to the cemetery with flowers from her garden and tell her how much I miss her...tell her how sorry I am for having taken her for granted.

I ask my sister if she would come with me but she declines. She says that last night she had dreamed about her; that Maman had come to see her.... all dressed up, and told her that she was going to stay with her in the new house.

"I wasn't even thinking about her," she insists frostily, "I don't know why I dreamed about her."

I am stunned... How could she not have thought of Maman on the day before Mother's Day? How could she not be regretting what she did to her last year? How can she have such comforting dreams when she caused   her   so   much   pain?

THERE IS a rocking chair in Sophie's room that Maman had bought for her. Last night, I saw it rocking in my dream. It was empty, but I could sense Maman's presence even though she was not visible to me. I called out to her several times: "Maman, please don't go...wait...please wait..." But she did not answer. I wanted to jump out of my skin and run after her... scream her name until she could hear me. Then I woke up with a searing pain in my chest and couldn't go back to sleep.

Sometimes, I fear that I may be losing my mind to grief. I am restless and anxious about everything-mostly worried about my daughter and how she would survive without me. I long so much to see my mother's family. I need *Daii jaan*'s embrace and my family's promise that they would not forsake my daughter. What if I die before she is eighteen? I need to know that my family cares; that they would be there to comfort and guide her.

In my mother's backyard, I feel blissful with the scent of her presence and the fragrance that emanates from her beautiful and colorful flowers. Last year, she had proudly and fastidiously planted the many seeds that she had brought from Iran. Now the seeds had blossomed into delicate cucumbers, luscious baby eggplants, and aromatic herbs. Her favorite flower, the divine and delicate *Gol-e Yakh*, Ice Flower, fills the air with its enrapturing fragrance. Everything here is a testimonial to the magic and grandeur of her presence, but she will not be here ever again to see and enjoy them. This garden was Maman's sanctuary, and the flowers were the seedlings that did not let her down.

I drive to the cemetery crying silently, not to disrupt the enthusiasm of my eleven-month-old baby who is flipping through the pages of her Dr. Seuss book in her car seat and articulating sounds to impress me with her pretend reading. But once we reach the gravesite, I can't contain my grief. I wail uncontrollably as I hold Sophie close to my heart for solace and reprieve. I know that she is the only reason I want to live.

On the way back from the cemetery, I stop at a neighborhood drug store to buy a pack of cigarettes. Maman used to come here and pick up little trinkets for Sophie on her way to my house. She used to say that the storeowner was a crook and charged her too much for everything. I steal an 89-cent lighter to get even with him. It is a small reckoning for all the injustices that were done to her and to me.

People expect me to stop grieving; they say I should get over my loss and move on. I know Maman would have never said that to anyone... she would have never neglected those who needed her love and her compassion.

I call my cousin Arella to let her know that I am thinking about her. She was barely three years old when I saw her in Iran in 1970, but she remembers Maman, her favorite *Ammeh* -her father's sister, her aunt Esther. She remembers the wonderful gifts she always sent her. She asks about her as if she is still alive and I am comforted to know that she remembers my Maman.

Papa says that he cries every night.... that he hears Maman talking to him, and he misses her all the time. It is a vile state of human nature not to appreciate others until they are gone, and it is a wonder that we can forgive those who have been vile. With all the pain and misery that my father has brought upon us, I still can't abandon him. Sometimes, I even feel sorry for him. I pity his pathetic ignorance and his excessive dependence on alcohol and cigarettes. I watch as he compulsively washes his hands and I wonder what sinful memories he has stored away inside his insipid mind. I have come to see his vulnerability and forgive what he has done to me, but I can't forgive him for his brutality against my mother. Now that my sister has moved away to Long Island-thirty minutes away, and my brother is moving to Florida to start a new job, my father is the only family I have left. He is the last person I should want to have by my side and yet, oddly, he is the only one who shares my pain. I ask him to come for dinner and I make him the Persian meal that I know he likes.

- Exile or Exodus? -

By June 1979, most of my relatives have left Iran. They have been granted political asylum by the United States and have settled in Beverly Hills.

Uncle Jacob, Papa's elder brother has recently moved to California with his family and now Papa with his youngest brother, Moshe, have gone there to visit him.

Daii jaan Nader, too, has arrived in Beverly Hills with his wife Marjan to attend the *Milah*, Bris of their first grandchild; Lidia's son. In spite of the political tumult and the revolutionary unrest in Iran, the orderly and stable foundation of my uncle's life has not been altered. He has managed to gather his assets in a timely manner and take time off for his leisurely visit to the United States.

I am glad to know that my family and many of my relatives are safe and I long to embrace them all. I know that my emotional wound and the resounding void from the loss of my mother can't begin to heal, unless I see my mother's brother. I have to believe that he is grieved by the loss of his younger sister. I want to believe that now, having come to America unscathed, he will call to tell me that he cares. But days go by and I do not hear a word from him. When I can't wait any longer, I call my *Daii jaan* at his house in Beverly Hills and anxiously ask to talk to him. When Marjan finally hands the phone over to my uncle, he talks only of his pleasure being with his children. He does not ask about his sister's last days or about our devastation. He wants to know how my business is and how much money I make. In a few days, he will be going back to Iran to collect the last and final scintilla of his fortune, and then he will return to the U.S., where he will live as a permanent resident.

"Will you stop in New York to see us, *Daii jaan*?" I ask cautiously to curb my enthusiasm.

"No, but I will call you from the airport." He says cavalierly.

Why, I wonder, is that necessary? What can he say or ask from the airport that he can't do from Beverly Hills?

Instantly I regret that I had ingratiated myself seeking his compassion, and I quickly say goodbye before he can hear my anguished cry. I remember just before Maman died, *Daii jaan* had come to the U.S. on his way to California, but had not stopped in New York to see his sister. Maman was heartbroken because she knew that all those times when *Daii jaan* stayed with her, prior to the purchase of his home in Beverly Hills, it was not a gesture of his affection but a matter of convenience. Still, disappointed and dejected as she was, she spent the last days of her life as a proud citizen of the United States, pleading with the

Immigration office to expedite issuing exit visas for her brother's family.

As I get off the phone, I am overwhelmed by disbelief and sorrow. "Doesn't Daii jaan care about us at all?"

I call my father at his brother Jacob's home. I tell him about my conversation with my Uncle Nader. I tell him how desperately I had bet against myself that *Daii jaan* would come through for us; that he would show at least a modicum of care and compassion.

Papa tells me that he, too, had called Uncle Nader earlier and pleaded with him to spend at least a day in New York to see his sister's children; to visit the grave and share their *gham* and grief, so they would not feel so disconnected and abandoned by their mother's family. But Marjan had taken the phone away from him and told Papa, in no uncertain terms and quite sternly, not to upset her husband.

"*Maaha aamadeem baraieh khoshee*, we are here to celebrate, not to mourn and grieve!" She had hollered.

I feel my chest tighten with anguish. I cannot believe what I am hearing. How can a family be so impervious to the grief of their kin?

My father's elder brother, *Amoo jaan* Jacob asks my father to give him the phone so he can talk to me. He knows that I am devastated and sobbing.

"*Azizam*, why didn't you all come here to be with the family?" He speaks with genuine affection and empathy, "Your mother was an extraordinary woman. She was loved and respected by everyone in the family."

Uncle Jacob's kind sentiments lift my spirit and soothe the pain of my grief. It is remarkable how profoundly a thoughtful gesture of humanity can alter one's state of mind and wellbeing.

I am astounded by the contrast between the empathic tenor of my father's brother and the cold and dispassionate tone of my mother's own sibling. I thank my *Aamoo jaan* Jacob. He is truly a man of nobility and grandeur. I tell him how deeply his compassion has touched me and I thank him for acknowledging my grief.... Knowing that there is kindness and virtue within my reach helps me survive the punitive ugliness of evil that surrounds me.

"Thank you, Uncle Jacob. I love you. I hope to see you someday."

"Come visit, *Azizam*. I would like to see you and your baby. Our home is yours. Come soon. We will all be happy to see you."

Some bonds are never broken, even with those who are not blood related and those who are separated by time and physical distance. Three nights ago, my childhood friend Ebi called. He is the son of our long-ago landlords, Mr. and Mrs. Ebrahimi. He said he had just heard about Maman's death and had searched everywhere to find me. He praised Maman and shared with me memories of her that gave me comfort. It was as if we were family and had lost touch, only briefly.

AUGUST 26, 1979 marks one Jewish calendar year since the day my mother died. My Aunt Atefeh and two of her children, my cousins Roshan and Kyan are here to share the conclusion of our mourning and facilitate our transition into a life of normalcy. My beloved Uncle Moshe has returned to Iran, leaving us all worried, and praying for his safe return.

We cut some roses and *Gohl Yakh* from Maman's magnificent garden and take our silent and somber ride to the cemetery. We cry together at the gravesite and I silently wonder how I can ever go on without my Maman. When we return to the house, I am overwhelmed by swirling emotions. Everywhere I look and in every corner, there are Maman's handprints and the empty spaces that she had once occupied. My mind mercilessly replays the memories of her last days.... how she thrashed her head against the wall and how she begged us to let her die. I pick up Sophie and hold her tight. I remind myself that she is the reason I have to be strong.

Aunt Atefeh and my father are cooking in the kitchen. They are using Maman's utensils and her spices to make us a meal to nourish us and help us through the last hours of our yearlong bereavement. It is time for us to end our mourning and cease asking "why?" We have to resume life and accept that there will always be the void of her presence in our lives, and the interminable longing for her in our heart.

IN SEPTEMBER, we learn that my Aunt Narges has died. No one wants to talk about it and it is not clear if she committed suicide. But the fact that her sudden demise coincides with the anniversary of my mother's death, points more to a probability than to a coincidence. I remember the letters she wrote to me soon after Maman died. Her despair and desolation was palpable through her words. I feel so badly that I did not keep closer contact with her, but I was in the dismal abyss of my own grief, struggling every minute of the day to remain sound and strong for the sake of my baby.

Aunt Narges had lived a pitiful life, much like that of my own mother. The two sisters were like a dangling participle at the end of the sentence that defined the glorious life of their older brother. They were like the flowers of spring that bloomed briefly and died, while the weeds in the desert lived on. My aunt's scars from the fire she had set to burn herself were grotesque, but they ran far deeper than her skin. Her unsuccessful attempt had only added to the humiliation and self-loathing that she had endured since she was sixteen. Now her children, too, will undoubtedly arrive at a tragic end of their own.

I feel infinite sorrow and unmitigated rage thinking about how two exceptional women became victims of a cruel and contemptuous verdict by their older brother... a decision that condemned them and their next generations to a life of relentless pain and suffering.

TODAY would have been Maman's 56th birthday. Jafar and Diana have come from Florida for a short visit and I have invited everyone to my house. After dinner, we all gather around Wayne's movie projector to watch old eight-millimeter films from Iran. Maman always looked vibrant and graceful in spite of her internal agony. Her smile and enthusiasm was contagious but lasted only briefly. As I look around and see the assembly of my siblings and our children, I see a ray of hope that we can build a better foundation for a new and cohesive family.

IN A FEW DAYS, Ruhie calls. She is distraught and frantic.

"I think I am going to have a breakdown." She bawls.

"What do you mean? What is wrong?"

"I wake up in the middle of the night crying and calling Mom. I want to go to the cemetery and dig her out of the grave and tell her how sorry I am."

It is a bizarre and disturbing thought but it does not surprise me at all. Ruhie has been trying to forget Maman instead of grieving her loss, so that she wouldn't have to face her guilt. I ask if she wants to go to the cemetery tomorrow so that we can both cry and apologize to Maman. She declines and I don't ask why.

The next day, she calls again, sounding frantic.

"There is something wrong with Jocelyn. She won't go to sleep at night...She is scared.... She cries and wants a picture of Maman under her pillow so she can fall asleep."

"Well, give it to her...She had a strong bond with Maman and she misses her."

"Jocelyn says she is mad at me because I didn't let her say goodbye to her Grandma."

When Maman was in the hospital and then when she was buried, I had suggested that Ruhie take Jocelyn to say goodbye, but she refused. Now Jocelyn wants to go to the cemetery. She wants to know if her Grandma can hear her in the grave. She wants to tell her how much she loved her and missed her. She wants to be buried next to her when she dies.

I break down and weep. My heart aches for all of us. We are alone...all drowning in a sea of grief. There is no family, no guiding light, and no lifeline to keep us connected to our roots and to safety.

Ruhie says she, too, is suffering from insomnia and anxiety. She is taking Valium at night to sleep, but the fear of death occupies her mind throughout the day. She worries that an imminent heart attack will leave her children motherless.

I tell her that I, too, have those fears everyday.

"It is natural.... once we lose a parent we have to face our own mortality."

"Don't lecture me, Goddamn it. I need you to be family, not a psychologist." She hollers.

"What do you need Ruhie? What can I do to help?" I sense the dark side of my sister rising to provoke a fight, and I am terrified.

"Just don't sound like you are so smart... that you know everything."

"O.K. I am sorry. Why don't you all come over for a day? Let the kids play together. Let's be a family."

"No, you just don't know how to act like a sister. I get sick being around you."

I say goodbye before she can hear me cry. I never know what my sister wants. No one ever does.

Later, my brother calls. His voice is muffled and agitated. His wife is leaving him and he fears an impending breakdown, and the ruination of his life. But he refuses to seek professional help. My siblings' inability and their lack of desire for introspection exacerbate my grief and leaves me feeling alone and hopeless. Now, Wayne, too, has withdrawn his support and compassion from me.

"It is not normal to be sad for so long. You should be done with your mourning after a year. Get over it."

He protests. "You have gone bonkers with your grief." He decries. Somehow, he finds it easier to admonish me and deepen my wound, rather than to comfort me and soothe my pain.

A VISIT WITH my obstetrician helps put my grief in perspective. Dr. Elahi is the archetypal physician every woman needs. I tell him about my unrelenting sadness and how everyone is expecting me to be done grieving the loss of my mother.

"You have gone through two major traumatic life events in a short time. It is very difficult to cope with such intense emotions all at once." He puts his hand on my shoulder and sets my mind at ease. He tells me that I am entitled to my grief, for as long as I need. Alas, there is someone who understands my pain...someone who acknowledges the gravity of my emotional upheaval and gives legitimacy to my persistent melancholy.

"Give yourself time." He says sympathetically, "It will get easier."

PAPA WANTS to go to Israel and bring home a new wife. His relatives have found him a Palestinian Jew who is poor, lonely, and eager to live in America. They claim that she is a good housekeeper and would be a good companion for him, but I am adamantly opposed to this preposterous proposition. I know it is hard for Papa to live alone and take care of himself. He has always expected women to serve him and tend to his needs, but I know that this venture will ultimately cost him dearly. I try to discourage him but he is adamant and ready to leave.

In a few weeks, when my father returns from Israel with a woman who now occupies the house my mother had lived in, I find it intolerable to visit him.

AFTER YEARS of trying to put together my broken family, I realize that my success, at best, has been dismal and incomplete. I had tried so hard to reconstruct the shattered foundation of our lives and build a safe and solid home for us all. However, at the end, my mother was dead, my father remained a punitive liability, and my siblings' dysfunction continues to consume and deplete me. Now that my sister has banned my daughter and me from her family, and my brother has isolated himself from his, I am left to believe that our only choice is to pursue our peace, not together...but separately. I have to find solace in my marriage, the love of my daughter, my career, and my friendships.

It is said that we are born twice: once when our mother gives birth to us, and once again when she dies. In my mother's absence, I discover more about the significance of her presence, and I discover more about myself. I am no longer her child and must become my own woman. I have to mother myself and nurture my own child. With the passage of time, I am coming to the end of a journey and arriving in a timeless place where my mother remains alive... not living here in the physical realm...but alive in me. She lives on through me, and by the lessons that she has left for me to pass on.

AT WORK, I am inundated with requests from Iranian applicants seeking student visas to come to New York.

Our homeland is in mayhem. Our Shah has fled to seek refuge and medical care in Cairo, and the country has fallen into the hands of a radical Eslaami government. Many families are trying to obtain exit visas for their children. Every day, I receive letters... even from members of my mother's family...those who had abandoned us, and those who I never knew. There are my mother's long lost cousins and relatives... even a girl named Roxie, the niece of Lidia's husband, asking that I urgently issue them I-20s, so that they can enter the United States. Now, precipitously and conveniently, they all want me to know that they are my family.

I am deeply moved and saddened by the heartrending stories and the desperate pleas of those who fear imprisonment and execution by the new government. I am an advocate of their cause and feel privileged to be able to help them save their lives.

WINTER OF 1979 brings to New York a massive amount of snow, a declining economy, and a rapid rise in crime. Wayne is disgruntled with his university position and wants to resign. We are both displeased with the diminishing quality of life and the forbidding cold winters. We have long hoped to establish our own private practice of psychology and the time may have come for us to contemplate moving to Florida for warmer climate and better career opportunities. I am reluctant to resign from my position. I enjoy working with my colleagues and know that my availability to my students, particularly the Iranian population, is urgent and critical. Nonetheless, and in spite of my own financial and personal success, I feel the need to move in a new direction.

As the summer of 1980 approaches, the massive exodus of Iranians shifts to the state of California and the number of student applicants seeking to enroll in New York universities decline. I work tirelessly past my regular office hours to expedite the processing of all the inquiries and applications at hand and by the summer's end, I feel sufficiently free from self-reproach to hand in my resignation.

IN SEPTEMBER 1980, Wayne and I pack our hopes and our troubles and move to Palm Beach, Florida, where we believe we can provide our two-year-old daughter Sophie a safer and better life. My brother has recently purchased a second house and will be vacating his two-bedroom condominium. He is quite pleased to have us rent his condo and become his loyal tenants.

"I know doing business with family is not a good idea." He quips, "Don't expect a discount and make sure you pay the rent on time."

"Don't worry, Jafar. I pay all my bills on time." I assure him.

In a few weeks, we learn that my brother is divorced and we will never see Diana again. I am very sad about this turn of events. I liked Diana and got along with her well. She was very fond of Sophie, and I had hoped that she would fill the void of an aunt in her life. Jafar is quite distraught and comes over every night to talk. Lately, he and Wayne have bonded over their mutual love of tennis and twisted discontent with women. Wayne is unhappy and guilt- ridden to have moved away from his parents. He blames me for

377

wanting to get away from his mother because I could not deal with the loss of my own. Jafar claims that my fierce independence and expressed liberal views had emancipated his timid wife and encouraged her to demand her autonomy. If it were not for the serious nature of these harsh and outrageous allegations, I would find them very entertaining, but this is not at all a laughing matter. The two men have conveniently formed a solid coalition in this regard and before I can object or appeal for a cogent explanation, my brother demands that I exit the room and leave them alone.

"Excuse me, I live here." I protest, "I am not going to lock myself up in the bedroom all night."

"This is a private conversation." Wayne takes my brother's side because he likes to impress him with his extreme psychoanalytic style: applying Freudian theories to everything, everyone, and no matter what the place or time.

"It's late and I need to put the baby to bed. I do not want you smoking in the house all night."

"Keep the bedroom door closed." Wayne instructs.

"You should be talking to an unbiased therapist, Jafar." I deem with good intention.

"I am... So leave!" Jafar sneers.

I take Sophie to her room and lay down with her. I have to believe that my brother is having a temporary lapse of good judgment; a rash of self-indulgence that he will overcome. I'll give him a chance to redeem himself. After all, we have moved here to start a new life. But then, what is going on with my husband... Why is he behaving like an adversary rather than a loving mate?

RUHIE CALLS to tell me that she is pregnant. She has had a dream about Maman and having perceived it as bad omen, wanted to share it with me. She is afraid someone is going to die... Maman had told her so in her dream.

"So, who do you have in mind?' I say cynically, knowing that if she thought I was the one at the gate of annihilation, she would not be calling to warn me.

"I've decided I am going to get an abortion." She announces glibly.

"You spent all those years crying because you couldn't have a baby. Now you are thinking about terminating your pregnancy... Does that make sense?"

"I never wanted her dead." She confesses hastily for fear that she would retract her words. "I just wanted her out of my life."

I know that her guilty conscience has led her to delusional thinking. I want to tell her to seek help, but I know that she won't do it and it may be too late, anyway.

"That is preposterous, Ruhie *joon*... Maman would never want you to abort your baby, and she is not going to punish you by killing your baby." I have to be blunt and to the point to convince my sister not to end her pregnancy. I know that I will not hear from her again, unless there is another emergency.

In a few weeks, my brother's evening visits and private sessions with Wayne end abruptly. He has met a woman that he sees regularly and he no longer has the time or the inclination to visit his confederate buddy. Wayne is displeased and our relationship begins to erode more rapidly. We are running out of money and our verbal feuds are escalating. Sophie hears our arguments and her mood and behavior is changing. When I ask Wayne to help me advance our career by soliciting the professional community, he is not interested. I have no choice but to do it alone and to establish a practice of my own.

We have gone for marriage counseling, but the costly therapy sessions have been ineffective. On the day that my therapist advises me to find a lover and offers to have sex with me to ease my distress, I decide it is time to leave him and ask Wayne to leave me.

I register Sophie in Nursery School part-time, and open an office for my private psychology practice. I work only when Sophie is in school. I will not leave her with babysitters or anyone else.

Jafar no longer visits, now that his girlfriend has moved in with him, but he calls me when he has a fight with her and fears that she'll leave him. Sophie loves her "Uncle Farfar" and misses him. I want desperately for my daughter to have a family and so, I show my brother immense gratitude on the rare occasions that we visit him and he pays attention to his niece.

IN FEBRUARY, my father informs me that my sister has given birth to a boy. I am happy for her and hope that the joy of a new baby...the son that she always wanted will turn a fresh and fulfilling page in my sister's life.

-Tehrangeles:
Where the Exodus Ends -

By 1981, the Iranian Revolution has changed not only the tapestry of culture and politics in that country, but has begun to alter the social and political landscape of California, particularly Beverly Hills. Most of the affluent Iranian Jews have left Iran not by expulsion but rather methodically and by their own volition. Their arrival has propelled what is undoubtedly the new age of the California Gold Rush. They have moved en masse with suitcases full of gold and cash; and have transported by ship, crates of their precious art, valuables, and furnishings. They pay hard currency to buy up the old Beverly Hills homes of movie stars and to erect in their place, extravagant mansions that flaunt their glaringly gaudy taste. They offer cash for depreciated properties and build luxury office buildings to rent or to sell with immense profit to the next wave of immigrants whose exit has been delayed because they have larger assets to liquidate.

IN 1982, my cousin Javid comes to Palm Beach to attend a conference. His parents and brother Daniel are still in Iran, but his youngest brother Kaveh and little sister Arella live with him in Beverly Hills. Although I am broken-hearted by his parents' dismissal of our loss and grief, I cherish the bond that I have maintained with Javid.   Amidst the chronic chaos with my siblings, it is uplifting to spend time with someone who is removed from angst and misery, and yet shares a common ancestry.

Javid has recently married Anya and has brought her along on this trip. She is lovely, beautiful, and down-to-earth, with a deep commitment to Judaism and humanity. She is clearly a good partner for my upward moving and brilliant cousin who has already gained international fame in medicine. I present Anya with an exquisite gold necklace to congratulate and welcome her to the family. I promise to stay in touch and visit them in California someday soon.

ON THANKSGIVING, my sister calls. She is once again distraught and in tears.   In the recent months, her husband's business has suffered a setback and financial loss, and he has been coming home late every night.

"I think he is gambling or doing drugs." Ruhie has surmised.

"If you can't get him to talk to you about what is going on, maybe you can talk to his father." I suggest cautiously and with great trepidation ... I never know what will trigger my sister's rage.

"I hate those bastards. They think their son is perfect."

"Come down for a visit? I say, "let's see what Simon does while he is here. If he is addicted to anything we will know."

In the winter, my sister, her husband and their three children come to visit. It has been a long time since we have all been together and I am delighted that our children will be acquainted with cousins who have been missing from their lives. I rent a car for them to use during their stay and give them my bedroom so that they will have privacy and comfort. I sleep in Sophie's bed and keep an eye on the kids who are happy to camp out in the small living room and play.

I have closed my office for the holidays and offer to take care of the kids so that my sister and her husband can spend a romantic weekend in the Keys. But, my suggestion is not well received. In fact, somehow, it has offended my sister's sensibility.

"Are you out of your mind?" Ruhie snaps. "You think I am going to leave my children with you?"

Simon looks at me in disbelief, but nothing about Ruhie should surprise him or me. We are always fooled by her tranquility, which proves to be fleeting, as something benign can instantly ignite her fury.

I try to remain calm and not let the discord escalate and ruin the day. I must watch every word and action not to get her upset.

"Would you like me to invite Jafar for dinner, then?"

"I am not talking to that bastard." She snares.

"Why? What has he done?"

"I don't want to talk about it. I know you have a relationship with him and he is letting you live here for free."

"Oh, no he is not." I say steadfastly, "I pay rent;

the same as everyone else... So, is that what is bothering you?"

"Isn't Wayne living with him?" Ruhie demands to know.

"I don't know...why would he? I am sure Jafar and his girlfriend want their privacy."

"Well, he said he didn't mind having Wayne there because now he can get rent from both of you."

I am flustered and exasperated with my sister's despicable attempt to manipulate the odds and set me up against my brother. She uses this tactic to alienate me from everyone. She always accused Maman of favoring me over her.... She made her feel guilty and hurled her into a state of abject despair. She can drive anyone over the edge.

I walk outside to smoke a cigarette and calm myself.

"Wait Azadeh, wait..." Simon has come out looking for me, and I am instinctively worried about my daughter who is left behind within the range of Ruhie's delusional reality. I turn around to go back inside.

"I am so sorry, Azadeh. Your sister is impossible to live with. You were so nice to invite us. You even rented a car for us and gave us your bedroom. You have gone out of your way to make us comfortable, but all she wants to do is fight with you."

"I feel helpless, Simon. It breaks my heart to have the kids witness such senseless disharmony."

"She does this to everybody. I feel helpless all the time... living with her is impossible. Now you know why I stay away from her and don't want to go home at night."

"It has gotten worse since Maman died, hasn't it?"

"Yes, but she has never been happy with anything. I give her everything she wants, but nothing is ever enough. I don't know how much longer I can put up with her. You are the wise and sane sister. Tell me what I should do."

I see tears fogging Simon's eyes. There is remorse but mostly a resounding resignation in his voice.

Now suddenly, I hear Ruhie screaming at the top of her lungs. She has something in her hand and is charging towards me, posturing to clobber me with it.

"You fucking bitch. Mind your own business and let me live." She shrieks, "You goddamn bastards... you talk about me? You should both drop dead."

I turn around to go back to the house. I can hear the kids crying inside.

"Stop it, honey." Simon pleads as if his kindness will quell my sister's disease.

"This is it, you bastards. I am leaving." She instructs her children who have now come outside crying, scared, and confused.

"Pack up your things... We are leaving."

"No Mommy, please.... We don't want to go. We want to play with our cousin." Jocelyn pleads. She is trembling fiercely...she knows her resistance will not go unpunished.

"Shut up, you idiot... I said we are leaving." She raises her hand to hit her daughter, but Simon intercedes and stops her.

I feel the weight of an ocean of sand on my chest. My sister has ruined another day and dashed another chance for us to be a family.

385

- Sandcastles -

Four years after our auspicious relocation to Florida and subsequent to frequent and futile attempts to keep our optimism and marriage intact, Wayne and I are divorced. My father's Israeli wife has left him, Ruhie and Simon are hopelessly struggling to keep their marriage whole, and my brother is engaged to his longtime girlfriend, Dolores who is aloof and by her own admission, "a gal no man wanted to marry."

On the afternoon of Jafar's wedding, Ruhie, Simon, their three children, and Papa arrive from New York and we all gather at my brother's to work out the details of transportation to the ceremony. Ruhie and I have not spoken to each other since that dreadful visit almost three years ago but today, I intend to be cordial to her and get through this reunion unscathed. Sophie is playing with her cousins in the living room where everyone has assembled. Perhaps Ruhie has not instructed her children to ignore their cousin or they have chosen to defy her. While we wait for the bride's parents, my father is concerned that he is running out of cigarettes. I, too, need to get some for myself. This is not a day to be without them.

"Please keep an eye on Sophie while I am gone. I'll be back in a half hour." I announce addressing my father. I don't want Sophie to wander outside by the pool, even though I have taught her to swim and she is well disciplined.

Suddenly, Ruhie screeches from across the room.

"You fucking bitch," she raises her finger pointing at me, "You are crazy... I have three kids to take care of and you ask me to watch yours."

A gloomy blanket of silence instantly shrouds the room. We are all frozen in our tracks...first with shock, and then with fright. The kids break the silence with their screams and Papa attempts to intervene.

"*Chi migi, dokhtar*, what are you saying, girl?" He appeals to Ruhie for reconciliation, "Azadeh didn't ask you to take care of Sophie. The kids are playing, and we are all here to watch them. You don't have to take care of anybody."

"You are defending her? Go to hell...all of you. I am not coming to the wedding." Ruhie bellows as she commands her kids to pack their stuff and get ready to leave.

Panic and protest overwhelm the room, but soon we are begging Ruhie to calm down and forgive us all for our transgressions.... her perceived and paranoid allegations.

"Please Ruhie. I am getting married today. You can't just leave." Jafar is pleading, his eyes burning with restrained tears.

I feel sorry for my brother... I know he is terrified and embarrassed. This is bound to cost him.... give his bride the upper hand when their marriage becomes a competition between who is sane and who isn't.

"See what you do, bitch? You ruin everything." Ruhie shouts, addressing me. "You just think about yourself, you bastard."

I am drained and exasperated, wishing I could leave. But I can't walk out on my brother's wedding. My chest is about to burst open. I have to go outside to cry and smoke a cigarette.

When I come back a few minutes later, Ruhie is sprawled on the bathroom floor, looking as if she is in a trance. As soon as she sees me, she begins to beat herself with her fist...just like Maman used to do.

"Goddamn you...you just want me to die...all of you."

"Please Ruhie, don't ruin my wedding." Jafar is kneeling on the floor, begging and crying. He is pleading with Ruhie to think of the special bond they share.

Finally, just before the ceremony is about to begin, Ruhie is ready to end the fiasco and come to the wedding. I clean up my face... smeared with make-up and tears. I know it will be a bad night, but I have to collect myself and get through it.

AT THE RECEPTION, the children are seated together at a round table. I have come to check on Sophie, who is all smiles, excited to be with her cousins. I stand at a distance when I see Ruhie going around the table with a pitcher of juice. She is filling every child's cup, but walks past Sophie without giving her a drop.

Sophie is looking up and following her aunt with her inquisitive eyes, wondering why she has passed her by.

"May I have some, Aunt Ruhie?" She pleads.

"Ask your fucking mother to get you a drink. I am not your maid." Ruhie snarls.

Sophie is scared and confused. She lowers her head and starts to cry. I, too, am reduced to tears, witnessing my sister's despicable cruelty to an innocent child. But for Ruhie, it all seems like a nice walk in the park. She saunters away smiling triumphantly, knowing that she has inflicted pain upon my daughter and me.

I chain smoke to calm my nerves, to fight the tears and the urge to take my daughter and walk away. I cannot wait for this affair to be over.

- A House of Our Own -

For weeks I have not been able to sleep, haunted by an eerie feeling that someone is hiding behind my bedroom window watching me. For a while, every time I heard footsteps, I thought it was a dog walker but lately, the occasional rustling of the leaves outside the window has me suspect otherwise.

Tonight, the screeching sound of the screen door on the patio jolts me out of sleep. I rush to the window and quickly pull up the vertical blinds. Suddenly, I am face-to-face with a large man standing just inches away and peering inside my bedroom. Instinctively, I raise my fist and with all the force of my pent up anger, after months of fear and frustration, I punch through the glass, aiming and hoping to injure the enemy. Then I run to get Sophie out of her room before I call 911.

"Mommy, Mommy..." Sophie cries.... "You are bleeding.... Are you going to die?"

I look down and see a trail of blood dripping from my wrist. The shattered glass has slashed my wrist, but I have been infused with too much adrenaline to feel it.

"I'll be fine, honey. Don't worry." I reassure her, "The paramedics are coming. They can stop the bleeding."

The medics arrive promptly and the police search the neighborhood to look for the man who has been stalking me. Outside, at the foot of the window, they discover a pile of cigarette butts beneath the bushes, but there are no footprints.

"This man has been coming around for a long time, judging by all the cigarettes he smoked." remarks one officer.

"He timed his visits when the sprinklers were on so you couldn't hear him... and the water washed away his footprints." Notes the detective.

When I realize the added vulnerability that I have inadvertently created by breaking the glass, I am terrified to stay in the house.

"He won't be coming back tonight, but you need to replace the glass and secure your window so he can't get in." The detective recommends, "And we'd like you to stop at the police station tomorrow and look at some photos. Maybe you can identify the perpetrator."

I stay with Sophie in her room awake all night, barricading us behind closed windows and doors that I have tightly reinforced with bulky furniture. I try to dismiss the stream of scenarios that could have ended far worse than a broken window and a bleeding wrist.

In the morning, I call my brother and ask if he would have security bars installed.

"Next time call the police instead of breaking the glass." He commands.

SINCE HIS MARRIAGE to Delores, my brother has isolated himself from me and we hardly speak. Unlike his first wife, Diana, who loved Sophie and always tried to nurture a relationship with me, Dolores is unsympathetic, grossly self-absorbed, and uncompromising. She is interested only in promoting her relationship with her own friends and family. Prior to her engagement to my brother, Dolores and her parents were quite solicitous towards me, believing perhaps that I had some influence in my brother's ultimate decision to get married. But since the wedding, all attitudes have changed and we are not included in any family functions.

Recently, my brother abruptly decided to end his longstanding relationship with a colleague whose family had treated him like their own ever since his move to Palm Beach. Bill and his wife Trisha's daughter, Chrissie, has become Sophie's friend and playmate, and the family has extended their support and friendship to me, as well. But now that my brother has severed his relationship with that family, he has forbidden me to see them or speak to them.

"How am I going to explain to Sophie that she can't see her best friend?" I question my brother's unreasonable demand.

"I don't know, but you have to choose between me and them."

It is hard to explain to a six-year-old child why she can't play with her friend. I buy Sophie a dog to soothe and distract her and try to explain to her my loyalty to my brother. However, ending my friendship with Bill's family does not mend or enhance my brother's relationship with me. He abandons us, even as we relinquish our solid and supportive relationship with Bill's family to please him.

It is time for me to move out of my brother's condominium. I have been his tenant for four years and his sister for forty-two, but neither my love, nor my loyalty has brought us close. I am ready to invest in a house and a home of my own.

I BUY a townhouse close to Sophie's school, not far from my office. I set up a room for her to do her schoolwork in the evening while I see my patients.

My brother has found a tenant and is impatient for me to move. I have donated most of my furniture but have to make several trips to bring my personal belongings to our new home. On my last trip to the condominium after work, I have come to empty the cupboards, pantry, and the refrigerator. But I see that everything has been removed and nothing remains. When I call my brother to find out what he has done with my food supply, he says that he threw them all away.

"I wanted everything out, in case my tenants ant to move in earlier." He explains.

In 1985, a few months, after Jafar's wedding, my father informs me that Ruhie is moving to Florida. She is convinced that ever since Simon's parents moved here last year, her husband has become addicted to drugs and pornography. Now that Ruhie has made amends with my brother, she feels that moving closer to him and to Simon's parents will enhance their lives and improve their relationship.

FOR MONTHS AFTER my sister's relocation to Florida, neither she nor my brother has attempted to contact me. Every holiday and each birthday, I fantasize having a joyous family gathering, but Sophie and I are always alone. My heart breaks every time Sophie asks about her grandparents, her Uncle Farfar, or her cousins. I am disconnected from my roots, my family, and my heritage. I feel insurmountable guilt and anguish that Sophie has no siblings and no one to depend on when I am old or no longer living. I put an ad in the local newspaper looking to adopt family grandparents who would fill the void in both my life and Sophie's. It is a pathetic act of desperation and I know quickly to withdraw my search. How can I trust anyone who is not my kin... not blood related? But what have I with those who do share a bloodline with me?

I think about joining a synagogue where I may find comfort and support. But how do I explain to them my family? Do I lie and say that I have none? I cannot lie, nor can I bear the shame and the humiliation of telling the truth. I must make peace with my siblings. I have to reach out to them, plead with them, and compel them to help me fix our broken family.

"Dear Ruhie and Jafar,
We loved Maman and miss her terribly. She did her best to give us all she could, in spite of the dreadful destiny that held her hostage her entire life. She wanted more than anything for us to love one another and have fulfilling lives. She wanted us to hold each other's hands and be a loving family. We will do well, only if we talk to each other and listen to one another with

compassion and care. We should support each other, not compete with one another. We cannot undo the misfortunes of our past but we can do better than our past. Let's make sure our children grow together, love one another and support each other. Let's make their generation better than ours. Let's do it in Maman's honor and in her memory. Let's do this for her, for ourselves, and most importantly for the sake of our young and innocent children. I love you both, Azadeh"

IN A FEW DAYS, I receive a call from a woman in New York. Her name is Gloria and she claims that my sister was her neighbor when she lived on Long Island. I don't know this woman, but I am compelled to listen because she knows my sister.

"I' ve been in touch with your sista since she moved to Florida. Her husband left her with three kids and no money. Why ain't you helping her?"

Now I hear a man's voice on the phone extension.

"Hey, this is Frankie here, Gloria's husband...I wanna tell you we's tired of your sista callin'... cryin' every day." He raises his voice a decibel or two, "What kinda family are yous. Why ain't yous helpin' her?"

"I appreciate your concern, but shouldn't she be calling me, instead of calling you?" I try to remain calm, in spite of the disparaging and offensive remarks launched at me by these strangers.

"She don't know I am callin' you." Gloria claims, "I hope you gonna do somethin' to help her cause it ain't our responsibility."

I call Ruhie to tell her about the phone call. "What is going on?" I ask.

"Simon has disappeared. No one knows where he is. As soon as his mother died, he left."

"When did she die? What happened?"

"She had cancer. Simon was spending every day in the hospital. I couldn't wait for the bitch to die."

I cringe to hear such severe expression of disdain and antipathy, but my sister's harsh language and callus sentiments should never surprise me. I do not know how she expected kindness from her husband when she pushed his tolerance over the limit; castigating him for spending time with his dying mother, and wishing her end to come quickly for her own relief?

"What can I do to help?"

"I want to sue the bastard for child support but I can't find him. I am sure his father knows where he is but when I call him, he hangs up on me. These people are sick."

"What can I do to help you, Ruhie?"

I want you to call his father and tell him he has to help his grandchildren. He has to support them or tell me where his son is so I can have him arrested."

"Putting Simon in jail is not going to advance your mission, Ruhie." I dare explain, "He can't work to support the kids if he is serving time behind bars."

I know there is more to the story than what she is telling me. I agree to call her father-in-law, Danny. I had known him to be a generous and reasonable man.

When I speak to Danny, I hear the voice of a man who is weary and broken. He has lost his wife, and lost his connection with his grandchildren. He assures me that Simon had left a good amount of money, bonds, and security for his children. He is currently in rehab and will not be able to work until he is clean. When I ask why he had severed his relationship with his grandchildren, he weeps.

"When I told your sister that I couldn't reveal my son's whereabouts, she got angry. Next thing we know, she comes to my driveway during the night and slashes all my four tires. She is crazy. I have a restraining order against her...I don't want her anywhere near me. "

I am appalled by my sister's behavior but again, not surprised. I call to ask her how she expects to get help from Simon's father after what she has done, but she is oblivious and remorseless

"It is best to wait for Simon to recover from his addiction.... wait until he is out of rehab. Then he can work and support his children."

"O.K. Never mind. I didn't think you were going to help me, anyway." She slams down the phone.

I HAVE PROMISED my daughter to take her to Disney World for her birthday, and decide to invite my sister and her children to join us. I am happy to make this my treat and take care of all the costs. I do not want to give up my hope for a family...I want to do my best for our children to have a relationship, even though my sister resents me.

To my delighted surprise, our excursion goes smoothly and is filled with adventure and fun. I am thrilled that our children have finally shared a joyful experience together without the usual tension and chaos. I am so grateful for this unprecedented show of unity that I am willing to do anything to keep my sister tranquil. Some time ago, she had told me that her jewelry was stolen. When we return home, I give her some of mine and then invite her to take from my china hutch any item that she wants. Ruhie casts a triumphant glance at me, and then casually proceeds to empty my china hutch of all its contents. I am left with a starkly barren piece of furniture, but still have hope for a better day and a new page in the tainted ledger of my relationship with my sister.

In a few weeks, Simon calls me. He reiterates what his father had told me and reassures me that he had not left my sister penniless as she claims. He pledges that once he leaves rehab, he will return to his previous job at the post office and resume paying child support so that he can see his children. He asks if I would write a letter to his supervisor and request that he be reinstated. I agree to do it because I know that helping Simon to get back on his feet would benefit my sister and her children.

A week later, Simon calls with the most bizarre and mind-numbing story.

"I made the mistake of telling your sister about your letter of recommendation. Instead of being grateful and happy, she cursed you and wished you dead for taking my side and wanting to help me. Then she called the post office and told them that you were a liar and I was a thief. Now, I don't have a job and your sister is out to get you."

I feel sick and my stomach heaves with fire in its pit. My sister's obsession and tenacity to pilfer hope and destroy relationships defies logic. She seems unable to connect the sequence between her behavior and its consequences. Now I am petrified of what she will do to hurt me. I know well that her capability and imagination to cause pain and promote injury are boundless.

Three days later, the management office in my building delivers a letter to me. It is in an old faded envelope that is not sealed.

"This was addressed to our office. So, we had to open it and read it. It must be from one of your patients."

As soon as I glance at the letter, I know who has written it. The letter is typed, but my sister's poor diction and grammar is the unique signature that identifies her writing. In the letter she claims that she has intimate knowledge of my sexual relationship with my patients, and that I should be put in jail for disgracing my profession.

That night, Jafar calls. He is enraged and out of his wits. His boss has received a letter from Ruhie that although Jafar was receiving a six-figure salary, his sister and her three young children were starving. The two-page diatribe continues to tell the tale of how Ruhie had taken care of Jafar; watched over him and worked to support him while he was in college, and now that she is in need, he is not willing to help her because "he's not a human being."

- Hope for Kinship -

In 1987, nearly a decade after my mother's death, I am lured by hope and optimism to reconnect with my mother's brother. The opportunity has arrived in the form of an exclusively designed invitation from my cousin Lidia, announcing the Bat Mitzvah of her daughter Nadia, at the Beverly Hills Hilton Hotel.

When we lived in Iran, I never knew anyone who had a Bat Mitzvah or a Bar Mitzvah. But now in America, Iranian Jews are celebrating the "coming of age" of both their daughters and sons with equal grandeur and delight. The paradox of transition in values from one generation to the next is glaring. The regal and festive affair; the extravaganza that commemorates the womanhood and independence of my uncle's thirteen-year-old granddaughter, looms as a patent injustice and a lurid contradiction to the merciless abolition of my mother's freedom at that same age. And now a generation later, having embarked on a journey to claim my own elusive independence day, I am alone and still on an onerous trail to remain bonded to my heritage but not bound to the legacy of my subjugated mother. Today, nonetheless, weary and anguished from the wretched events that have defined much of my life, I have come to escape and celebrate this cause...without any acrimony or malice in my heart. I have come here with great hope and anticipation that in the company of my mother's family, I will find just enough love and compassion to help me expunge–however briefly- my desperate loneliness and longing for a family.

When I arrive at my uncle's house in Beverly Hills, I feel my mother's presence in her brother's embrace. The home that my uncle has built for his wife and his children is filled with bliss and prosperity. It is the home that I never had, but always coveted; and the home that I wish I could have made for my daughter. There are young children frolicking and laughing; they are free from the fear of loneliness and longing; they do not know of loss and have never grieved. They know that they belong here; they belong not to one, but to everyone. They know that they will never be abandoned because everyone is here to nurture them and keep them safe. They are a family... and Sophie is captivated by the commotion and the excitement that is entirely unfamiliar to her. She has never seen anything like it. Whenever she has been amongst her aunt, uncle, and cousins, she has seen only discord and disharmony. Here, everyone is fussing over her and she feels as if she, too, has a place in their heart and with their family. My youngest cousin Arella boasts about how she submitted Sophie's baby photo as her own to register in school.

"Look how much we look alike... we are like sisters now." Arella gushes and hugs Sophie, giving her hope that she will be like a big sister and forever her family. She tells me about Maman and how she had bonded with her in Iran. She remembers her warmth and her abundant generosity. "Oh...I loved the beautiful gifts she sent me on my birthday every year."

I am delighted to see my cousins, and thankful that I had dismissed all my reservations about this visit. I am looking forward to the Bat Mitzvah celebration the next day, where I am certain to see many of the relatives that I have not seen in decades. I have so profoundly missed my family and our traditions: the communal nurturing, the embraces and the voices, the sound of Persian music: the soulful melodies, the traditional tunes, and the vibrant music that stir the instinctual desire in every Iranian to dance and sing. I have missed the aroma of the delectable Persian cuisine and the sheer joy of celebrating the way only Iranians can bring life to a party. This is the essence of existence; the life force and lifeline that is so common place and ubiquitous here, but absent and inaccessible to me. Tears have flooded my face, remembering... realizing how much I have lost and how brief this reprieve will be.

THE NEXT MORNING, *Daii jaan* is pondering a decision about the persistent leak in the shower of his master bathroom. He says that the estimates he has received are exaggerated and untrustworthy.

"They want three thousands dollars to cut through the marble shower wall, remove all the plumbing and replace it with new ones. " He grumbles.
"Let me look at it *Daii jaan,* I bet I can fix it." I say enthusiastically, as I watch brows rise and jaws drop

in awe of my audacity. No one, let alone a woman, has ever dared to challenge my uncle, and they do not know that all my life I have been dared to fix things out of need, or just to test my survival skills… And now invigorated by the warm reception of my mother's family, I would do anything…even tear down the wall myself, to be forever endearing.

Daii jaan is bemused.

"*Shoma mohandes hasteed ya inkeh ravanshenaas*, Are you an engineer or a psychologist?" He asks with derisive curiosity.

"Actually, I have a knack for fixing things…" Every thing except my family, I murmur as I survey the shower assembly.

"O.K." I announce cheerfully, "You don't have to pay thousands of dollars to some charlatan to break the walls and fix this leak. I know how to fix it easily."

Daii jaan displays a faint smile. It is not easy to read his emotions, but I am certain he is jeering inside. Everyone has been standing by silently, questioning my judgment and wondering what my uncle would say.

I ask my cousin Daniel to drive me to the hardware store where I find the small versatile tool I need. Then within minutes after we return, I have tightened two concealed loose screws and verified that the leak is sealed.

My uncle is in awe against his will. Everyone applauds, promising to spread the tale of my feat throughout the city. I know they are secretly enjoying their father's minor defeat.

"*Aafareen*, bravo." *Daii jaan* concedes, speaking my praise, albeit reluctantly.

"How did you become so methodical and skilled?"
"I have inherited my mother's genes." I declare boisterously, making sure that everyone hears me.

"You remind me so much of your mother, Azadeh." *Daii jaan* muses, "She was resilient, intuitive, and vibrant... just like you."

I am at once shocked and delighted. For the first time, I have seen a flicker of my uncle's humanity; a trace demonstration of feelings that I have never seen. He has finally acknowledged my mother, albeit too late, but perhaps through me... and because of my courage. And now, this minutia of faith is all that I need to believe that we are at last one blood –bonded family.

ARELLA and I have bonded and I could not be happier. She has also formed with Sophie a genuinely warm and caring relationship. I know that she shares with me the most basic need: a yearning to belong without dependency and a desire to define herself without losing her foothold and her family. We both have been mired, albeit a generation apart, in the quandary of conflict between independence and loyalty. She secretly covets my audacity to live freely without conventional restraints, and I aspire to have the sustenance of her traditional family that protects her from despair and feeling lonely. I know without a doubt that unlike me, she will eventually find a viable balance between her freedom and her family because although she shares with me the same bloodline, she does not share my history. In a few months, she will graduate from high school and will be asked to choose a man from the countless eligible suitors who have expressed their wish to come for her *Khastegari*. She is regarded as a highly desirable woman in the elite Iranian community of Beverly Hills. She has beauty and poise, excellent lineage, prime reputation and an unrestricted dowry. I invite her to come to Florida for a taste of 'freedom' before matrimony. Her parents grant her permission and she is delighted.

Late in June, I close my office for a week and travel up the East Coast of Florida with Arella and Sophie. We visit historic places and play on the sandy beaches. We stay at luxury hotels and savor exotic dishes. We share our memories of Maman and stories about our grandmother *Khanom jaan*, whose soul she is told, she bears.

In St. Augustine, the oldest city in the nation, the magnificent Spanish architecture reminds me of my extraordinary ventures in Europe. I tell her the tales of my journey and the delight that I had felt visiting the land of our ancestors in Spain.

"Oh... I will be doing a lot of traveling, too. The man I plan to marry likes to travel."

Arella has already chosen her future husband. Navid is a kind and gentle man from a philanthropic and highly respected family. He has more than ordinary compassion and an inordinate amount of wealth... personality traits that are often incompatible and rare. Arella knows that marrying a man whose fortune exceeds her father's is the ultimate level of success; guaranteed to get her father's respect.

LATER IN THE YEAR, Sophie and I are invited to Arella's engagement party and subsequently to her wedding. We attend both events; in spite of the enormous cost of traveling, extravagant gowns and valuable gifts...those that Maman would regard as 'worthy of remembering.' Now in keeping with her tradition, every time I visit her family, I find myself making an extensive shopping list...bringing gifts for everyone: young and old, children and the elderly, even the housekeepers and those who are remotely related to me. I am determined to nurture my bond with my mother's family at any cost- hoping that through Arella, Sophie will stay connected to her roots and her heritage when I am gone.

As it is customary in the Iranian culture, the bride's parents arrange and organize the engagement party, and Arella's *shrini khori* celebration is the most exulted that I have ever seen. Everything from food and flowers to entertainment and gift offerings is the glorified production of a fairy-tale fantasy. Dancers in traditional clothing emerge with trays of jewels from each corner of the expansive hall. They dance their way to the bride and groom and offer them a taste of the lavish abundance that will satiate their lives.

Just as the bride and groom begin to survey the exquisite contents of one jeweled platter, another tray is delivered, piled with gold, and dripping with diamonds and precious stones. Each time a piece of Jewelry is removed from the tray; a jeweled or diamond necklace to hang on Arella's neck, or a gold watch for Navid to wear, the guests roar with awe and the thunderous traditional cheer..."*gilli lillilli*" rises to the sky.

I do not know why anyone needs so many articles of jewelry, but this is not a feast for the display of needs; it is a pageantry of affluence and cheshm hamcheshmi, the trumping of the next family in extravagance and one-upmanship.

Arella's bosom is soon burdened by the weight of her prosperity. The multiple layers of substantial gold and bejeweled necklaces have strained her neck, obligating her to lower her torso and compromise her poise and dignity. It is a sizable price to pay for someone who seeks independence from conformity. As Marjan runs to rescue Arella from the gravity of her multi-million-dollar jahazi, her friends, too, gather around her to remove the necklaces and free her delicate body from the hefty load. This extraordinary opulence, however glistening, means little to me. What matters is that I am celebrating my connection with my mother's family.

I give Arella a modest crystal bowl:
"Let the brilliance of this vessel behold the clarity of your vision and your purpose; let it remind you that compassion and humility will be your richest assets. With love, Azadeh"

IN NEW YORK, Papa is alone. He can no longer tend to the house or get around to see anyone-including his doctors. It is time to move him to Florida, where we can take care of him and he can see his grandchildren.

In the summer of 1990, I close my office and go up to New York with Sophie to clean out the house my mother had once lived in. After twelve years, I can still feel her presence. Every thing reminds me of the last time I saw her here alive. I cry and once again I say good-bye, as I dispose of her meager possessions. I cannot deny my disappointment for having to tend to my father in his final years, instead of my mother.

407

Maman would have thrived living in Florida...walking along the beach...reminiscing about her childhood and about the precious days we used to spend on the shores of the Caspian Sea.

In ten days, my brother arrives at the house to claim its ownership. He has already drawn up my father's Trust and Will, appointing himself and his wife as the Trustees. He is going to make all the decisions about my father's finances and where he should live. He has consulted with an attorney but not with any one of us, including my father. Once the house is sold, I suggest that we all meet and discuss Papa's options as to where and how he wants to live but clearly, the only option is to abide by the plans that my brother and his wife have conceived. Jafar wants nothing less than total control over everything.

"We are putting him in assisted living and investing the proceeds from the sale of the house to take care of him."

Jafar claims that both Ruhie and I have taken advantage of our father; that he has helped each of us financially, but has not given him anything. Ruhie and Jafar are yelling and cursing at one another. It is the legacy of our family to live in this nightmare. Papa is the only link that we have left to be a family but now, he has become the cause of more hostility and contemptuous conflict.

"Get the hell out of my house...all of you. I don't want to ever see you again." Jafar howls so violently that all four children tremble and begin to wail in unison.

I take Sophie in my arms and leave. She is confused and heartbroken. She wants to be with her cousins, and it has been just a few weeks since she started to call my brother "Uncle Farfar" again.

Ruhie calls *Daii jaan* and asks him to intervene. He is baffled by Jafar's lack of foresight and ingenuity.

"Even the wealthiest people here hide their money so that the government would pay their bills."

- Home Wrecker -

It is winter of 1990, and I am struck with a malady that has challenged my physicians and defied their expertise. I have been feeling progressively tired, irritable and melancholy. My energy has diminished substantially, my sleep is disturbed, and my days are replete with anxiety. I cry for no apparent reason – albeit I have ample cause to cry. I drink at night to get through the overwhelming responsibilities of the day and to deny my despair. Sophie hears me in the middle of the night crying and saying things that she doesn't comprehend. I try to ignore my symptoms but their progression is undeniable and alarming. I have consulted numerous specialists and have been diagnosed with everything from Chronic Fatigue and Lupus to chronic depression and menopausal insanity.

ON A FRIDAY EVENING, feeling alone and distressed, I decide to go to the local synagogue. I am not going to pray to God for his mercy. I will not be asking him to change my destiny or to fix my family, nor will I even ask him to cure my malady. I am going there to hear the sounds and prayers that once comforted me.

When I was a child, the temple was a place of peace and unity. I saw my relatives and everyone that I ever knew...all gathered in one place and under one roof, which was often the open sky where we huddled together because the small synagogue could not accommodate all the patrons. There...in that space and time, we were all one and the same. We were all connected; bonded as if we were one family. Now I am here in this unfamiliar space filled with strangers, and I yearn for a sense of safety and belonging. I long to hear the echoes of common voices that resonate under one roof and assure me that I belong somewhere.

I call Sophie from the phone booth in the hallway. It is Friday evening; the rare occasion that she visits her father. As I step out of the booth, a distinguished looking man walks over to me. He introduces himself as William Beck and wants to know what my name is.

I am Azadeh...pleased to meet you."

William looks me in the eye and smiles.

"I am going to marry you." He says spontaneously and with alarming conviction.

I stand speechless and stunned but mildly amused. I have never heard of an 'icebreaker' or a pick-up line so intriguing and blunt. This is a madman-without a doubt.

"Would you mind meeting me for dinner so that we can work out the details?" He speaks in a serious tenor.

"You are funny, William. I like that." I respond with

trepidation and mild intrigue.

"I am not at all joking, dear. You see... I have known your face all my life. I just didn't know where and when I would find you."

Now I take a step back, certain that I am talking to a certifiable lunatic. However, as patrons walk by and greet him with utmost reverence and respect, I surrender my doubt and agree to go on a date with him.

WILLIAM HAS SURVIVED the Holocaust with a remarkable story and a few odd habits. I am in awe of his resilience to have lived his youth in a cold Siberian prison, alone and often hungry. He had finally managed to escape to America when he was twenty, and made a fortune buying and selling oceanfront property. He is bright, charming, and competent. But he is obsessed with physical fitness and a diet that consists of meager calories. It is as if in spite of his wealth and physical freedom, he has remained faithful to the regimented life he had once lived as a prisoner.

In a few days, William takes me to see all of his properties and asks me to decide which one I would like to live in. I tell him that we need time to know each other and that I am not willing to move and uproot my daughter until I am certain that we get along in every respect. However, without a firm commitment from me, William has faithfully begun to renovate his current house to provide Sophie with her own private quarters and amenities.

"This house will be ready for you in case you decide to move in and marry me."

Men of William's caliber and intensity have not

crossed my path in decades – not since I left New York and abandoned its dynamic and infinitely diverse culture; and not since I merged into the reclusive life of private practice. William is decisive, energized and competent. He is on a mission and nothing can stop him. He has already drawn up a prenuptial agreement, leaving me a portion of his assets for every year that I stay married to him, and has found a tenant for my townhouse so that I would have additional income of my own, even after we are married. His newly renovated house is on the East side of town, in an elegant neighborhood and a favorable school district.

I feel vulnerable because of my undiagnosed illness, and although reluctant to relinquish my fierce need for unencumbered independence, I agree to move in with him but postpone our marriage until a later date.

William has asked to meet my family but I am reluctant. I try to avoid the subject but I know that eventually I have to tell him the truth.

SINCE THAT DREADFUL night at my brother's house, my sister and I have maintained a civil dialogue and I have once again renewed my hope and optimism that we will have peace. It is a bizarre phenomenon that the three of us can never maintain a relationship simultaneously. We are like a three-legged table with one leg always missing. Now that my sister has extended her rare civility towards me for over three months, I am so grateful that I have offered to pay her tuition and all her academic expenses if she would return to college and get a degree. Then a month ago, when Jafar sent each of us a check for three thousand dollars, stating that it was all the inheritance we should expect to receive, I turned my share over to my sister because I thought she needed it more than I did.

When William insists on meeting my family, I tell him that my brother is currently upset with the family and as soon as he has cooled off his heels, we will get together with him.

"How about your sister and your Dad?" William inquires. "Why not invite them over...it is time for me to meet them."

In a few days, I invite my father, my sister, and her children to the house for dinner. William bonds with Papa immediately. He had lost his father in the concentration camp and is thrilled to pamper mine. He even lights Papa's cigarettes, even though he can't tolerate anyone smoking around him.

"Don't smoke in the house, Papa." I warn my father, "William is a health addict. He doesn't like the smell of cigarettes."

"It is O.K., dear." William concedes, "I like your Dad. I can make an exception."

While I am in the kitchen preparing dinner, the children play in the pool and William has engaged Papa and Ruhie in a conversation about our family. He is appalled to learn that my brother has not spoken to us in months and that we don't have a fond and close relationship. He had been deprived of sharing his life with his relatives and cannot fathom severing ties with any family members- let alone one's own siblings.

When William asks my sister about our childhood and about me, I become anxious. I hope that Ruhie uses discretion and does not volunteer unnecessary and damaging information. I have known her to speak and act recklessly, often without regard for the impact of her words or the consequences of her behavior. However, having had a peaceful relationship with her for the last three months has given me reason to hope that she has changed.

In a few minutes, I am alarmed when I realize that the conversation outside has suddenly become subtle and incoherent. I am fraught with stifling dread and know instinctively that my sister, just like a sly snake, has been waiting for an opportunity to strike and malign me again.... to expel her venomous diatribe of accusations and delusions to ruin me.

I quietly wedge myself behind the sliding door to eavesdrop, and my suspicion is instantly confirmed.

"She is the worst sister and human being in the world. She is a selfish whore.... She took everything from me; even my boyfriends...I don't know why you want to get married to her."

I feel the ground slipping away and I can't catch my breath. A cold sweat permeates my skin. I let out a cry and collapse.

Hours later, I am released from the emergency room, dazed and despondent. I spend the next few days at home and in mourning. I can't work, nor am I able to cease my relentless cry. My daughter is distraught and William is inconsolable. He can't undo the wreckage that my sister has made of his dream, and he can't mend the heart that is broken beyond healing. He has become impatient, irritable and irrational. He wants me to get rid of Sophie's dog because he barks too much. Sophie is cognizant of the change in my relationship with William, and mad at him for wanting to take away her dog. She refuses to talk to him, and now William has decided that he wants to have a child of his own. He wants to know if I will be willing to give him one.

I am devastated and on the brink of a breakdown. I can't think clearly and I don't know what to do. But I am certain that I can't undo the damage that my sister has inflicted upon me.

One day, I hear the neighbors screaming:

"Stop her, stop her."

I run outside and see Sophie behind the wheel of my massive 1984 Mercedes. She has released the emergency break and is rolling down the street, progressing towards the Intracoastal waterways. I race to take hold of the steering wheel and engage the emergency break to stop the car. Fortunately, the enormous mass of the vehicle and its idle speed has prevented its climb over a barrier and into the water stream. I embrace my daughter who is visibly scared and surprised with the outcome of her mischief. I know she has not been happy and the recent events have made her feel confused and insecure. I know it is time for me to rise from the rubble of my haunted life and start all over again; this time with the firm commitment to abandon hope to resurrect a family with my siblings.

When William leaves for Canada to visit his relatives, I realize that our relationship has been irrevocably damaged. I am sick and exhausted, but mostly humiliated. I have to tell my friends and family that my marriage plans are cancelled. Now, I have no choice but to rebuild my life on my own, once again. I have to be strong and move forward.

On the weekend, I find a house a few blocks away from the ocean and decide to move out while William is away. I believe it is best for both of us to end things this way.

IN DECEMBER, while I am overcome by exhaustion amidst doing repairs, unpacking and settling into our new home, Marjan calls from Beverly Hills.

"We are coming to visit you during the Christmas holidays. *Daii jaan* was offered a couple of free tickets, so we thought we come to see your new house."

I am thrilled that my uncle and Marjan are coming to see us. However, the house is in disrepair, and I am negotiating to collect a large debt that will require court appearances.

"We want to see Jafar and Ruhie. So make sure they know we are coming." Marjan stresses.

I have not spoken to my brother since he banished us from his house and from his life five years ago. I have also pledged not to ever again be lured by the illusion of a relationship with my sister. However, I cannot let my uncle and his wife know the devastating depth of our dysfunction. It would be far too humiliating and a shameful assault to my mother's memory and honor. I have to allow just one more time, for my loyalty and honor to override my right to self-preservation. I call my siblings and invite them to my house to see their *Daii jaan*- the patriarch of the family and the seminal essence of our mother's existence. They have not seen each other in decades.

On the day of their arrival, looking forward to *Daii jaan* and Marjan's visit, I am infused with optimism and memories of my mother and feel an unexpected surge of energy to clean the house, shop for groceries, and prepare dinner, just minutes before I pick up my guests from the airport.

After dinner, we reminisce about life in Iran and how theirs has transformed since they arrived in America. Daii jaan, his children, their extended families, and many of their friends live in the opulent mansions of Beverly Hills, where they frequently entertain hundreds of guests. The Iranian community has established every conceivable service and amenity to make them feel at home...everything from their own synagogue and television station to authentic shops, restaurants and grocery stores with Farsi-speaking Mexicans. Then of course, there are the prestigious hospitals and medical centers...all staffed with renowned and brilliant Iranian doctors. The world is their oyster, and life could not have turned out any better.

As the long night of conversation concludes without any remembrance of Maman, or how her loss has impacted our lives, I realize that nothing has changed at all. Nonetheless, *Daii jaan* remains the singular and most intimate connection to our Maman. He is the cherished consanguine whose presence, in some inexplicable way, acknowledges and validates my mother's life. This is the bond- the vindication that I cannot and do not want to sever.

On the weekend, we embark on a two-day cruise to the Bahamas. My brother will not be joining us, but he will pay from my father's account for Ruhie and her children, so long as Papa can go with us and share a cabin with her son, Dustin. It is a bizarre irony of fate to have me on a cruise with family members who each have caused me irreparable harm. But little in my life has ever been explicable or normal.

I buy tickets for my guests, plus an array of souvenirs for them to take for my cousins. Just like my mother, I have a tenacious need to prove to my uncle that money is of little value to me and that I am far more generous than he is.

Once on the ship and away from the shore, Ruhie obstinately denies my father access to the cabin he is to share with Dustin. I cannot let the weekend turn into another catastrophe designed and delivered by my sister. I have no choice but to share my cabin with my father. I give him my bed and squeeze next to Sophie in her bed.

By the time their visit ends, *Daii jaan* and Marjan have seen the best of what Palm Beach and my hospitality can offer, but I have neglected my work and my failure to appear in court has cost me thousands of dollars.

IN A FEW DAYS, I receive a six-page letter from Ruhie replete with the usual random expressions of hostility and delusions. My 'nerve' to book a cabin for her son to share with my father has inflamed all of her past grievances and unleashed a torrent of her memories of adversity and misfortune for which I have been responsible.

I know I have to accept the fact that my sister is ill. She is the saboteur of every relationship, not just her own but those of others. She instigates conflicts by fabricating delusional scenarios and accusing others of the cruelty that she herself inflicts. She has filled her children's minds with lies and hatred for anyone that she dislikes -including their own father. They can't question and challenge her because she will threaten them and bring them more anguish. She abuses them verbally, strikes them, and then calls the police to take them away. She has even threatened to put her children up for adoption. I know she needs help, but the very nature of her illness denies her access to insight and awareness. Once, I even made an appointment for her to see a psychiatrist because she said she wanted to kill herself. I thought she was beyond psychotherapeutic intervention and instead needed to be put on medication.

When Ruhie came out of her session, I asked her how it went. She said that the psychiatrist wanted to know why she spent the entire hour complaining about the sister who had brought her there, paid $250.00 for her session, and was waiting outside to make sure she was O.K. She related this information to me in such a matter-of-fact manner that I was stunned and scared. Is she so disconnected from a discriminating conscience? I have always been caught in an agonizing quagmire: feeling sorry for her on one hand, and yet despising her for her reckless torment. That day, I bought her the medication that the doctor had prescribed, but she refused to take it. She said there was nothing wrong with her.

ONCE MY father's ability to take care of himself diminishes, Jafar shuttles him to a nursing home where Papa's desire to live rapidly declines. When he refuses to eat his favorite Persian meal that I have cooked for him, I know that he will not have long to live. Now every time I visit him, he tells me that he is waiting for his life to end. As my father's funds dwindle, so do his health and the quality of care he receives. One day, a man calls from the nursing home to tell me that my father is dying. I rush to see him and arrive just as his lifeless body is being removed. I kiss his forehead and say goodbye to him. I am now an orphan, never having had a chance to hear my parents' last words or to give them comfort when they took their last breath.

- The Sky is Falling -

As the episodes of my undiagnosed affliction continue with the added dimension of dizzy spells, rendering me unstable on my feet and incoherent in my speech, I am frequently rushed to the emergency room and referred to a multitude of specialists. On two occasions, I was hospitalized for observation, x-rayed, tested, poked, and spinal tapped with no remarkable diagnoses or remedy. The frustration of not knowing what is wrong with me ads to my misery, and I feel dismissed by the medical community. During the day, I work between the episodes of my malaise, but at night the walls close in and leave me fraught with panic.

Amidst all the challenges that consistently test my strength and resilience, there is a rainbow of hope in my life: watching my daughter become a well educated, poised, beautiful, and independent woman gives me vitality and optimism.... confidence that tomorrow will be brighter than today.

I know that Sophie is burdened with conflicting feelings of sympathy and anger towards me while she confronts her own pressing challenges of puberty and adolescence. However, she is quite competent, well adjusted, and seemingly unscathed. She has been the top student in every grade throughout the years, has excelled in all her subjects, and has achieved an exemplary status in every endeavor, including her extracurricular activities. She is a star tennis player, a talented actress with an exceptional singing voice, and a prized and popular community-service volunteer. I never miss any of Sophie's activities or performances no matter how badly I feel, or how many times I trip over myself because of fatigue or relentless dizzy spells. I always pick myself up and record every one of her performances with overriding pride and a large video camera that I carry around.

IN A FEW MONTHS, the debilitating episodes of disorientation and dizzy spells escalate, first with increasing frequency and intensity, and more recently with severe headaches. Suddenly, everything begins to spin around me-swooping up and down and sliding side-to-side. I feel weak and unsteady, as if I am about to black out. I no longer rush to the emergency room. Instead, I read and research my symptoms and have insisted on an MRI and MRA of my brain.

In less than twenty hours, I receive a phone call from the hospital.

"Hello, this is Dr. Levine. I am the radiologist at BRC. I have just read your MRI and MRA. I tried to call your neurologist, Dr. Stein, but he is out of town. So, I decided to let you know what I found."

I light up a cigarette and brace myself in the chair. I am certain that the radiologist has bad news.

"You have a cerebral aneurysm, and there is evidence of a mild stroke."

My heart skips a beat, and my mother's image flashes before me. Tears rush to flood my face, but I take in a large dose of nicotine and quickly compose myself. I have a patient waiting outside and he needs my help.

Dr. Levine is on the phone waiting for my reaction.

"Thank you. I appreciate your call."

"I suggest you make an appointment to see Dr. Stein as soon as possible."

I am relieved that I have time to draw up my Will. Perhaps my demise is not as imminent as I initially feared. I make an appointment with Dr. Stein, and then set up a meeting with an attorney to discuss my Will. I call my brother to ask him about the deed to the burial plot that I had left with my father. We have not spoken in a long time. He is cold and impassive when he hears my voice.

"It looks like I have inherited Maman's aneurysm." I announce irreverently.

"So, are they going to operate?"

"I have not seen the neurologist yet, but it is time for me to get my legal affairs in order."

I explain to him that since my daughter is not of legal age, I have to assign an executor for my Will and appoint someone as my Trustee to carry out my wishes.

"So, who's gonna be the executor?"

"I don't know yet." I say dismissively. I don't know why he cares. Does he think I would want either one of my siblings to be my executor?

"I just want you to know that when Maman died, I

bought two burial plots next to one another. I want to make sure that neither you nor Ruhie put a claim on it because even though it is under our family name, it is a plot I bought for myself."

"Well technically, it is a family plot. So if you want it, you have to consider that real estate values in New York have gone through the roof. So you have to buy it out from me and Ruhie according to the market value."

I feel as if I have been dunk in a sea of ice…. frozen with angst and shock.

"Well, good luck. Let me know when you're ready to buy me out."

I hang up the phone and pour myself a double shot of vodka. Then I light up a cigarette and call my cousin Javid. I need his compassion and his medical advice, but he is nowhere to be found.

BEFORE I RUN OUT OF TIME, I have to find someone who can act as the executor of my Will and Trust. When I tell Arella of the gravity of my condition, I am hopeful that she will volunteer to be my executor but more than anything, I want to know that she will not desert my daughter; be a vital part of her life when I am gone.

"You can have a bank as your executor. They will do a good job managing your assets and dispersing it according to your instructions."

I tell her that I am worried mostly about my daughter's psychological health and that furthermore, banks do not accept the responsibility of managing an estate worth less than a million dollars…it's not worth their while and not profitable.

She is stunned to know that I can't leave the welfare of my daughter in my siblings' hands; and she can't fathom an estate worth less than seven digits.

"Arella, you are the only one I have; the only one that I can trust to stay close to Sophie for emotional support."

"I am sorry, Azadeh... You shouldn't have put all your eggs in one basket." She advises.

In a few days, Marjan calls, and it is clear that Arella has discussed our conversation with her. She is wondering why my siblings and I are not talking again.

"You have to make peace with them. You are the oldest sibling and *fahmideh*, intuitive. You should all try to help each other. You have no one else."

"I have tried everything, Marjan Khanom. I am tired of trying and failing...I can do no more."

"Arella is tired, too," she retorts, "Can you imagine how hard it is to furnish a fourteen-million dollar house?"

I tell her no, I cannot imagine.

- The Last Wedding -

Daniel is my uncle's middle son and the only one who has disappointed him. Unlike his brothers, he has shown little desire to attain higher education and even less loyalty to the family's competitive standard of wealth and success. Lately, however, my uncle's family have marshaled around Daniel and set up a unique business with the potential to earn him a lucrative income and place him in the same exclusive rank with the rest.

My uncle's status in Los Angeles is supreme. He continues to awe his compatriots with his acumen, immense fortune, and the professional reputation that his sons have achieved. His daughters, too, have married well, live lavish lifestyles, and are envied by women of their community. In addition, the donation of large sums of money; philanthropy in the service of fame, has brought praise and accolades from the best of the Beverley Hills community, sanctioning their ostentatious claim to Royalty status.

Now that Daniel has been elevated to the ranks of his family's extraordinary wealth, he has selected a beautiful girl to be his bride, and his father is offering him the most elaborate and extravagant wedding by far.

My invitation to the wedding arrives as I prepare to leave for the New York Presbyterian Hospital to consult with an intracranial surgeon. But before I can mail the RSVP, Marjan calls to find out if I plan to attend the wedding.

"You know we have a very large family now.... *maashallah*, God bless them; and there are so many people we have to invite. This is not like the affairs at the Beverly Hilton with seven hundred guests. This one is at Beverly Wilshire and your *Daii jaan* has to pay for it. It's going to cost him three hundred dollars a person...*baavarkona*, you must believe me. So, we don't expect everybody to come just because we sent them an invitation."

I am speechless. It is abundantly clear that Marjan does not want me to attend the wedding. Surely, she is not sharing this information with others. It would be a monumental taboo in the Iranian culture...an etiquette faux pas and a blunder, even for the least cultured to divulge such information to an invited guest.

"Don't worry, Marjan Khanom. "I say solemnly. "I was not planning to come, anyway."

He set the world aflame,
And laid me on the same;
A hundred tongues of fire
Lapped round my pyre.
And when the blazing tide
Engulfed me, and I sighed,
Upon my mouth in haste
His hand He placed.
RUMI

- A Day of Pride and
Decades of Shame -

In June 1996, Sophie graduates from high school with copious awards and honors. She plans to pursue medicine and has received full scholarships from several elite universities across the country. I feel as if I am riding on top of the world. I want to share my pride and my profound happiness with everyone in my family because now, in spite of all the adversities and overwhelming hardships, I finally have come to a place of restoration and fulfillment that is healing me.

At Sophie's graduation, Wayne and I are her only family members in attendance. All other graduates have an entourage of friends and family cheering their graduate; they wonder about the beautiful and elegant young girl who is called to the podium each time an award is presented, but there is no crowd of relatives to cheer her.

To share my pride and happiness and perhaps to fill the void of my family's absence at my daughter's graduation, I compose a letter to our friends and family, highlighting a newspaper clipping and a photo of Sophie receiving the top award in science. Sophie never wants me to brag about her, but I convince her that anyone who knows her would be happy to celebrate her achievements.

In a few days, I receive a small manila envelope from Beverly Hills and recognize on the cover, the distinctive style of my uncle's handwriting. As soon as I open the package, cold chill sweeps through my veins and my body shudders. Inside, there is the fragile gold watch that my mother always wore ... the watch that kept the chronicles of so many sad memories and witnessed her years of torment.

"What is wrong, Mommy?" Sophie asks fretfully, noticing my quivering hands as I hold the memento of the freedom my mother never achieved.

"What is this?" She takes the watch from me to examine it...to assess what has caused me so much anguish.

"What is this, Mommy?" She repeats, anxious and confused, "It is rusted...looks very old.... I don't get it."

I remove Marjan's letter from the box and begin to read it through the haze of tears that flood my eyes. It is a lengthy note, but I want to decipher every word and sentence and put him or her in context so that I do not misunderstand its content. Marjan's simple language is redundant and rhetorical and only when I reach the bottom of the page, do I find a reference to the inauspicious message:

"This is your mother's watch. She gave it to me as a gift and now, I want to give it to Sophie."

I am baffled and broken. I know my mother never parted with her watch. Why would she give it to

Marjan as a gift? I need to talk to her and ask for answers, but I must wait until midnight to call her. I want to make sure Sophie has gone to sleep because I anticipate a devastating conversation.

I take a large dose of my vodka tranquilizer and light up another cigarette before I dial her number.

"Thank you for your congratulatory letter." I say with coerced civility. I have been taught to overlook a violation rather than protest, to be polite and graceful no matter how unbearable the pain.

Marjan is quiet...so I continue.

"I am confused, Marjan Khanom. This watch meant a lot to Maman. How was it that she gave it to you as a gift?"

"The truth is Azadeh, that the watch was not a gift. When your Maman was in Iran, she needed money and she sold us her watch. We bought some other pieces of her jewelry... I am keeping those. I didn't want to tell you the truth because I didn't want to make you *naarahat*, uncomfortable."

My heart has constricted ever since I heard Marjan's first words and now, it feels cleaved and shredded into thousand pieces. Blistering flames rise from my stomach to burn my throat and surge through my brain. I feel nauseous, unsteady and faint. I lose my grip on the phone and fall to the floor... sobbing and asking why... Who is this God who allows cruelty to persist... allows evil to live on with impunity?

The celebration of my triumph and the moment of my pride has been viciously pilfered.... replaced by memories of my mother's life of anguish. I am alone and consumed by grief... numbing my pain with

431

alcohol and choking it with fumes of nicotine.

FOR WEEKS, the ominous cloud of loneliness and depression darkens my world and leaves me drifting into the path of ruination and remorse. The joyous celebration that I had envisioned for my daughter is drowned in sorrow and sadness. The malicious message from Marjan, disguised as a 'gift' of good will has opened up a floodgate of wretched memories. The salves that time and I had finally congealed to protect my psychic wounds from bleeding have now been scraped away, leaving me naked with pain and bleeding again.

Every night, the horrific scenes of my childhood and the suffering that my mother endured haunt me. I am besieged by the memories of her abuse and my own in the hands of my father. I can't fall asleep and when I do, I am awakened by the deluge of nightmares that plague me for the rest of the day.

I am helpless against humiliation and hopelessly lost and disconnected. I do not know why my family has caused me such cruel and brutal distress... just at the moment when I was at the summit of my pride and happiness. I had wished for nothing more than words of validation. Instead, they had offered me a souvenir of my wretched yesterdays.

"You put so much faith in them, Mommy." Sophie offers me her clarity. Perhaps her intuition has never been fogged by her desperation to conceive a family hatched out of delusions and deceit. She doesn't know whether to worry about me or to detest me for being weak...suffering because I have failed to give her a family. All these years that I have dragged us through a roller coaster of hope and disappointment has made her question my sanity and lose respect for me. She once said that I lived a "carpet-life existence," allowing my family to abuse me and walk all over me. She said that she would never want to live the life I lived.

"When I graduate from college, I am not coming back home." Sophie warns me. "You can keep your family, I am going to find a family of my own."

Now, as my daughter leaves for college and my last remnants of hope pulverize into a pulp of debris, I know that I am alone and abandoned by everyone that I have ever loved, and all those with whom I had yearned to build a family.

I need to talk to someone... someone who knows me and remembers me when I was a child. I had long concealed the sad memories and buried the tragedy of my mother's life to survive my own but now, I need to find answers to old and new questions. I need desperately to make sense of my relationship with my uncle and his family...how their words and actions have undone and devastated me. I need to know if there is something I have missed...a benevolent purpose that I have failed to see beneath their deeds of atrocity.

I seek the wisdom of my Iranian elders... I talk to people of all ages and creeds...I search desperately for an explanation to help me redeem my trust in my mother's family. But, the resounding consensus is that this malevolent act was meant to diminish me...to remind me of my past, and my mother's dishonored status... a deliberate message to remind me that I shouldn't dare claim the prestige and prominence that belonged exclusively to my luminous cousins.

433

AS THE NEWS of my devastation reaches Beverly Hills, *Daii jaan* calls to tell me that I have upset his wife, "complaining about her gift." He says that they are distressed because their name and reputation is being marred, but he can't tell me how that is possible if their action was not meant to malign.

I hear the echoes of the familiar theme from my childhood, when my uncle never took responsibility for creating the tragedy that defined the lives of his sisters. He was only concerned that no one would hear their voices of discontent for it would tarnish his prized public image. And now again, there is no concern or remorse for how this "gift" has devastated my life.

Marjan is on the extension line proclaiming her wisdom and declaring her authority, as if she has just led her soldiers to a well-deserved victory.

"*Khobkardam, khaili khobkardam*, I did good and I am proud of it.... my deed was very well justified." And then recklessly and sanctimoniously, she pours burning insult to my already wounded heart.

"You wanted money from us and we didn't give it...that's why you complained."

IN AUGUST 2001, Javid calls to tell me that *Daii jaan* had died. A few months earlier when I heard that he had fallen ill, I called to talk to him but Marjan would not let him get on the phone.

"He is taking twenty pills a day. You'll upset him," she had growled, "I'll tell him you called."

Once when I called, *Daii jaan* answered the phone. He was home alone and able to speak to me freely.

"Everybody here is feeling fine these days except

434

me." He said acrimoniously. Perhaps for the first time in his life, he knew that he was vulnerable.... He had realized that neither his enormous wealth, nor his acumen or his status was going to save him. He was going to depart this temporal life like everyone else, and leave all of his fortune behind for others to enjoy without him.

When I call Javid to comfort him after his father's death, he tells me about the burden that he has carried alone for twenty years...the knowledge of his father's cardiac ailment that he had kept secret from his siblings all those years.

"He would still be alive," he laments, "had he not picked up the smoking habit from your father."

I am incensed by the irony of this supercilious comment. I want to tell him about all the burdens that I have carried and all the secrets that I have not shared... I want to tell him about the rapacious and merciless deal that his father sealed; the singular decision that wrecked the lives of his two younger sisters and devastated the lives of their children and their next generation.... I want to tell him how his father celebrated his egregious transaction of greed by sharing my father's Gorgaan cigarettes as a promise of collaborative solidarity that destroyed the lives of so many... But I do not want to hold Javid responsible for his father's sins. Instead, I tell him that his father was always proud of him.

ON A RECENT TRIP to Los Angeles, I quickly discover that everyone is avoiding me like a scorned leper. It is as if a divine decree has descended from the Holly Hills of Beverly to command and demand my resolute alienation. But when I run into my mother's cousin, Yasmine, she is glad to see me, though our encounter is intentionally brief. It is obvious that she doesn't want to be seen talking to me. She asks if I could meet her later at a remote restaurant outside the city.

Yasmine and I meet at a venue just north of Los Angles, far from where relatives and acquaintances typically congregate. We give each other a long and warm embrace and then shed copious tears as we exchange our last memories of my mother.

"The saga of the watch has dispersed all over the city of 'Tehrangeles,' Yasmine confirms, "Marjan has banned everyone in the family from contacting or acknowledging you."

"Thank you for not indulging her folly."

"Truthfully Azadeh *joon, I* was quite surprised that you had maintained a relationship with your uncle and Marjan in spite of their cruel treatment of your mother...specially when she came to Iran in 1970."

"Maman seemed to hold no anger or animosity towards them, and I followed suit. Once she died, my uncle and his children were all that I had to feel connected to her. "

"Your Maman was a very generous and forgiving woman. She never held her brother responsible. She suffered terribly, but always blamed herself for her dreadful destiny. She felt she did not deserve better. Even when her brother sold her and kept the money, she never complained."

"He had told her that the property was worthless and she believed him. She loved him unconditionally and wanted to please him, no matter how hurtful and costly."

"We knew the man who bought the land...He paid over a million for it."

"I think Maman suspected it all along. I found a letter from Nader tucked away in her wallet next to her last one-dollar bill and a lottery ticket. The letter was dated a few months before her death. In that letter, Nader chastised her for inquiring about the land and warned her not to ever mention it again. The teardrop stains on the letter left the indelible message of pain and desperation that Maman suffered. It took every ounce of strength for me to restrain my rage. Instead, I cried and wrote him a letter, which I never sent."

I wipe the tears that have flooded my face. I light up my third cigarette in less than an hour and take a long swig of my vodka tranquilizer. The memories are too painful to bear.

Yasmine looks at me with fret, as I take a long drag from my cigarette. She knows that I have a brain aneurysm and shouldn't smoke cigarettes.

"It is heartbreaking to see so many lives shattered because of one man's Machiavellian action"

"Some people make an effort to redeem themselves; try to do the right thing to rectify the damage they have caused. But denying the truth and victimizing the victim has always served as an effective modus operandi for my mother's family to justify their self-serving and iniquitous behavior. When I told them how devastated I felt, receiving as a "gift" the watch that my mother had sold them to feed herself, they said that I was ungrateful and deranged. I encountered the same reaction, when I asked *Daii jaan* about Maman's land and her Stradivarius violin.

He dismissed it with such derisive arrogance that I felt foolish and contemptible.

Yasmine's eyes open wide with curiosity. She inches her head closer, as if about to snag the clue to a pressing mystery.

"You asked him about the violin? Aah...tell me, *azizam*. I can't wait to hear this."

"Well, Maman used to tell me how much her father enjoyed having her play the Stradivarius that he had bought her when she was a little girl. Then a few years ago, when I heard about the value of the rare instrument, I wondered what had happened to it."

I take a swig of my drink and inhale another ration of nicotine.... remembering vividly my conversation with my uncle, as we sat at his dinning table in Beverly Hills.

"I was asking *Daii jaan* about their childhood days in Rasht, and then I casually asked about Maman's Stradivarius violin."

Yasmine is anxiously waiting for me to continue.

"And...what did he tell you?

"He was surprised that I knew about it and annoyed that I asked. Then he said, quite impassively, that it was stolen en route to America."

Yasmine suddenly lurches out of her seat and throws her hands up in the air in disbelief. She is livid.

"Uh...*laamassab*, the immoral one! That is a lie... Nothing was stolen from their valuable collection of furniture, rugs, arts, and antiques. Everything that was shipped from Iran, arrived without a dent or a scratch... and nothing was missing."

"Unless they had put a sign on it to identify it as a four million dollar treasure, who would have known to steal it?" I say cynically.

"Stolen Stradivarius?" Jasmine snickers with sheer and obvious contempt, "Believe me, they would not have kept it a secret. Marjan would have moaned about it all the way to the Interpol and the UN."

"The history of every Stradivarius violin, including its value and its owners, past and present, is well-documented. The profile of the missing and stolen Stradivarius violins reads like the list of the FBI's most wanted."

"*Azizam*, even if someone stole it, knowing its value, it would have been akin to stealing the Mona Lisa. It would have raised global attention and controversy."

"Yasmine *Joon*, You can always tell when someone is not telling the truth... they offer the most outlandish explanation and excuse. He could have said it broke, or even denied that he had it at all, but to claim that it was packed amongst all of their treasures and happened to be the one item stolen, cracks the lie wide open."

"Your mother left her violin with *Khanom jaan* when she got married but your uncle took possession of it, as he did with all other family assets...he did it without any reproach or guilt. He believed he was entitled to everything."

I feel sick to my core and now, Jasmine is apologetic for deluging me with such disturbing facts and narratives.

"Greed has no heart and no conscience, Azadeh *joon*. What was done to your mother ranks as the most heartless and inhumane acts committed against one's kin. I loved your Maman. Everyone loved and

439

respected her. Now, I am heart broken more than ever because Marjan has tarnished your mother's name.

"She has always accused her husband's family of being unfit, *divaneh* and genetically impaired. Isn't it ironic that the only family members spared from the ravages of this 'insanity gene' are those who reside in the exclusive zip code of Beverly Hills? I say to deride the myth.

"Azadeh joon, she parrots those words without knowing what they mean. She can't hold a conversation beyond the mundane, but now has your uncle's fortune to speak volumes for her. Money is all that matters to most people in this community. Everyone pretends to be Marjan's *doostar,* the fans who will be invited to her lavish parties, as long as they curtsy to her will. Do you know that she held a memorial for your uncle every month for the entire year? She catered an extravagant banquet for hundreds of people…. those who would say and do anything to be on her roster of privileged guests. Money buys loyalty and unfortunately, everyone's allegiance in this town is for sale."

Jasmine takes a deep breath…a mixed sigh of relief and exasperation. It is as if she has just fulfilled a burning moral obligation by offering me her fidelity and now, she has to redefine her loyalty to suit the pretentious reality that she has briefly betrayed.

"I understand that your relationship with my uncle's family must remain intact. I am grateful that you took a chance and stepped out to let me know how you feel about this charade of shameless lies and greed."

I tell Yasmine about the phone conversation that I had with Marjan after I received the watch.... How flagrantly and smugly she had declared that she was still in possession of other items that my mother had sold to pay for food and shelter.

"I wonder, Yasmine...how much money would Marjan need to release my mother's possessions, her *yadegari*. I will pay her on her terms so that I can restore my mother's dignity."

Yasmine sits sullen as her eyes flood with tears, soaking her face. I reach out to hold her hand and offer her my last tissue. We have wept into five packs of Kleenex since we sat down two hours ago.

"*Azizam*, don't be naive. She has plenty of money. What she lacks is nobility. It used to drive your *Khanom jaan* to tears, watching her hoard food when there was no shortage of it at your uncle's. Keeping what belonged to your mother makes her feel superior."

I empty the last few drops of vodka down into my throat...it burns from the fumes of my incessant smoking. Then suddenly, a scorching flash of intuition strikes to paralyze me with rage.

"Was my uncle the pawn broker who bought and sold my mother's possessions all those years?"

I look into Yasmine's eyes with agonizing despair, hoping for redemption, eager for her to dismiss my caustic suspicion.

She is quiet and then, her eyes reveal the searing secret that she is about to share.

"I am sorry, *azizam,* you have the right to know the truth."

441

WHEN I call Marjan, I am shut down and dismissed as soon as I say hello. Her incessant rant of incoherent babble immediately drowns my words.

"I don't know what you want from us," she roars, "We have no money to give you."

I am stunned. Does this woman actually believe the lies that she herself has conceived and fabricated? This convoluted and irrational thinking process is so akin to my sister's that I am practically immune to its consequences.

"I am not interested in your money.... I want to make peace and have a relationship with my cousin. They are my family."

Marjan is silent for a moment, and then she calmly delivers a most malicious injury.

"We are not your family. Now that your uncle is dead, we have no ties with you and no reason to talk to you."

I am stunned and speechless, as I try to assess the implications of Marjan's coldhearted statement. But before I can gather my thoughts and regain my senses, she strikes me with yet another scorching jolt to guarantee my ruin.

"If your mother was a good woman...if she cared about her children, you and your siblings would not have turned out so defective."

-The Final Chapter-

It is the dawn of Noe Rooz 2008. I have come to Beverly Hills with the ashes of my dream and the glitter of all the gold that I could carry. I have come to pay ransom to the woman who in spite of her colossal fortune, holds hostage the remnants of my mother's misfortune; the mementos that she had taken to her homeland as badges of her tormented legacy... the relics that she sold to her brother to buy herself food.
I have come to claim my mother's honor and the name that she cherished with pride until the day she died.

AS I STAND atop the remote cliff in Beverly Hills... lost ... longing for that safe refuge that will never be... yearning for the family that I will never have ... and grieving the hopes and aspirations that I have buried, I am shadowed by a dark menacing cloud that looms over me.
   Pages of my life flash before me and with each

memory, a searing pain soars from my core to mercilessly pummel me.

My vision leaps from bygones to now, and then forward ... forward to that terrifying moment when the aneurysm in my brain will rupture and lay me dying alone.... alone without a family ...alone with my secretes and without someone who has witnessed my life and can tell my story.

I look down below and once again ponder the ultimate freedom to choose my end on my own terms... to let the silent canyon bear all my secrets, and my life's final chapter.

WHEN I LOOK UP, I see the ominous clouds in quiet retreat.... they seek to vanish in deference to the glow of the Caspian Sun that is rising majestically from the East...It is soaring splendidly and fastidiously to triumph over the evil of darkness, and to wither the greed of a tainted earth.

In the distance, I hear the roar of the Caspian Sea and I know that my mother is here with me. ... I breathe in the air that is infused with her scent and I am instantly transported to a place of fairness and lucid tranquility... a realm of timeless harmony where one life ends and another begins.

I know that this cannot be where the last chapter of my life ends... but where it begins... where it lives on to illuminate the path of those who will survive me, and   those   who   know   my   name.

IT HAS BEEN thirty years since I last heard my mother's melodic voice and now, she is summoning me again.

"Come home *azizam*... Take the ashes of your shattered dream and build with it the pillars of a new one. Tell our story to the world...tell it in your words before you run out of time. Tell your story because once the silence is broken and your voice is heard, you will be free and never again the victim of your destiny."

> And all the land will talk of me:
> I shall not die; these seeds I've sown will save
> My name and reputation from the grave,
> And men of sense and wisdom will proclaim
> When I have gone, my praises and my fame.
> -Ferdowsi-

ABOUT THE AUTHOR

J.M. Sandler was born in Tehran, Iran, where she began to document her life since the age of eleven. She left her homeland alone at the age of seventeen with the mission to educate herself and save her family. Her heartrending and extraordinary journey was often impossible to endure, but she was enriched with empathy and empowered by her own sense of pride. She transformed her pain into compassion, and her tragedy became the catalyst that helped many others through their life's journey. She hopes that her story will offer inspiration, insight, and promise.

Contact:
jmsandler.caspiandiary@Gmail.com

10/27/12

Ebi 3 copies
Parviz 1 copy — Purchased
Parvin Sahim 1 copy
    Purchased

Proof

Made in the USA
Charleston, SC
18 October 2012